d'artiste™

DIGITAL ARTISTS MASTER CLASS

MATTE PAINTING 3

Detail: Hidden Valley, David Luong, USA

Ballistic Publishing

Finest digital art in the known universe

134 Gilbert St | Adelaide SA 5000 | Australia
correspondence: info@BallisticPublishing.com
www.BallisticPublishing.com

First Edition published in Australia 2013 by Ballistic Publishing
Softcover Edition ISBN 978-1-921828-96-6
Special Edition ISBN 978-1-921002-78-6

PUBLISHER: Ballistic Publishing
CO-EDITORS: Paul Hellard and Mark Thomas
SENIOR DESIGNER: Mark Thomas
GLOBAL ARTIST LIAISON: Paul Hellard

PRINTING AND BINDING: Everbest Printing (China)
www.everbest.com

PARTNERS: The CGSociety (Computer Graphics Society)
www.CGSociety.org

Visit www.BallisticPublishing.com for our complete range of titles.

COVER IMAGE CREDITS

Front cover:
d'artiste: Matte Painting 3 Softcover
Milan Schere, GERMANY
page 156

Front cover:
d'artiste: Matte Painting 3 Limited Collector's Edition
Milan Schere, GERMANY
page 142

INTRODUCTION

FROM THE TEAM AT BALLISTIC PUBLISHING AND THE CGSOCIETY

Welcome to the eleventh book in our *Digital Artists Master Class* series. The *d'artiste* range of books is designed to uncover the techniques, thought-processes and robust decision-making that produce world-class digital art across all genres and platforms.

Our artists are united in their dedication to creating matte paintings that are indistinguishable from reality, through a commitment to intricate detail, a rigorous and continually refined technique, and a humility that allows them to continue to learn and improve. This stands as a clarion call to all artists to pursue their art with the same commitment and determination to aim for excellence every time they switch on a monitor or put pen to paper.

d'artiste: Matte Painting 3 is a stunning showcase of three highly acclaimed matte painters – David Luong, Damien Macé and Milan Schere. These three master artists have worked on a remarkable number of high-profile movie and game projects including *Diablo® III, StarCraft® II, World of Warcraft®, Game of Thrones, Avatar, Harry Potter, Sherlock Holmes, Dredd* and *The Three Musketeers*.

In this book, each master artist presents insights into their matte painting techniques in a gallery of personal and commercial work, and in a series of tutorials on personal or commercial digital matte paintings (dmps). Each artist has also compiled their own Gallery of Invited Artists – each an extensive showcase of dmps featuring pieces from some of the most talented artists involved in matte painting working today; our master artists offer comment on each piece.

Along with extensive biographies of our three master artists, this all combines to present a comprehensive and personal insight into each artist's techniques, approaches, influences, future goals and, of course, their incredible artwork.

We are fortunate to be able to include a foreword by Michael Pangrazio – one of the film industry's matte painting icons. In his foreword, Michael describes his early days in the industry, reminding us to be ready to capitalize on any opportunity that presents itself (however incongruous it may seem); you never know where you'll end up!

Michael also very generously gave his time to our three master artists in a wide-ranging question and answer session, during which they plied him with all manner of questions – about his early days at Industrial Light & Magic, his transition from traditional oil paint and brushes to an all-digital workflow, about some well-held industry secrets, his advice to artists wanting to break into matte painting, and his thoughts on where matte painting is heading in the future. The transcript of this Q & A session is a fascinating read.

Ballistic Publishing continues to expand the *d'artiste* series to encompass all aspects of digital content creation. The series also includes *Digital Painting, Character Modeling, Character Design, Concept Art* and *Fashion Design*. Look for new *d'artiste* title announcements on Ballistic Publishing's website at www.BallisticPublishing.com

We are confident you will love this new title. On behalf of our master artists, David, Damien and Milan, the team at Ballistic is proud to present it to you. We trust that it will help educate, challenge and stimulate you to aim for excellence in your personal and professional art endeavors now and into the future.

/ BALLISTIC /

FOREWORD

MICHAEL PANGRAZIO
Senior Art Director
Weta Digital

The film industry has always seemed magic to me. From my early days working on the iconic pictures at Lucasfilm to the groundbreaking work we do at Weta Digital, the alchemy of matte painting has never failed to capture my imagination.

Having the opportunity to write this foreword has allowed me to reflect on my career as a matte painter and the creativity, talent and skill I have witnessed along the way. When I started out in matte painting there were only a handful of people in the world who did it. I now work with many accomplished craftspeople with the creativity, knowledge and technology to create just about anything you can imagine.

It seems like it was all predestined, the way I slipped into this business. I was working in an art store in Pasadena, California, when one day a gentleman called John Eppolito came in asking if anyone knew airbrush technique and could teach his wife. I volunteered for the job and met with him at his house.

In his attic he had a matte painting by the great Albert Whitlock. It was a beautiful image of a castle on a hill painted in the center of a pane of glass, the rest of which was painted black. I asked why it was black around the castle. John explained the black area was used to mask the live action footage that the painting would become part of. He asked if I thought I could do that. It was an ironic moment – meeting a stranger with something so obscure as a matte painting in his attic, which almost prophetically made me ask myself, "Could I do that?" It was the beginning of a series of unlikely situations which, when strung together, led me to my career in matte painting.

I started working for John at Introvision, learning the techniques and principles of matte painting, and in a week or so I started working on my first film, *The Hazing*. A few weeks later *Battlestar Galactica* went into production. I was sent down to a meeting with the producer Glen Larson on behalf of Introvision with just a few weeks' experience under my belt.

I met with Ralph McQuarrie and Joe Johnson and they asked about my background as a self-taught artist. I offered to show them some of my work, which I had fortuitously stuffed under my sweater prior to the meeting. It was not the most conventional way to present a portfolio, but Joe remembered me and called me three months later to invite me up to Lucasfilm to be interviewed by George Lucas and Richard Edlund for a job as an apprentice matte painter. I was hired and moved up to Marin County a few weeks later. This cemented my new career, and with Lucasfilm I worked on many great films including *The Empire Strikes Back* and *Return of the Jedi, Raiders of the Lost Ark, E.T., The Dark Crystal* and *Labyrinth*.

When I started out at Lucasfilm I worked as an apprentice under Alan Maley who taught me the early techniques of matte painting, which were very meticulous and perilous ways to produce visual effects because every time you exposed a negative you risked making a mistake that could destroy the original. Sometimes the matte painting would have several re-exposures or some kind of light effect, double exposure or a hold-out. Because it was all done on the original negative we had to do it with great care. The advent of the digital era has relieved us of the pressure of destroying the negative. Although, out of hundreds of paintings I was

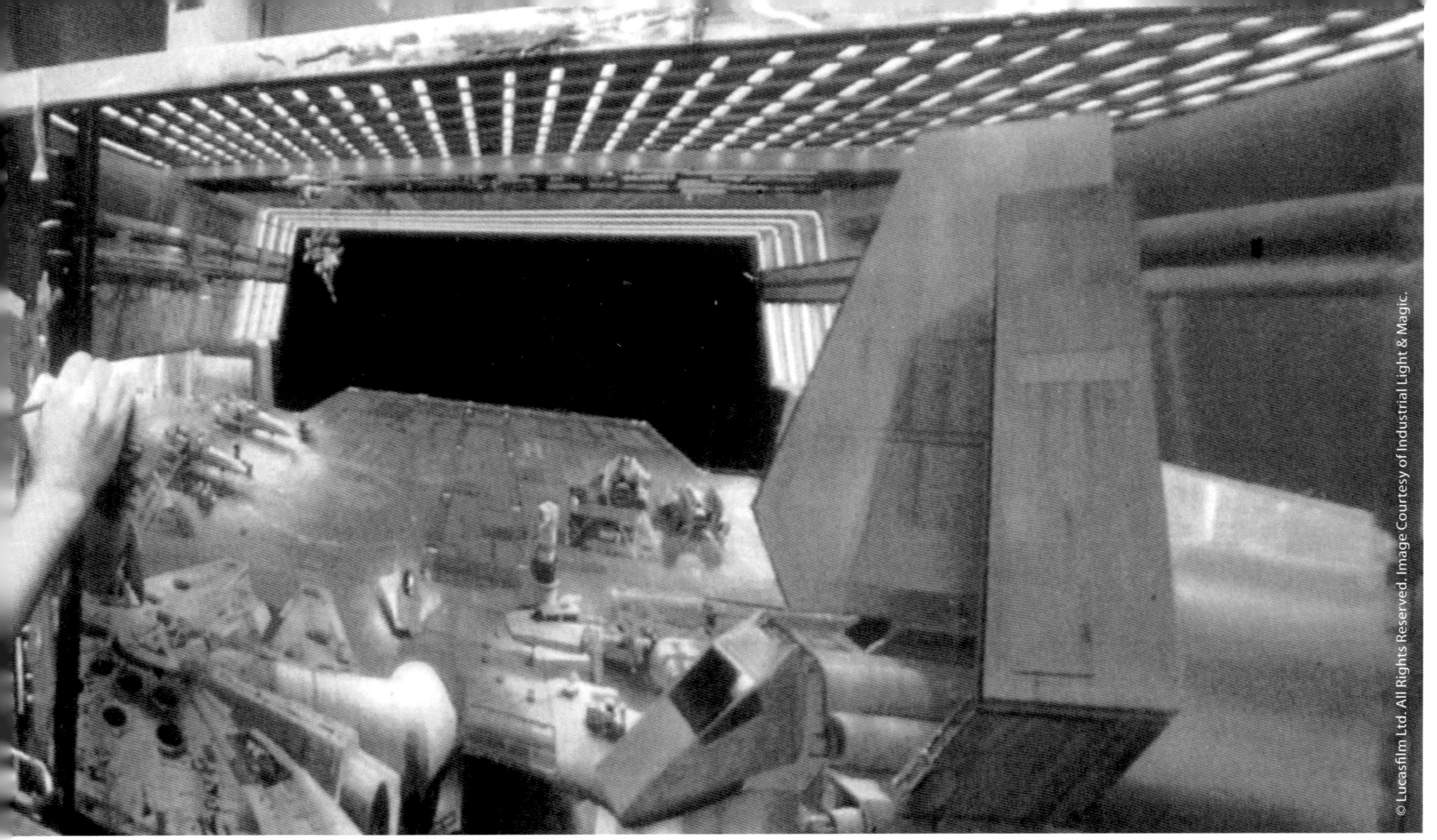

involved with back then, we never destroyed a single shot.

After seven years as head of the Matte Department at Lucasfilm, I began my own company, Matte World Digital, with Craig Barron. We started in an empty garage and within seven years we had worked on 27 films (including *Dracula* and *Batman Returns*) with several matte painters. This was an incredibly rewarding time for me.

I took a hiatus from the industry at this point to spend some time with my family. During this period the industry changed dramatically and when I returned to it, I found that the digital revolution had taken hold. My artistic talent was still relevant but my technical experience had become obsolete. It was agonizing making the transition to the new paradigm, but I wanted to do well and I had a duty to produce good work. I ploughed through and managed to teach myself how to work digitally.

I saw that the convenience of the modern methods had been a huge evolution in the matte painting process. Changes that would have once taken weeks, I could now do in seconds. I could replicate and manipulate digital footage without fear of destroying the original film. A whole new level of opportunities had been opened up. But the principles that I had learned through experience and through watching the great artists – the core ideas of composition, color, light and simplicity – still applied.

I got to know Ralph McQuarrie when he was living in Los Angeles and I would go over to his house and show him paintings, which he would critique. He was a great influence and a real gentleman. I would bring him sketches and he would suggest something like I had overstated the highlights, so I would understate them and realize that suddenly my work looked more real. Being understated and less fussy makes it easier for the eye to look at. A great artist once told me that it is not what you see, it's what you don't see that makes a painting work. What you leave out of an artwork makes it visually softer and easier for the eye to accept.

Another one of the best pieces of advice I have ever received came early in my career. As an apprentice I was told not to fall in love with my work. That really stuck with me and prepared me psychologically for the realities of working in film. Things can change at the drop of a hat and if you are attached to your work you can get very upset about that. Knowing this, and remembering that your work serves the interests of your client and not yourself, will help you survive the instability of the creative process.

When creating a painting I always ask myself what I want the audience to see first. They only have a short time to see it, and making this decision is an important principle of composition and emphasis. Learning these principles has guided me through my career and I have found that they always apply regardless of which techniques I'm using and medium I'm working in.

The modern digital matte painter is a creator of unique worlds just as he or she was 30, 50 or 90 years ago. The new tools and work techniques may seem very different from the days of glass painting but the main tools are still the trained eye, the capacity to tell a story or convey an emotion through image making, and the ability to make that image alive.

Digital matte artists find the most extraordinary approaches to shot making these days. Now we 'paint' 3D sets, have multiple camera projection set-ups, sliced-up images, and little digital dioramas. We continue to play and experiment with new techniques, and we have taken the new tools and made them work for us instead of being too distracted by the technology. We use software but go back to the brush, the photo, the miniature, and then back to the software again. If we encounter a problem we come up with a solution. It is still smoke and mirrors.

I've had the opportunity to see the work of the artists who will guide you through their approaches and techniques in this book. They are masters of their craft and wonderful artists, and I know that this book will be a source of inspiration. The art of matte painting brings wonder and excitement to cinema. It can transport us to another place or time, or to a world beyond imagination.

After 40 years, the film industry is and always will be magic to me.

Q&A WITH MICHAEL PANGRAZIO

Michael Pangrazio's career in the feature film industry has spanned more than 30 years, with his early work becoming some of the most iconic matte paintings of all time – the warehouse interior set extension at the end of the movie *Raiders of the Lost Ark,* and many of the *Star Wars: The Empire Strikes Back* mattes. As a traditional and then digital matte artist, Michael has been in the vanguard of the movie industry, transitioning from working on oil-on-canvas to cutting-edge digital mattes. Now Senior Art Director at Weta Digital in New Zealand, Michael generously gave his time for this interview with our three matte painters.

DAVID Q **You were prominently featured in Craig Barron's matte painting book *The Invisible Art*. How do you think matte painting has evolved from the time of that interview – which was around the time digital matte painting took off – to what it is now?**

MP: It's similar in some ways, in that you still have to follow all the traditional artistic principles. Overall it still takes the same talent, skill and experience to get a good end result. Instead of using supplementary tools like miniatures and photography, and then texturing and painting them, we've ended up with a digital version of the same technique. We've left behind the physical world in visual effects and evolved to a fully virtual approach.

I think it is easier today in some respects because in the old days you had to physically create the painting on glass, and if changes were required you had to physically re-paint it. The technological tools we use today offer greater flexibility and speed.

DAVID Q **A lot of miniatures were used for *The Lord of the Rings*. Do you think there is still any use for miniatures in matte paintings these days? Like for *King Kong* or *The Hobbit*.**

MP: That is an interesting question. I think the Weta Workshop is still in business over here making miniatures. Some of them might be just a prototype – sometimes things are done in a physical way just to let people kind of walk around and talk about them. I know that set designers make little models, so miniatures can still be involved in the process but they don't play the traditional role that they did back in the pre-digital age.

DAVID Q **As a digital matte painter these days, some artists work from the concept, to the matte painting, to modeling, lighting, rendering and compositing the entire shot. Do you think this model is better than being strictly a matte painter in a big studio?**

MP: Well, if you are going to do your own shots you have got to know all the technical requirements, in order to be self-reliant. I think it is important to have a single vision, or at least bring to bear a single vision in a shot. Sometimes things are not better when you have a large committee-type approach or a strict hierarchical system. You have to compromise, I guess is my point.

I think sometimes as work gets done with a single vision, that person is responsible and their enthusiasm drives the project, pushes the boundaries, and maybe they put in a lot of a little extras or a little extra time to make it look right because they have their reputation at stake. So I am a believer in individualism.

Now sometimes when things get so large you might have a show with 2000 or 3000 shots or something, this is where you need a different model. In that circumstance I think you have to compromise that individualistic approach, and coordinate with other people. You have to have a structure around you that ensures that everything gets done. It is amazing how movies get made because you are always pushing the envelope and doing changes right up to the last minute. There has never been a time that I have worked on a film that there was extra time at the end of the project, like, "Oh, we finished a month early." I don't ever remember anybody experiencing that.

DAVID Q **How was it co-founding another studio? Was it hard on the creative side to handle the business or did you have someone else to help you?**

MP: Well, we were pretty naive back then when Craig Barron and I started Matte World, which after a time became Matte World Digital. While at ILM there was an evolution in our thinking about wanting to be independent. We started looking at our clients and thinking, "Well, we did well with our clients through ILM, but I wonder what it would be like to work with them directly?" I think many people have thought of that after working for some time at a place; that breaking away would be risky but exhilarating. It is not being disloyal or anything, it's natural to want to be more responsible for your own decisions and destiny.

We didn't have any assurance that we would be successful, but we solved problems as we went, which made it a very organic process and it worked out fine in the end.

DAVID Q **Do you ever go back and do matte paintings since you've been in your role as Art Director?**

MP: Once in a while I will be asked to do something. Maybe they are really busy and so I'll jump on board and do an element of some sort. When I say 'element', it is not a piece of finished art; I just do a concept piece or something. So yes, I have jumped back into matte painting, but I prefer doing what I am doing now.

As Senior Art Director, how does your art direction compare to other art directors at Weta who haven't specialized in matte painting?

MP: Well, Weta is a very interesting company; it's a very large company. I think at peak times we have 900 or 1000 people here. It reminds me of the building of the ancient pyramids, with 1000 people all pushing in one direction.

I mostly work through concept art here at Weta. I produce concepts to convey my art direction. I have created thousands of concepts over the years. I interact with other people verbally but I find visuals are a more eloquent and efficient way to work. Sometimes reference images are used to elaborate on the look I'm developing. I think that is the way to go because it is so self-explanatory.

It is an advantage that I have been a matte painter in the past because of all the disciplines and problem-solving that I have had to go through to be a good matte painter. My work experience has prepared me for my current role. I think that after you do something like matte painting for 30 plus years you want to grow and move on and try something different. I really enjoy the art direction side of things.

As far as the specialization of matte painting goes, are we all converging towards being environment artists these days rather than just being strictly matte painters?

MP: Yes, that is a really good question. I think not everybody could be a matte painter, and not everybody who is a CG artist is suited to matte painting. I think it is a right brain/left brain issue. The left brain is all about logical things. People who are predisposed to thinking logically work out of that side. But I think the artistic side, the right side, is important to have, primarily, for a person who is going to make aesthetic judgments because they are looking at the creative side of things. I think it is important to have an artist-driven vision also, and not just focus on technical considerations.

Here at Weta we have a new Environments Department where all these disciplines are interacting with each other and merging into one department, as opposed to a more compartmentalized approach.

I think this is where your question is relevant. It is merging because of the amount of shots you have to do, and how big they are. They are bringing people together to communicate with each other across all these disciplines.

David: Yes, I think that is definitely good because I know there are a lot of people who just do 3D, and they do their painting entirely in 3D, and then do some touch-ups on top of that, but some just do painting and have some 3D to support that. But the definition of what matte painting is these days is almost blurring into environment art.

MP: I agree with you. It is blurring, but in the end it's really not the processes that show up on the screen. I feel like there are no rules; if you can find a way to solve a problem you should do it. Some people think that's cheating, but I think if it looks right on the screen that is all that counts. There are no rules except that it has to look real.

David: Definitely. I agree with that. I have been teaching matte painting online with the CGSociety for five years now and I tell all my students, "Whatever it takes to get the shot done." They might need to do photography or miniature shots or paint a 3D concept – just whatever it takes.

MP: Yes, that is how I always approach things; I'm not a purist in that way. It is just a problem to be solved. There is no moral issue here, it is a matter of how you can trick the audience into thinking that it's real.

It is the ultimate magic trick and it still has to look real. I mean, that is what is so interesting after all these years, to still be struggling with that same issue.

How has it been working at Weta Digital compared with a studio like ILM or even Matte World Digital?

MP: Well, I think the main difference is the size. Weta is the biggest, ILM I think is the second biggest, and then Matte World was just a blip on the radar screen compared with them. Weta started as a small effects studio to work on New Zealand productions. It was primarily expanded to work on *The Lord of the Rings* projects as far as I understand. So it was specific to a style, and about solving a set of problems, like, what Middle Earth looked like. Since then it has evolved to tackle the problems of creating CG effects for a variety of film genres. ILM followed the same pattern – where *Star Wars* started the effects studio, which then branched out and diversified.

I think Matte World allowed me the most freedom as I was able to work directly with the directors to solve problems by listening carefully to what they said and then following through within my solution.

I understand that large companies need to be structured that way, but I have enjoyed my little shop and a 10–15 person crew. It really is a delight to work on that level.

How many shots did you guys usually finish when you only had a 15 person crew for a movie?

MP: It depends on how many shots they wanted of course, but in the old days to hand-paint something usually took a week or two, or more if it was very complex.

It reminds me of that warehouse shot at the end of *Raiders of the Lost Ark*. That took three months to paint. That included all kinds of experimentation and trying to develop a look, but it could still take that long. Nobody would tolerate that today; after three months you would probably be out of business.

Now it is a week or so to do a completion, and you have the aids of great software and technical developments to really help you accomplish that.

***The NeverEnding Story* is one of my all-time favorite childhood movies. How much were you involved with the matte paintings in that movie?**

MP: I worked on it when I was with ILM. I went over to Germany and to the various studios with the director Wolfgang Petersen.

It was pretty humorous as I remember, because it was during their winter and they had put me up in a big old building that was pretty much abandoned and didn't have any heating. I just sat there and tried to do concept work, and I was just really, really cold. They treated me really well though, and I enjoyed myself over there.

I remember all the sets were made of

styrofoam, and I found out the production designer owned a styrofoam company. It was a great movie.

The ability to go on location, and to interact with the crew, even go to a foreign country, it is all part of the beauty of the job. At least, perhaps, it was more like that in the past than it is today.

DAVID **Q What are your thoughts on the current state of the VFX industry, and especially the implosion of the industry in Los Angeles?**

MP: The market is sort of decentralizing. That is how I see it anyway. I guess somebody has decided that expenses are so great in their present form that things have to be broken up, and that it has to go into smaller units to compete, or to other countries. I am sorry to see that.

It happened to Hollywood. They go up to Toronto and Vancouver and other places to shoot now, and, I guess, why would VFX not change as well? The center of gravity eventually has to change. I don't know where it's going, perhaps to other countries, but I'm not really sure of what the plan is. I know that people need work and there are a lot of specialized people still there.

I am hoping people will form smaller companies, and maybe specialize a bit. If they coordinate themselves into a little guild where they can work together in loose, small companies they could present work at a price that is attractive. I don't know. What do you think is happening?

David: Yes, it is happening all over the place. We saw Rhythm & Hues studios close up recently. I do think there is a lot of globalization, and subsidies for industries all over the world. London has a lot, and I think in New Zealand and Canada – it really seems to be siphoning a lot of work from Los Angeles.

The other thing people are thinking about here is unionization, as a lot of other parts of the film industry are part of a union. Do you think having a union in the VFX industry would help?

MP: You used the word 'global'. I think that it would be more difficult because every jurisdiction has its own problems to overcome. In New Zealand, for example, it just wouldn't happen. And it may not happen in other countries either. There is always pressure from another area saying, "Okay, we don't need those union rates, so you can come over here and do it cheaper" – and that undermines the market in countries where you have unions. It is self-defeating in that way, although I think it is a noble idea.

DAMIEN **Q Time is money, and in this industry time and money are everything. It is common now to have to deliver a matte painting within a week – sometimes even in a couple of days. As I understand it, back when you started, your process included not just the actual matte painting but doing your own layouts, concepts and preparation before even starting with the brush.**

MP: I think that is a great statement. Let me elaborate on that. I think it shows a different approach. Back then there were only a few matte painters in the world, so there was a mystique about it. At some points there were probably only two or three people working as a matte painters in the world.

Nowadays people know textures, and they all know a little modeling, and they know each other's workflow a little bit, whereas back then nobody knew what a matte painter did – even within your own company. So that mystique and mystery allowed you to be able to set your own working parameters. It enabled you to ask yourself how long this painting really would take to accomplish, and you could pad it out a bit to make sure that the quality was good.

It was certainly less regulated back then, because of the mystery and the rarity of doing that job, and that made the scheduling a bit more appropriate. I think we had more time to really solve the problems on our shots. Plus we were working by hand and that process just took time.

And if you were using original negatives you still had to match everything perfectly, which took a long time and often you couldn't predict how long it was going to take. Since nobody knew how we did things, we were able to work under a cloak of secrecy.

DAMIEN **Q People might think that matte painting is more technical than it used to be, but even back then it seemed to be a very tech-heavy task. How do you feel about it from your experience?**

MP: Often today people are so highly technical in their approach that they may think back on the way it used to be done as sort of primitive. And I don't think that perception is accurate.

If you look at the classic approach to matte painting, it was done on original negative, and the original negative was the one and only first-generation image capture of that scene. So you didn't want to *ever* lose that. If you worked on original negative, you had to preserve the original from destruction.

You had to implement procedures that were strictly followed to ensure you wouldn't make a mistake that destroyed the original. So from that point of view we had a lot of protocols to follow, we were very cautious, and we never did destroy a negative.

Also, we only had limited test footage back then. They might have run, say, 30–40 feet extra at the end of a take to start to work with, and that diminished all the time as you tested. So there was a kind of fail-safe where, if you ran out of test footage before you finished your work, you knew you were getting into trouble.

From a technical point of view of course we just didn't have the kind of computers we have now. We did have some computer-driven motors for the cameras. We could use stop-motion frames with long exposures, and we could do motion-control things if we wanted to capture something – maybe partially use a miniature and do a motion-control move to a painting later when you merged the two in Comp (what used to be called Optical).

So it was certainly very technical in its own way. A person couldn't just walk in off the street and do any of those disciplines. You had to learn quite a bit about them to do them well. So from that point of view I think it had a lot of technical aspects to it.

DAMIEN **Q You mentioned Comp. Even back then did you guys do compositing? I mean, did you iterate, and change color and grade as well – or is that unique to the digital age?**

MP: We had an Optical Department where they would reproduce the film, but they just didn't digitize the film – they would copy the film to second generation. And use hold-out mattes, and grade it, and do all the things Comp does now, but we didn't use it all that much.

Once in a while we would integrate, but it was on a case-by-case basis. We would sometimes composite matte paintings and just supply an element, basically just the matte painting itself with a hold-out matte, then send it to Optical and they would put it together.

It never looked quite as good though, because in those days we had a lot of film grain problems with second- or third-generation copies, and it really showed up or degraded quickly. The ideal was to cut with the live-action original photography and use original negatives so it would seamlessly cut together. We always tried to push for that when possible.

DAMIEN Q **You mentioned there were so few of you doing matte painting back then that it wasn't so much like a team. Did you have a VFX supervisor or some kind of department that you reported to? How did you get the modifications for the pieces that you were painting?**

MP: We were very independent, though we did have supervisors; Dennis Muren was one of them. They were busy doing other things for the most part, and we were charged with solving a certain part of the problem.

We would go out on location oftentimes, if there was original negative, and put up a big black box with black cloth, and inside was the glass that we shot through making our matte. We would be on a platform, and be inside the box with the camera, and nobody knew what we were up to.

So I think that is kind of a metaphor for all the rest of it – we just had a lot of freedom, and we worked directly with the directors and I thought it was fantastic.

I was a supervisor at ILM for seven years back in the early days of their Matte Painting Department, and we had our own dailies and we were pretty independent. We mostly tried to solve our own problems within the department. Sometimes we wouldn't show our work until it was a final, which is a very different approach than we have today.

We would all of a sudden be finished, or at least be satisfied, and say, "Okay, we'll screen this." And by that time it was too late to do anything else, oftentimes because we had burned the original negative anyway, so nobody could go back and reverse it.

And that was it. But, most of the time people loved what we were doing.

Damien: So you were directly working with the directors back then? Your comments came directly from the top?

MP: Yes, that's right. Again, because of our process, we would go out on location where the director was in charge, and shoot with the live-action crew.

They would set up a scene or a set outdoors, and we would be out there and be scheduled to come in and shoot an original negative. We were part of the film crew.

And so, of course you are going to meet the director. And you're all out there and he is wondering what exactly you're doing; not every director understood it. So we had an opportunity to really interact with them. We went all over the world doing this. So yes, things have really changed now.

MILAN Q **As an Art Director at Weta, what do you do, and how is it related to your earlier matte painting work?**

MP: I had done a little bit of VFX art direction before at ILM. I don't think I was credited as such, but I was a VFX art director on *E.T.* and worked with Dennis Muren. I had an opportunity to give my opinion about what I thought things should look like.

I think sometimes the opportunity to express yourself, to give your opinion, is best done through an illustration or a concept work, because while there is a lot of talk that goes on, to actually see it in front of you really helps.

Also, I think especially because of my matte painting background I was able to get pretty close to a specific and realistic look. When you show that to somebody, they can react to it and see a lot of great detail and hopefully it looks like a frame of film – that would be the ideal. So I think the matte painting training has definitely helped me to develop the kind of style where I can be very specific.

In fact, what is ironic about this whole thing is that now I am trying to go the other way – to get more impressionistic. It's because I notice how beautiful some of the concepts from these artists are. We work on films from Twentieth Century Fox or other studios, and they are always supplying us with concept work from their side, from the production side of things. And usually it has the loose kind of impressionistic brushwork that makes concepts come alive. They have such a lot of energy to them, a lot of life, and are not so stiff.

I am trying to learn how to become more loose with my work, as I'm so conditioned to make my pieces look like a photograph.

Milan: Apologies, but you are talking about the general feel of a piece? Do you think that something as loose as what you're describing works for VFX art direction in such a professional work environment?

MP: I am talking about the general feel.

Let's just say that you have got a building behind on the background. You do not need to put in every single window on that building to give the impression that the building is lit a certain way. You can express a lot of lighting and convey a lot of information with a lot less detail.

I think it is the same way with language. You can express yourself and say something in a very long-winded way with a lot of complexity. Sometimes the genius of an idea is to boil it down to the least number of words required to express that idea. It is the same way with art. I think you can really edit the artwork down.

A great artist once told me that it is not what you *see*, it is what you *don't see* that makes a piece work. I really believe that. It is not putting in every little detail because it becomes too fussy, and can look contrived and stiff. But when you give an *impression* of something, then somehow the human mind can accept it even though it is softer-looking and easier to look at.

MILAN Q **So, the production art that you currently produce in your normal work environment, who would it go to? Who do you directly interact with? Is this something you provide to matte painting or to another department?**

MP: Here at Weta I would say that it mostly goes – if I am working on *The Hobbit* – to Peter Jackson, though I would go through Joe Letteri sometimes. Then Peter would give us his comments, and if it was acceptable it would then be promoted, so-to-speak, to a level of approval.

I would encourage any department that has an approved concept and responsibility to contribute to the final shot to think, "Let's make it look worse than the concept, make it look better than the concept."

Then it would go to the various departments, and then it's looked at as production artwork that has been approved, or it has a hold on it that gives a characterization from the director. Then the rest of the disciplines follow – they look at it, and the Texturing Department looks at it, and so on.

There is an inertia in a big institution where everybody has got their own style, so they take something, and they will tend to start moving it in their stylistic direction, and so you often end up with a completely different look at the end – but hopefully it is better than when you started.

MILAN Q **With your matte painting background do you primarily do environment work, or do you also venture into doing creatures or anything character-based?**

MP: I do everything. Sometimes I feel like I can do anything – there is such an abundance of reference material out there that it is like getting yourself educated on a visual problem to solve. You can always go out and educate yourself, you can look at lots of imagery.

Let's say you have to create a creature and it has got a certain base characteristic, like it looks like a rhinoceros or something. It's easy to know where you start. Then you just begin building on top of that.

I am also a believer in happy accidents. You take reference of a rhinoceros and a giraffe and you start combining them into this new kind of creature, and you end up with something you had not thought of before. And then you say, "Okay, I like that part, I didn't think of that. I'm going to use that." It is often a surprising journey to go on because sometimes I have no idea what it will end up like. I cannot envision everything.

MILAN Q **What is your day-to-day routine like now compared with when you worked at ILM? I know you were specifically a matte painter then, and the industry has changed so much. Here, we have dailies once or twice a day now, or sometimes even three times, and then we need to go back to review our mattes each time. What was it like for you in those early days?**

MP: Well, back then ILM was kind of like the Wild West. I'd just moved up from Los Angeles to Marin County, and the structure of the company was pretty sparsely staffed at that stage, and it had a really great dynamic.

When I say Wild West, it was a really positive thing, because people would communicate freely with each other to solve their problems rather than have a structural hierarchy to go through. It really wasn't a top-down sort of approach. If you needed to rig something because you wanted a model, you'd go to the Model Department and talk to somebody.

And you know, you just got your work done – if you had a problem, you just worked around it, you talked to people and got to know them, and they got to know your problem, and together you solved it. I love that model.

But then the work got so big, you couldn't do that anymore. But back in the early times it was really fantastic. I really enjoyed working in that kind of setting for the first three years, and then it became a little bit big for me.

It was at that point I wanted to leave and I started Matte World. I wanted to experience that sort of ease of communication again, because all companies have that kind of spark. If they are successful, they get big – it's just natural.

MILAN Q **Would you be able to answer a question about *Indiana Jones and the Temple of Doom*? I have seen images of the cliff face where the characters come out through an opening in the cliff after the rollercoaster ride. I believe you worked on that sequence with Caroleen Jett Green at ILM. I've seen images of the cliff face where the lighting was different. There are rumors that you had to basically re-paint some of those cliff face mattes because they wanted the lighting changed. Is that true? Can you remember back to what happened with those images?**

MP: It was a long time ago – the early eighties. I think it did have to be redone. As her supervisor I would have probably come in and said, "Do you mind if I get the brush and try to show you a couple of ideas?" I probably did have some input over it, but I think that she was probably primarily responsible for those pieces. She was great then, but she was kind of an apprentice. So I probably painted on it, but she did the majority of the work.

Milan: Nowadays if the same situation happened, my supervisor would just add a new layer in Photoshop and do the same thing you did. But back then, you had to paint right on her image – she must have just been there standing and looking at what you were doing to her work.

MP: Yes, I guess if you have a Photoshop layer you can always turn it off after your supervisor leaves if you don't want to see it anymore. But I left something that she would have had to erase by painting over and over it again. But hopefully it was always an improvement, maybe it wasn't, but hopefully it would be, and it would stay in there to the end if it was appropriate.

Milan: That is awesome. In my opinion, matte painting is just a series of decisions. You have to be able to see the reality – be able to identify what is going on with the way things look in your painting. They are the same kinds of decisions that you have to make when you're painting with real paint.

MILAN Q **Michael, you are an amazing individual. After you left Matte World, for some years you were not active in the film industry and when you returned the whole industry had gone digital. You transitioned from being an amazing traditional painter to a digital painter. In theory, one should always apply the same techniques digitally as in traditional painting, but it is not that easy. I am very curious about how you made the transition practically.**

MP: I will try to be brief about it. After I left Matte World, I just needed a break from the industry. My kids were eight and nine and a half then.

This industry is often very demanding and I felt like I wasn't getting a chance to be with the children. I didn't want them to get to be young adults and leave home, and then suddenly realize I never really participated very much in their lives.

So I left the industry for nine years and I stayed home and homeschooled them. I was with them every day for those nine years.

And then I saw *The Lord of the Rings*. I was so impressed with that movie. It made me yearn to get back into the industry again because I was so amazed by it visually. It was just so beautifully done.

I went to The Orphanage, at the Presidio in San Francisco, and I had been working with CorelDRAW at home a little bit, not very much, but I wanted to get back in the industry. I approached that company because I was living in Monterey, which is pretty close to San Francisco, thinking that I could move up there pretty easily.

I think my past reputation helped carry me through, because technically I probably was not qualified to work anywhere at that point, but they gave me a job.

I really struggled for the first three or four months. It was really hard. I just kept asking all the stupidest of questions of my workmates, some of whom were matte painters, and they were very patient and tolerant with me. Sometimes I wouldn't even ask because I thought I might have hit my daily limit of asking other people – I just didn't want to be a pest. So I would just sit there and agonize through the whole thing, and I finally began to solve my own problems. That is, afterall, probably the best way we learn.

After those initial months of struggle, I kind of had a breakthrough where I was able to at least function and produce work, and then it was great. I really enjoyed it and thought that way of working was such an improvement.

In the past I used oil paints to airbrush with, and sometimes I would use Cartoon Colour or Cel-Vinyl paint. We just ended up having to breathe the fumes from the airbrush. We didn't have a great spray booth or anything at ILM so we would be breathing the fumes. We would wear a mask but it wasn't that comfortable.

And I never had any clothes that didn't have paint on them. I'd buy new clothes and go to work in them and get paint on them. So that was solved by this new technique, and I was able to start to paint digitally. From a health point of view, the transition was probably pretty advantageous.

From then on I have learned incrementally more and more about the technical side, but I am still not a big whiz when it comes to technical things – I guess I am a right brain kind of person. I just want to intuitively work my way through problems, rather than do it intellectually, so that is part of my artistic creative process. I don't try to push myself too far into the technical thing.

I happened to meet Paul Campion, who had worked on *The Lord of the Rings* in the Texture Department. I told him that I loved the movie and asked what New Zealand was like, and he said it was great … so I applied, and I was able to get a job down here as a matte painter.

After a couple of months at Weta, I got a chance to meet Peter Jackson, and he asked me to do art direction on *King Kong*. I was being honest and told him that I had only done a little art direction, and also that I wasn't very technical either – so he kind of took a risk with me.

MILAN Q **It is great to hear that *The Lord of the Rings* held the same inspiration for somebody like you as it did for the three of us. Also, that back then you had the same experience with the industry as we do now, and it was just as demanding. My wife and I both work in the industry, she is also a matte painter, and we have a two-year-old son. We value every second with our son. It's really great to hear that other people have basically been going through the same experiences as us.**

MP: How can you be married to a matte painter? How does that work? Do you ever stop talking about work?

Milan: You'll have to ask her. It works well for us. It's actually great – anyway, we are always just talking about our son, and that is basically it. He just takes up all our attention I guess.

MP: That is interesting to me. There haven't been that many female matte painters, so to find a female matte painter that you fall in love with is amazing – the odds are absurd – so, congratulations!

Milan: Thank you very much. She will like to hear that.

MILAN Q **Michael, I have one more specific question about *The Hobbit*. I have heard that Peter Jackson is drifting more into a full 3D digital environments approach. Maybe it's because there is an option for moving the camera around? I think the goblin cave environment – which was most impressive in the movie – was mainly done digitally, and I was just wondering if you knew how much matte painting was done on such a large-scale environment, and how much of it was completely 3D? Would you be able to address that, or is that too specific a question?**

MP: I can answer that. There was one matte painting and that was in the trailer. I went through the goblin sequence and all the rest of it was full 3D.

Computing power today has gone way up, and we are probably going to see that trend as the software improves and computing power increases. You are able to make it possible – from a timing point of view – to actually do a full 3D environment. That one, though, still never reached full infinity because there was atmosphere in it.

You will still have a lot of matte paintings to work on, but I think the trend is probably going in the opposite direction, which is to do more full 3D environments.

Chris White, who is very talented, was a supervisor in charge of that. He is a brilliant guy and a gentleman, so he deserves all the credit really.

MILAN Q **You have been quoted in other interviews mentioning the software package Vue, which is not a commonly used software across the industry. I have tried using Vue but it takes a bit of getting used to and a fair amount of fiddling to get a good base render out of it within an acceptable render time. Have you personally been using it?**

MP: I haven't used it all that much. Some of the matte painters here are using it, but only at the beginning of a project to get one more angle on solving a problem looking at the lighting or the environment, and then mostly they paint over it. You probably don't see very much of it left at the end of the process as it's been covered up.

I enjoyed working with it, I just thought it was kind of clever. This was about two years ago. I don't really use it on a daily basis.

Also, with concept work you don't have the stringent requirements that you do for film, which is one thing I love about it. I can work with a crummy 8-bit jpeg, all compressed and looking terrible, and then just paint over it. I don't want to say that it is a bad or good piece of software – we just don't use it that much.

Milan: I was just really curious about it, because it is always somehow mentioned in connection with you online.

MP: I would think that is probably not an accurate reflection of the situation. I don't use much software, though I use Photoshop of course, and sometimes Artrage. Adobe made some big improvements in Photoshop CS6 with the brushes, which I like, and I'm able to get a painterly feel with those. I often start off my concepts that way.

I am not actually rendering much of anything, though. I work with a young assistant technical director called Olivia

Adams. She does some renders for me because I will be asked to do something that is already built as a model; for example, on the movie *Tintin*.

They required a few scenes that were already built, but they wanted to have alternate creative choices about how the buildings were composed, the time of day, and things like that. So of course I would get somebody to render it for me. I wouldn't paint all that from scratch. Plus it is not as accurate as using the renders in the model, so I have my trusty little pipeline kind of working for me.

At a point in production where you have no plate yet, would you just start with a blank canvas or do you ever use a photograph as base to paint on top of?

MP: Sometimes it depends on exactly when you are asked to do something – and if it is really pre-production. At the beginning you know there really aren't any assets out there to use. You might get a rough environment but they haven't really built anything yet, so you are the one who is defining things at the beginning, which is kind of neat. I like doing that when I have the opportunity.

But after things get established, like in the middle of a film when they have built a bunch of things, of course you have to pull them in and use them. If you have a ship or something that has got to be that specific ship, it is silly to start over from scratch. So, yes, I would use that. I think that is part of the matte painting approach.

In the old days we used to have stacks of books like *National Geographic* that we would go through looking for elements we could use. "Hey, that's a nice sky, we can paint that, and, that's a great looking wall." It's the same process now. We are still taking bits and pieces and putting them together into a single picture that hopefully ends up as an image that catches your eye and looks dramatic.

And we had to learn how to deal with making something eye-catching and dynamic in a really short period of time. You have to catch the viewer's attention and direct them to the thing in the frame that you want them to look at first. You've got about three or four seconds, so you have to know what you want them to see first, second and third. By the time they've seen the third thing, they're off to another shot.

So I did bring all that matte painting experience to doing concept work, and I think that has helped me a lot.

Milan: So it is basically the same approach as today, it's just that now it's all on two screen sets and it is all digital. But it is still the same thing now that you did back then?

MP: That's right. And that's what I was trying to express earlier, in that in the old days, like at ILM, we had a Model Department. And here at Weta Digital we have a Model Department, but they are not making anything physical anymore – but they are still making models.

So you have the same sort of studio functionalities and the same categories, but they are not really new. They are really working the same way they were – in terms of subject matter – back even in the 1920s and 1930s as they do today. It is just that they are using a different set of tools now to get the same kind of results.

Michael, I'd like to ask your advice for any students and artists who will be reading this. It seems that your path into the industry was not really a textbook approach. Knowing what the industry is like today, what would you advise for somebody who has their mind set on matte painting?

MP: I think my opinion has changed about that, because if you had asked me that 10 years ago I would have said that you could teach yourself anything you wanted just by talking to people that were doing it.

In the last 10 years or so, the courses they teach at universities are amazing. Olivia, my ATD, went to Massey University here in New Zealand. Oftentimes I'll say something like, "Hey, can you put a texture on this", and she'll say, "Oh, I did that at uni. Yes, I'll do it for you."

I think it's really valuable that you can spend four years going to school, learn these techniques, and have something practical to take into an industry.

I didn't go to school to learn what I did, I was an apprentice at ILM with Alan Maley, which was a different approach. But nowadays there are schools that you can go to and learn these things, and it is a great route for people. And you make connections and then you can network with people with common interests. But I think that is the key. I know it sounds like a cliché, but, "Hey kids, stay in school!"

I read a story about your fake studio 'sting' with HBO on the film *By Dawn's Early Light*. Could you share with us what happened?

MP: Okay. Well, it is probably not something I would recommend somebody do, but it was kind of innocent because we were qualified to get the job, it was just we didn't have a facility.

Craig Barron and I were working out of a tiny room; it was like a garage next to a Domino's Pizza – which was convenient because if you wanted to eat you could just go next door. But it was not a great location for meeting executives flying up from LA to meet with us because they were doing a film.

I think it was because we had a good reputation in our field that they were taking us somewhat seriously. We just did not have the facility to bring them to, and they probably would have turned us down if they saw where we were working with paint all over the floor and oil stains and stuff like that.

We ended up renting an industrial bay really short term. It didn't have any power, or any phone lines, and we had to rent some office furniture to fill it up. We actually bought outlets and glued them on the walls with hot glue to make it look like we had electricity, which was really pretty shameless.

If I remember right, we had a whole group of friends and family in pretending to be workers to make it look like we were busy. You do what you can, you know?

And we had a successful meeting with them, and we must have pulled it off because they didn't say anything. And they did give us the job, which was enough money to start actually renting a real place to work from – a real location with real people.

You have to have your first break, the first real step. So we just did what we thought was worth doing.

I was wondering if you still do personal drawing or painting in your free time?

MP: Yes, I do a little bit of Photoshop painting. I am really fascinated with the turn-of-the-century kind of painting, particularly the French, and sometimes Impressionistic.

Sometimes I do it in Photoshop first and then try to do it with a real brush. I just don't have all that much time. If I ever have the opportunity to retire, I will probably do a lot of painting.

And learning how to be looser with Photoshop allows you to be looser with a real brush.

If you had to pick just one, what would be your best professional memory?

MP: The Disney logo comes to mind. I was given the opportunity in 2005 at Weta, in New Zealand, to design and supervise a new logo for Disney. I had the privilege of interacting with Mike Gabriel and his staff at Disney in Los Angeles. We completed the logo after several months of intense artistic collaboration. Now, when I see the logo it brings back so many happy memories of working on that project. The logo is seen by millions of people everyday, so has a wider reach than anything else I have worked on.

Another favorite memory is from when I worked on *Empire of the Sun*, a Steven Spielberg movie. I flew down to Los Angeles and met Steven at his screening room, and I'll always remember he had this old-fashioned popcorn maker in the corner. I felt like I was in the center of the movie-making world. That was really something.

Can I ask another question about *The Hobbit* … What was it like to do art direction on that?

MP: Well, *The Hobbit* was concept based, so whenever I have an opportunity to do some concept stuff it is great.

Also, what can you say about Alan Lee and John Howe – those guys are the consummate representors of Tolkien's work in art. They worked on the original films and really are the driving force, justifiably, in that area. I get to latch on and do some work with them, and I feel pretty privileged to do that. But they are the primary motivators, and when they move forward it is so natural to them – even the way they draw their trees and roots and rocks.

When I first met them about two or three years ago, they were constantly drawing – even in our meetings you would see them with paper and pencil, and while everybody was talking they continued to draw. I know they had a huge workload, but they were conceptualizing constantly in pencil. And they just recreated Tolkien's world. They've done probably tens of thousands of images to craft this consistent look. I am able to get close to that at some points, but not with the same consistency.

I work on all the shows here that need conceptualizing and art direction, and I get busier when we do an in-house show like *Tintin* or something we produce ourselves.

In those years that you were gone from the industry, you illustrated some children's books. I have been able to find two, *Glim the Glorious* and *Once Upon a Time: A Treasury of Modern Fairy Tales*. Were there any others that you illustrated?

MP: Well, those are the only two that I worked on with Random House. I also did a lot of posters and little cards back in that era, this was about 20 years ago, maybe even 25, with Visionary Publishing.

I would work at ILM during the day and then come home. I had an art show that included elves and fairies that sold out. They then produced posters and distributed them worldwide. I don't think they're available any longer. But I especially loved the elves riding on snails and doing all kinds of other quirky things. I really enjoyed that.

Maybe if I can retire someday I can get back to that sort of thing. To me that subject is very magical – the idea of elves and fairies is charming. I think the world could do with a softer, nicer, more pleasant view of things, and a bit more wonder and magic.

Do you have any spare time to play video games? A lot of the game cinematics I work on approach film quality. Have you seen any of these cinematics and what do you think of them compared with ones from recent films?

MP: I am pretty ignorant about games. I had a computer but games were never something that I played nor did my kids. It is probably shocking to people, but when my kids were young they never watched TV, we never had one.

I do know what you are talking about, though, and I would love to see how things become more refined. I see that capabilities in computing power and software are shifting to some point in the future where all kinds of projects can be done virtually in a simplistic way with a lot fewer people.

I think we are five to 10 years away from a situation like that – similar to the way they can make some music today where they digitize the sounds and have a singer and a producer together in a room making a record. I think that is going to happen in games and film production, and it will all be of the same quality at some point. What do you think?

David: I think it is getting very close. I work in the Cinematics Department for Blizzard and we work on pre-rendered stuff that is nearly film quality.

And then we also have the in-game cinematics work that just uses a game engine. The quality is nice and almost real-time, with a high amount of assets in the 3D space.

I think it is almost there with the next-gen consoles such as the Wii U and the to-be-released Xbox One and Playstation 4. The stuff is looking amazing, like the shaders, the textures, and they do it all in real-time in the game engine.

Michael, we were all really looking forward to talking to you. The three of us have realized that your matte paintings have been a great influence on us, and have really encouraged us to get where we are today. So, thanks from the three of us.

MP: That is great to know. Thank you.

1

DAVID LUONG

Diablo®III, StarCraft® II, World of Warcraft®, Night at the Museum, Superman Returns

93

DAMIEN MACÉ

Game of Thrones, Sherlock Holmes, Avatar, Harry Potter

135

MILAN SCHERE

Tron: Legacy, Dredd, Mama, Robocop

'The Three Musketeers': Image from The Three Musketeers, provided courtesy of © Constantin Film Produktion GmbH

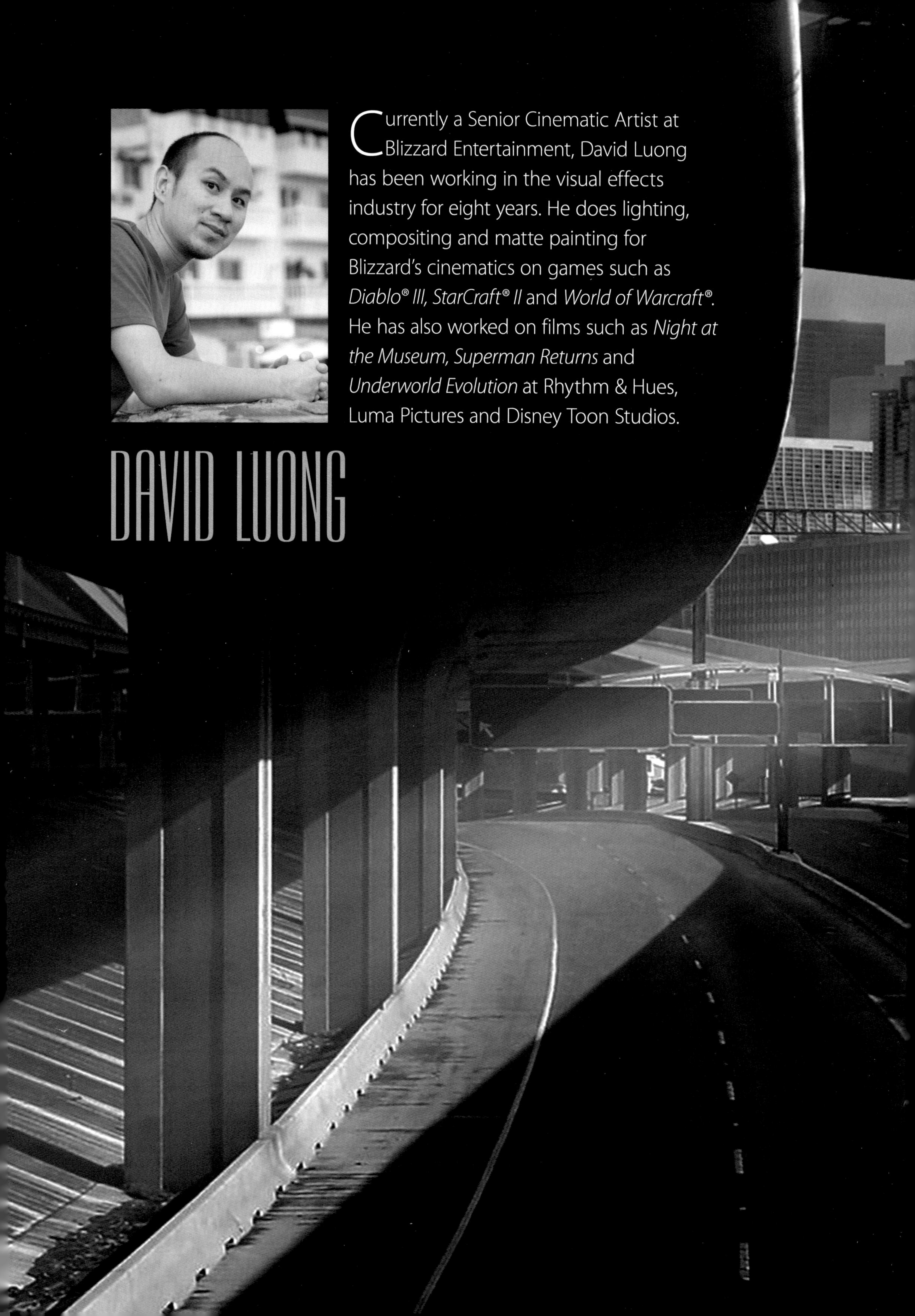

Currently a Senior Cinematic Artist at Blizzard Entertainment, David Luong has been working in the visual effects industry for eight years. He does lighting, compositing and matte painting for Blizzard's cinematics on games such as *Diablo® III*, *StarCraft® II* and *World of Warcraft®*. He has also worked on films such as *Night at the Museum*, *Superman Returns* and *Underworld Evolution* at Rhythm & Hues, Luma Pictures and Disney Toon Studios.

DAVID LUONG

Claustrophobic Overpass
A matte painting I created for a music video called 'Chains of Humanity' by God Forbid. After painting out the cars and the signs, I added in the additional overpasses in the top, right and left sides, as well as a cityscape in the background with strong light rays pouring in. CG people would later be added on the ground.

DAVID LUONG

CONTENTS

DAVID LUONG BIOGRAPHY

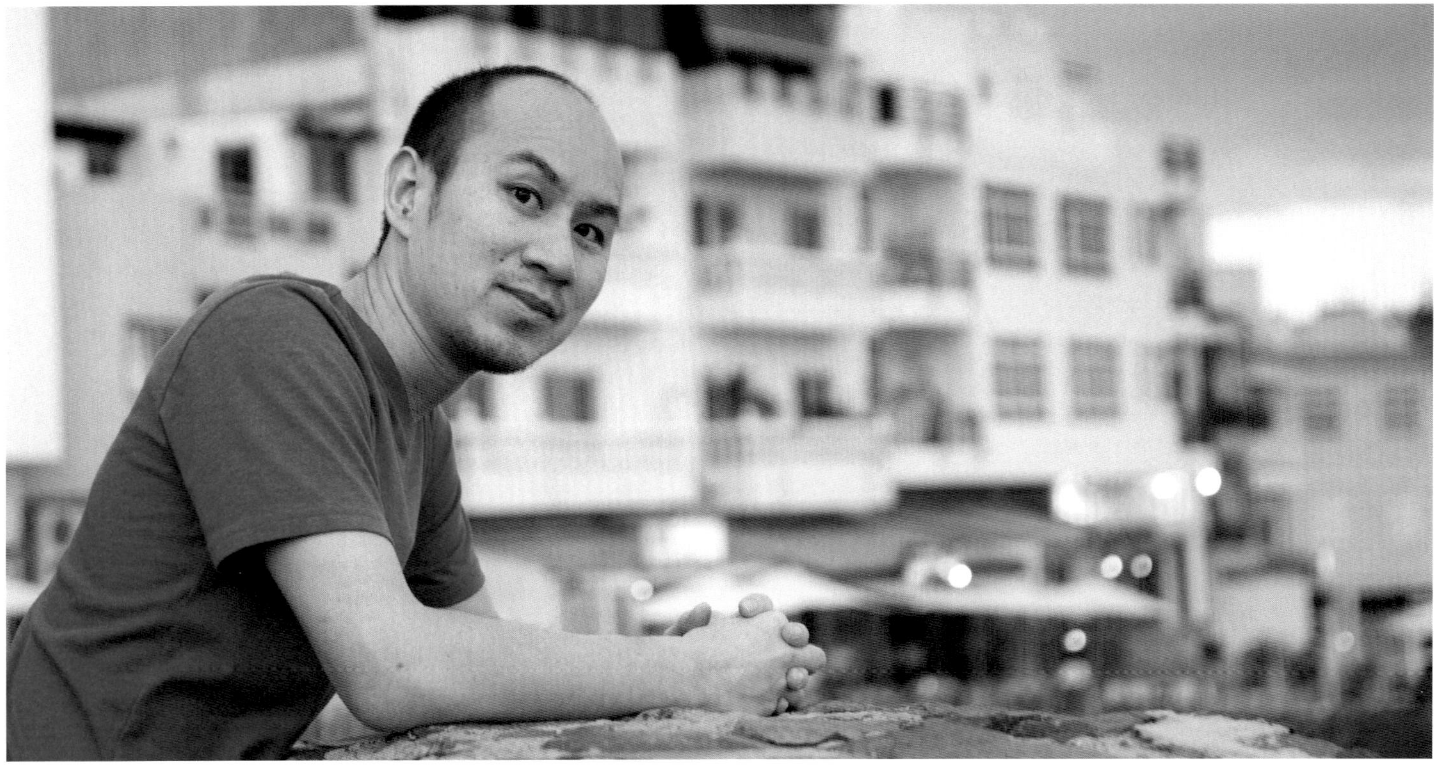

MY EARLY YEARS

My family is from Vietnam. Like many, they were heavily affected by the war and by the middle of the 1970s wanted to escape the country. Things were very hard for them, and I remember my dad telling me the craziest stories about how they tried to make ends meet.

By the early 1980s the family had finally saved enough money to leave, and wanted to get to America to make a better life. Many of my relatives left Vietnam also, but were scattered across the world to places like The Netherlands and Australia. I was born just a couple of months after my family arrived in Orange County, California – the first of my generation born outside of Vietnam.

When I was six or seven, I played Nintendo games such as *Legend of Zelda®*, *Final Fantasy* and *Mario Brothers* all the time with my friends and family. Later, I played lots of PC games – *Warcraft® II*, *StarCraft®*, *Diablo®*, *EverQuest* and *Ultima*. Playing these games inspired my interest in computers and how they worked, which naturally became my hobby. I also loved movies and watched a lot of them growing up. One of my favourites was *The NeverEnding Story* from way back in 1984. I watched in over and over again, losing myself in its fantastical world. I just loved the visuals – the matte painting and other visual effects – and it opened the door for me to other fantasy movies.

In early high school I took a journalism class and began to get interested in the graphics side of the school newspaper. During this time I was introduced to Photoshop, and I taught myself typography, graphic design and photograph manipulation, and created some headlines for the newspaper. The newspaper's editors thought my headlines were good enough to enter them in national competitions for high school journalism; I won a national design award for a website I designed and built.

My brothers are dentists and my family wanted me to be a dentist also. So I took biology classes at university and minored in other subjects like music, which I enjoyed. But I was depressed about where I was heading, and I realized that I need to follow my heart. I combined computer arts, movies and games and thought, "Why not try animation?" In my second year of college I applied to the Academy of Art University in San Francisco. My brothers and sisters helped me convince my parents to let me go to San Francisco to attend the Academy. Luckily I had relatives living there, which helped my cause. I started a four-year program, beginning with perspective drawing, figure drawing, anatomy, art theory and clay modeling. I loved it!

TEACHERS

In the second half of my four-year course we were introduced to computer classes. I took a lot of 3D classes, compositing classes, particles/fluid simulation classes, and had my first matte painting class with Aaron Muszalski. I started doing graduate-level classes even though I was an undergraduate.

I was so inspired by the city of San Francisco and the beautiful culture there. I began combining everything I knew and started creating my own video projects. I would rent time at the Green Screen Studio at the Academy and bring together a little crew of friends and shoot videos. I did all the

compositing and matte painting myself, which was a great learning experience. One of my productions, *Temple of Knowledge* (2004), is on my website. It was used by the Academy to promote the school on national cable TV. The matte painting I did for this production was my first.

While playing Blizzard games like *Warcraft® III* and *World of Warcraft®*, I'd watch the cinematics and get super excited and feel the need to work in that industry one day. I had the same feelings when I watched movies like *The Lord of the Rings*, which is my second favorite fantasy movie. I was also inspired by films like *Jurassic Park* and *Terminator 2* from the early 1990s and *The Matrix* in the late 1990s – films at the pinnacle of movie VFX at the time. I told myself that if I ever graduated I would apply to work at either Blizzard Entertainment or Weta Digital, two of my favorite studios – one for games and one for film.

STUDIOS

After graduating in 2005, I applied for positions all over the world. My first response was from DisneyToon Studios at Burbank in California, offering me a two-week stint on the movie *Tinkerbell*. After that I was interviewed by Luma Pictures, who reviewed my reel and said to come back the following Monday. I drove the hour and a half up to Santa Monica ready to start that Monday, but when I arrived the VFX supervisor asked me why I was there – the producer hadn't hired anyone yet! I had thought they had given me the job. Anyway, after a lot of phone calls, they finally decided to take me on.

Then came Rhythm & Hues, where I worked on a number of productions including *Garfield 2, Night at the Museum* (compositing) and *Superman Returns*. Here, I met Dylan Cole – an awesome artist (you can see some of his matte paintings in my and Milan's Gallery of Invited Artists). Dylan shared a secret with me about how he'd made a lot of snow in a matte painting using mostly baking soda, then photographed it in miniature scale and painted over it in Photoshop.

After Rhythm & Hues I updated my reel and submitted my matte painting/compositing reel to a number of places, including to my friend Jason Hill who I worked with at Rhythm & Hues. He had recently started working as a lighting artist at Blizzard Entertainment. After seeing my reel he said, "Oh yeah, this is cool, this is the kind of fantasy style that we want for the next cinematic. I'll definitely try to help you out."

In October 2006, Blizzard called me for an interview for my dream job. At the interview I walked around the studios amazed and inspired by everything hanging on the walls. Two weeks later I was hired and I've been there ever since.

SOFTWARE

At Blizzard I use Photoshop for painting and textures, Maya for lighting, Renderman for rendering, and then NUKE for compositing. I do use After Effects a bit, but not to the same extent as NUKE, which is just so much more powerful for bringing images together. I do a lot of my projection paintings in NUKE as well. I paint them up in Photoshop and then project them back into NUKE using some simple geometry or some cards (flat planes that represent a vertical space in the 3D scene for the camera to project on to). It's the same when I create something in Maya – I can create it quickly then fold it up and export it as a .obj file into NUKE, where I can control it better and faster.

PROJECTS

My first project at Blizzard was the teaser trailer for *StarCraft® II* in 2006. My second project, from 2007 to 2008, was on *World of Warcraft®: Wrath of the Lich King*. I worked on the cinematic from the beginning to end. I was very excited about this project because I have always loved the game franchise. I put all of my years of passion into my work on it.

The director, Jeff Chamberlain, was really

Chicago set extension
I shot a photo in downtown Chicago and gave it a new skyline with towering buildings based on other parts of downtown Chicago. It was interesting to play with a new composition here, and follow the correct perspective and colors of the new painted buildings into the original ones. *[left]*

cool, and directed me to do lots of field tests and color tests and wedges to see what he liked as far as environments and skies, and I added my own concept work as well. I would take Arthas, the main character in *World of Warcraft*®, and draw on top of him, adding hair and capes and snow, to see what he looked like. I also did the lighting, matte painting and compositing for Arthas where he holds up his sword and where the dragon pops up out of the ground. This was the first time I had worked on the big marketing posters. Arthas was rendered in gigantic 6k resolution and I painted on top of him and matte painted the background. This was the first big poster image I worked on at Blizzard.

Recent projects I've worked on at Blizzard have been *Diablo® III, World of Warcraft®: Mists of Pandaria* and *StarCraft® II*. On *Diablo*, I did a lot of compositing work including on the shots of Diablo fighting the angel Imperious (the main bad guy in the game). I worked with Nick Carpenter a lot, trying to nail down the look and feel of the environment in the cinematic. I also worked on the environment for the church, which was the introduction cinematic for that game (you can see a couple of these images on pages 6–7). It was great working with the environment team, who would build up a fresh model for me to paint on and enhance, and then I would put in the practical effects, composite my own layers of atmosphere, and do the matte painting.

During the *Mists of Pandaria* project I collaborated with the director and the art director on the three main characters, the Panda, the Orc and the human, and helped establish their final looks. At the same time, I worked on the matte painting for the mysterious island, which was a big camera move, starting in the top left-hand corner and panning down to the island.

TYPICAL WORKFLOW

Usually we have a concept from a concept artist and we take that and do rough mapping with textures, taking references from photographs or paintings, anything we can find, and then we work on it in Photoshop. We get that approved by the art director and the director. If they say it's good to go then I start to model out anything I need as far as simple geometry in Maya or NUKE, and then start testing it back and forth from Photoshop to NUKE to Maya and back again – to make sure it projects correctly. Then I get feedback from the art director/director and iterate until they're happy.

INSPIRATION

In 2005 I was still in school when the first *d'artiste: Matte Painting* book came out, which featured Dylan Cole along with Alp Altiner and Chris Stoski. Dylan was my favorite because he had just worked on *The Lord of the Rings*. I emailed him and asked if he could take a look at my portfolio. He actually emailed me back, which really inspired me to continue with my work. I had thought a lot of top artists might be too busy to talk to me because I was just starting out, but Dylan's response showed me that many artists want to give back to the community. I am so thankful that Dylan did that for me, and now I make sure I do the same for people who ask me for advice.

THE FUTURE

I think matte painting is going much more towards a totally 3D world. A lot of matte paintings are now fully 3D, and I really have to push myself to keep up with it. The software releases are always exciting, and that is good for matte painting.

In the future I'd like to move into an art director role, where I establish a vision of my own and supervise other artists, working with them as a team to figure out visually what is appealing for a cinematic or film.

WOULD YOU RATHER

Slay the dragon, or rescue the princess?
Slay the dragon. There is a bunch more loot to be had when you slay the dragon!

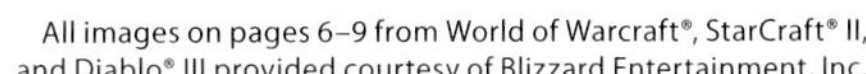

Diablo® III: Church side-view final composite still
The church was modeled/textured by Seth Thompson, and the ground was modeled/textured by David Lesperance. I created the background matte painting and added additional texture onto the castle, as well as lighting the 3D environment, rendering and compositing the matte painting to final.
[below]

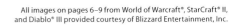

World of Warcraft®: Wrath of the Lich King® mountainside poster
A high-resolution poster I created with the help of Reo Prendergast (modeled/textured the Frostmourne sword), Tyler Hunter (modeled/textured Arthas), and Jeff Chamberlain (art direction). Final color correct by Jonathan Berube. I did the lighting, rendering, compositing, additional texture work and painting, as well as the matte painting background. This poster was created to be used in marketing material for the game.
[far left]

StarCraft® II: Raynor above the clouds poster
Marketing came to us to create a new kind of cardboard cut-out stand that could be used to advertise the game's release. It would also be used for many other marketing materials for *StarCraft® II: Wings of Liberty*. The character Raynor was posed by Aaron Chan; Raynor modeled/textured by Fausto De Martini; battlecruisers modeled/textured by Jeremy Gritton; and art direction by Jeff Chamberlain. I did the lighting, rendering, additional texturing of Raynor, matte painting and compositing for this large-scale image.
[left]

StarCraft® II: Heart of the Swarm™ Kerrigan victory poster
This is a matte painting based on Fabio Zungrone's and Levi Peterffy's work. Buildings modeled/textured by the Cinematics Environment Team; the character Kerrigan modeled/textured by Xin Wang; and Kerrigan lighting/rendering by Kaz Shimada. I took these assets and painted on top of them then re-lit Kerrigan and some of the city, and added in the additional explosion element and mutalisks flying. This matte painting was created to be used in marketing material and behind the box image for the game.
[above]

StarCraft® II: Raynor above the clouds poster background
This is the background matte painting by itself for the *StarCraft® II: Wings of Liberty* poster. The inspiration for the multiple planets in the back came from watching *Avatar* just before creating this matte painting.
[left]

Personal short film – 'The NeverEnding Story: The Renewal'
These images come from a short story I wrote during my early years of matte painting. I created all of the matte paintings in a 360 view for an all-green screen shot set. Eloise Honrada played the Empress and Ron Coloma played the Bearer of Auryn. It was a pleasure to work with principal photography that had consistent texture, lighting and colors on all four sides of the environment.

Top row, left to right: The left side of the environment with the actors, showing the golden colors of the sky with the deeper blue colors of the shadows; close-up shot of the left side of the environment with the actors; wide establishing shot of the matte painting with the Ivory Tower lit. *Bottom row, left to right:* The behind matte painting for the actors as they walk up the steps to the plateau; the left side of the environment matte painting by itself; the right side of the environment matte painting by itself. I photographed a rock that had the same outdoor lighting as the matte painting and color corrected it to match the existing matte painting.
[above]

Moonlight of a Chinese Night
A personal matte painting based on a photograph I shot during the daytime in China, which I then converted to a night-time shot with a replaced sky. Making the moon a little bigger surrounded by moonlit clouds brings a fantastical feel to this piece.
[above]

Temple of Knowledge
This is an image I created some time ago, inspired by *The Lord of the Rings* movies. I wanted the adventurer in the foreground – an elven archer played by my friend – to look outwards at a temple full of the wonders and knowledge of the land, in a golden dusk setting with strong contrast and light rays pouring down from the sky.
[left]

Horizon of Heaven
The inspiration for this piece was to show what the entrance to Heaven might look like. It would be high up in the sky between a layer of big, voluminous clouds, nearby to an enlarged sun in an endless sea of sky. The colors would be always golden, the sun casting strong, warm orange light fading into violets and blues of complementary shadow tones.
[facing page]

Overlooking the City
I made this matte painting for the music video 'Chains of Humanity' by God Forbid. The original base photo was shot by Mark Duckworth high up on a building top in San Francisco. I painted out the signs in the buildings and replaced the sky, as well as added new buildings to support the downtown area.
[above]

Hidden Valley
This matte painting was created specifically to enter into the *d'Artiste: Matte Painting 2* book and I was happy to know that it was accepted. It goes to show that this book series does inspire other artists greatly, and now it's come full circle. The inspiration behind this image is the idea of finding a valley that is as majestic as it is untouched by civilization. As far as the eye can see, there exists a blanket of trees and water providing a home to many things.
[above]

Origin, Nature's Reclamation
I created this matte painting for a short film and as a study of plants/overgrowth painted on top of buildings. Humans have left this place to rot after a corporation has run it into the ground due to greed. Now all that's left is the organic life that was previously there, reclaiming its reign on the land.
[left]

TUTORIAL 1: The Ivory Castle

My partner Steve and I went to Germany in 2011. It is a magnificent country and I was able to take some great scenic photographs near the Neuschwanstein Castle that I intended to use for a matte painting, which I will go through in this tutorial.

For the matte painting, I chose a base plate showing Steve in a dried-up gorge, with Steve looking out into the distance. I wanted to create a lush mountaintop that he would be standing on as a warrior from a time long past, with his pet dog Xena resting with him after a long journey. After fighting many battles the warrior seeks sanctuary from the darkness of the land. A great castle lying in the distance represents a safe haven for him and Xena.

This tutorial will cover putting together a forest and mountainous landscape with some waterfalls, as well as integrating 3D elements and an entirely hand-painted castle using Photoshop. All will match the lighting and color of the plate and overall scene. Final output resolution is 1920 x 1080 pixels, but we'll be painting at double resolution so the paint work will scale down well.

I am a big geek when it comes to J.R.R. Tolkien's Middle Earth. I also grew up loving *The NeverEnding Story*. In this tutorial I incorporate visuals from these two fantasy worlds to create the following scene – beautiful waterfalls surrounding abandoned elven-like structures, serene in late afternoon light, offsetting the centerpiece, the Ivory Castle, which was built by people who engage in pure and expressive forms. The Ivory Castle is inspired by the Ivory Tower from *The NeverEnding Story*.

Software used: Photoshop CS6, CINEMA 4D R14

1. I start with the base plate positioned compositionally, with the castle on the right and a rough horizon line to guide the piece. I'm planning to have my warrior standing on top of the ground here in the foreground, like in the base image.

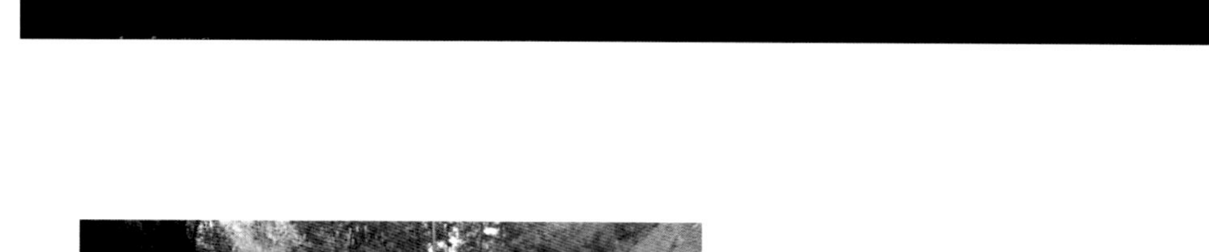

2. Here is a secondary plate looking down from on top of the Bavarian hills. I paint in some values and a silhouette of the castle, which I will later refine. This will sit nicely on top of the forested hill complete with a little curvy path winding its way towards the castle (the path will also be refined later). The houses and structures in this base image will be painted out.

3. Some photos I took around the area give me a base reference of what I envisage in terms of lighting, color and texture. The waterfalls will also be integrated into the painting, falling down from the mountains.

4. I mask out Steve (my future warrior) using the Lasso tool. I do a rough placement of where I want the cliff to start tapering off, positioning it so the lighting will match the background plate. The idea is to have the foreground in shadow.

5. I do a quick paint out using a soft Eraser tool on the edge of the trees to blend them in with the sky. Using any automatic tool such as the Magic Wand or Channels results in very fringey and white edges on the trees, so I will blend them in later with a sky that is compatible with a bright sky from the tree line plate.

6. This is a reference photo of one of the waterfall elements that I'll be incorporating later. Notice that it's in shadow; later we'll be justifying this using trees on the right.

7. Here I roughly place the previous photo, connecting it to the cliff line. Right now the water looks like it's coming out of nowhere, but I'll be addressing that later.

8. I found another photo in my library that will match the time of day, angle and texture for the left side of this piece. The light is a little strong, and the ground textures aren't lining up yet, so I'll need to grab some more photos to fix this.

9. Here is another element of waterfall I'm going to use that will make for a more interesting composition rather than just having one waterfall element. Again, I choose roughly the same lighting, angle and texture to match the previous ones.

10. I fill the gap between the left side and the waterfall's original location. This will be my base waterfall look for the piece. I'll support it later with an additional waterfall in between the peaks at the cliff in the middle. There's some bounce light of warmth coming into the top of the waters that will match nicely with the texture right above it in the hot sun spot.

11. Here are some trees I'll be using on the right-hand side as blockers of light, and the suggestion of many more trees on off-screen right will shadow the foreground.

12. Due to the nasty edges of the tree against an unkeyable background, I use the Eraser tool coupled with a frayed custom brush and pen pressure sensitivity to achieve the edges needed here on both trees.

13. Here is the third and final waterfall, cascading down the cliffs between the two trees at the end. This waterfall will supply water to the main waterfalls in my piece.

14. Because the cliff is still in shadow here, the element I chose works well. But now I lack mist spraying up from the waterfall. I need some further lighting paint work in front of the waterfall, to imitate the way light rays would reflect off the water's spray.

15. Here I'm going to use the previous waterfall image's details of mist and spray and paint them back in with a frayed brush, similar to the one used on the tree.

16. This is the result of the paint-back, with some supporting mist and spray on the third waterfall as it falls down to the ground.

17. I do a general clean up of matte edges, painting them to blend with other images between borders, move around some elements to make more sense compositionally, and adjust some black levels. The left side now has a conclave, with some shafts of light hitting the middle cliff hill, then going through and hitting the trees on the bottom left. For optimal silhouettes, I place a shadowed tree against a lit tree.

18. Now I can go into C4D and get to some lighting and rendering of stock elven buildings. I position them to about the same horizon line and angle them according to the lighting of the base matte painting. The late afternoon warm light is coming from off-screen right. After lighting and rendering the 3D models from C4D, I bring them into Photoshop for color corrections and paint work to integrate them into the environment.

19. I boost the elven buildings' black levels depending on their surrounding black levels, mostly lifting the reds and blues. Then I give them an overall green mid-tone, but with slightly more blue the farther they are from the camera (due to the atmospheric perspective such as in the far-right building). I paint in areas of vegetation and mask the trees back on top of the buildings so they sit in naturally.

20. I found a picture of my dog Xena that I will use for this piece. Xena will be sitting there taking a rest, looking at my warrior, who will be looking across to the castle.

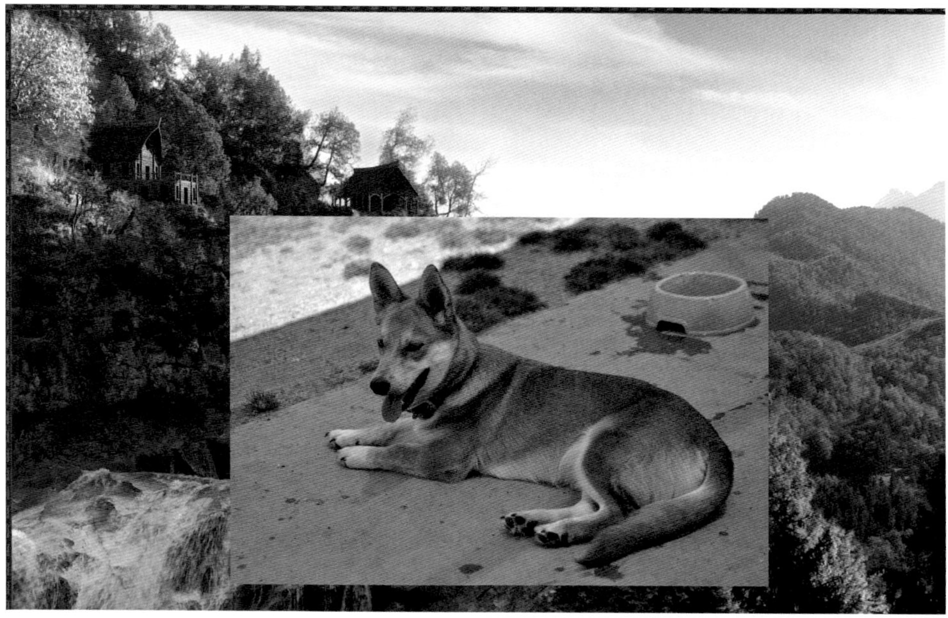

21. After masking out Xena, I place her on the rock that fits her angle, paint in her shadow and the reflection occlusion from the environment from her onto the rock, and do overall color correction of more blue tones using Curves. Then I paint in some blue sky reflection on Xena's back to match what's happening with the rocks she's lying on.

22. I'm going to work on the sky some more as it's a bit plain blue. I will use this photo of a baseball field nearby my house as I like the wispy clouds in it. I'll later reinforce it with more light-hearted puffy clouds on the horizon near the castle.

23. Using the Eraser tool again, I carefully mask in the clouds and blend the new sky in with the previous sky. This should match the color and lighting of the base plate.

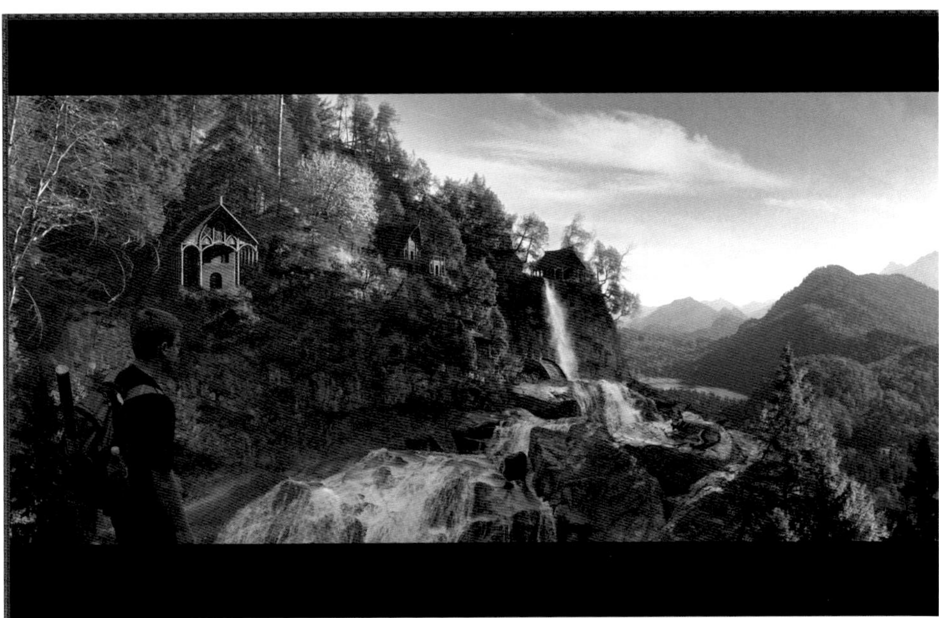

24. To transform Steve into a warrior, I photograph him holding a shield at roughly the same angle as the backpack on his back in the original photo, in the same type of lighting and environment.

25. I mask in the shield and then paint in the shadows to integrate the shield on to Steve's back, and remove the backpack.

26. No warrior goes with a weapon! Here I follow the same process as with the shield. The sword will be placed between the shield and the warrior's back.

27. I mask the sword, and place, color correct and paint in shadows for ambient occlusion on the bottom of the sword.

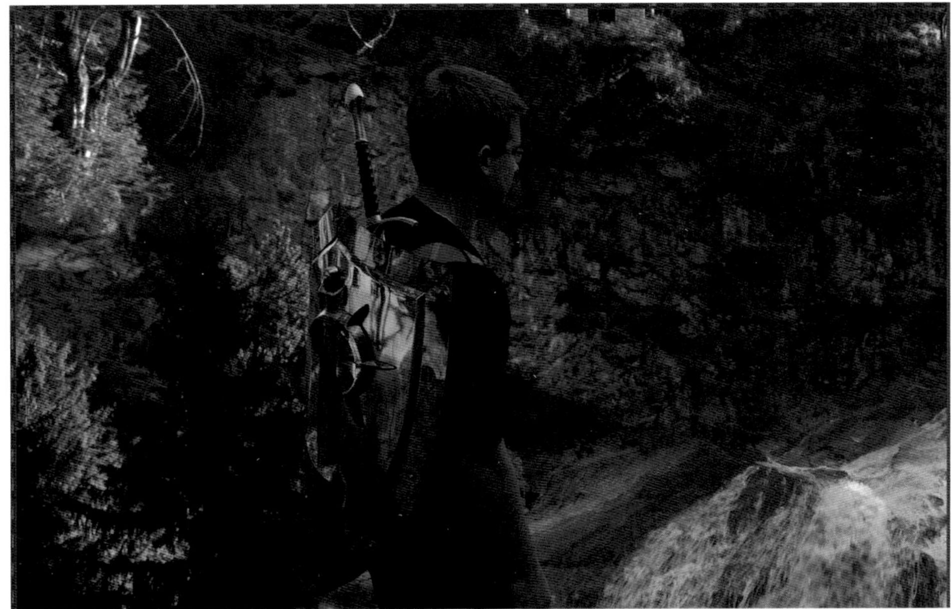

28. Now I go back to the wide angle of the piece, and I can see everything in place in the foreground, as well as an additional sword the warrior is holding as a resting sword. Here the rough concept of the castle is back, as well as the little painted-in pathway and some watch towers on the castle.

29. I begin by laying down more correct values on the concept, sampling the color of the shadows nearby. I won't worry about lighting or texture now, just some base values.

30. After painting in the values, I turn off the outline layer of the castle to do some final painting and texturing work. I'm mostly using the default round brush with pen pressure for the opacity setting. I've got each of these building elements on a separate layer, so later I can move them around, duplicate them, and further paint on them with ease. Notice that the domes are curved upward according to the horizon and our eye level. Be sure to pay attention to these types of things while painting.

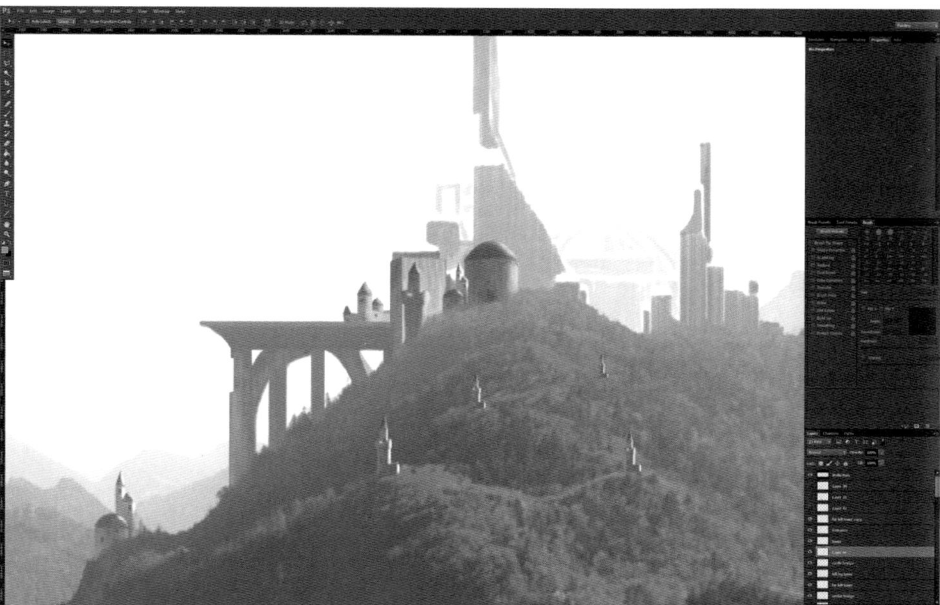

31. I take some of the same structures on the left and use them as new buildings on the right. I paint in additional texture, value work, and transform them to fit into my earlier concept.

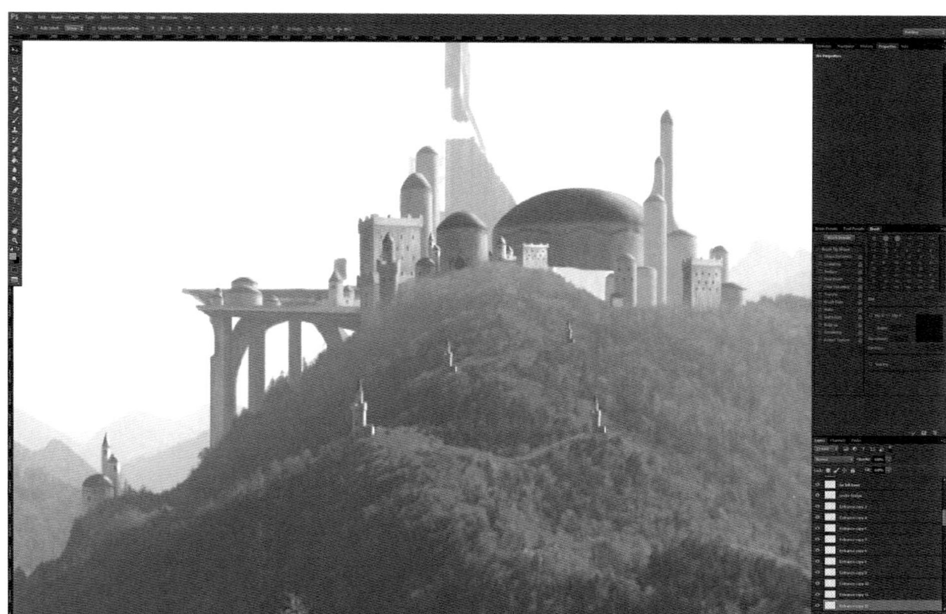

32. I continue adding in the value work of the entire castle, fully realizing the original concept. I take some of the dome-shaped buildings in the foreground, duplicate them, and move them behind, and paint them more on top to match the atmospheric perspective as well as the lighting. I am zoomed in about 300% so the full resolution won't be this close. Since our target is 1920 x 1080 pixels, painting at double resolution such as this is highly beneficial. Shrinking it down later will be photo-real as long as I have the right values, texturing and lighting.

33. Here I paint in the final rooftops of the castle, and the curvy nature of the tallest tower. Because the main tower wasn't exactly straight down due to its curves, I have to take particular care in painting this, using Lassos as a guide and a feathered edge to achieve a consistent look for the curved surfaces.

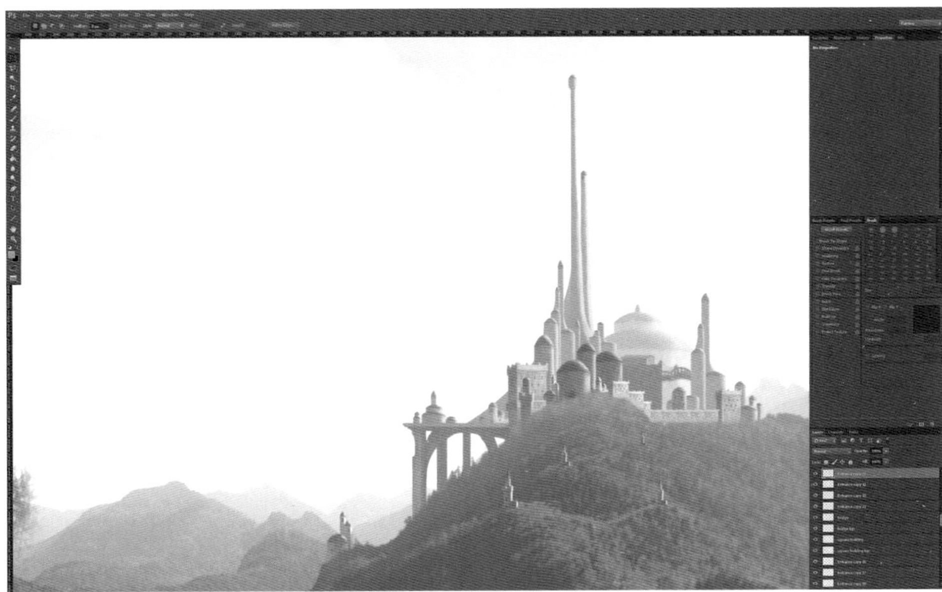

34. Zooming back out, I add in additional curved support structures for the bridge on the left and a curved buttress on the right, as well as some buttresses on the main tower support.

35. Now I refocus back onto the sky and add in the puffy cumulus clouds I mentioned earlier. This photo matches the lighting and perspective well after positioning, so I'm going to use parts of it as additional texture for the sky.

36. I erase out the areas I want to keep for the puffy clouds, making sure the lighting and values match after color correcting them in. They will frame the castle nicely, so I make a gap between two puffy clouds with a tapered look to give them a nice composition. I also do some general clean up of both the tree line edges and the overall image.

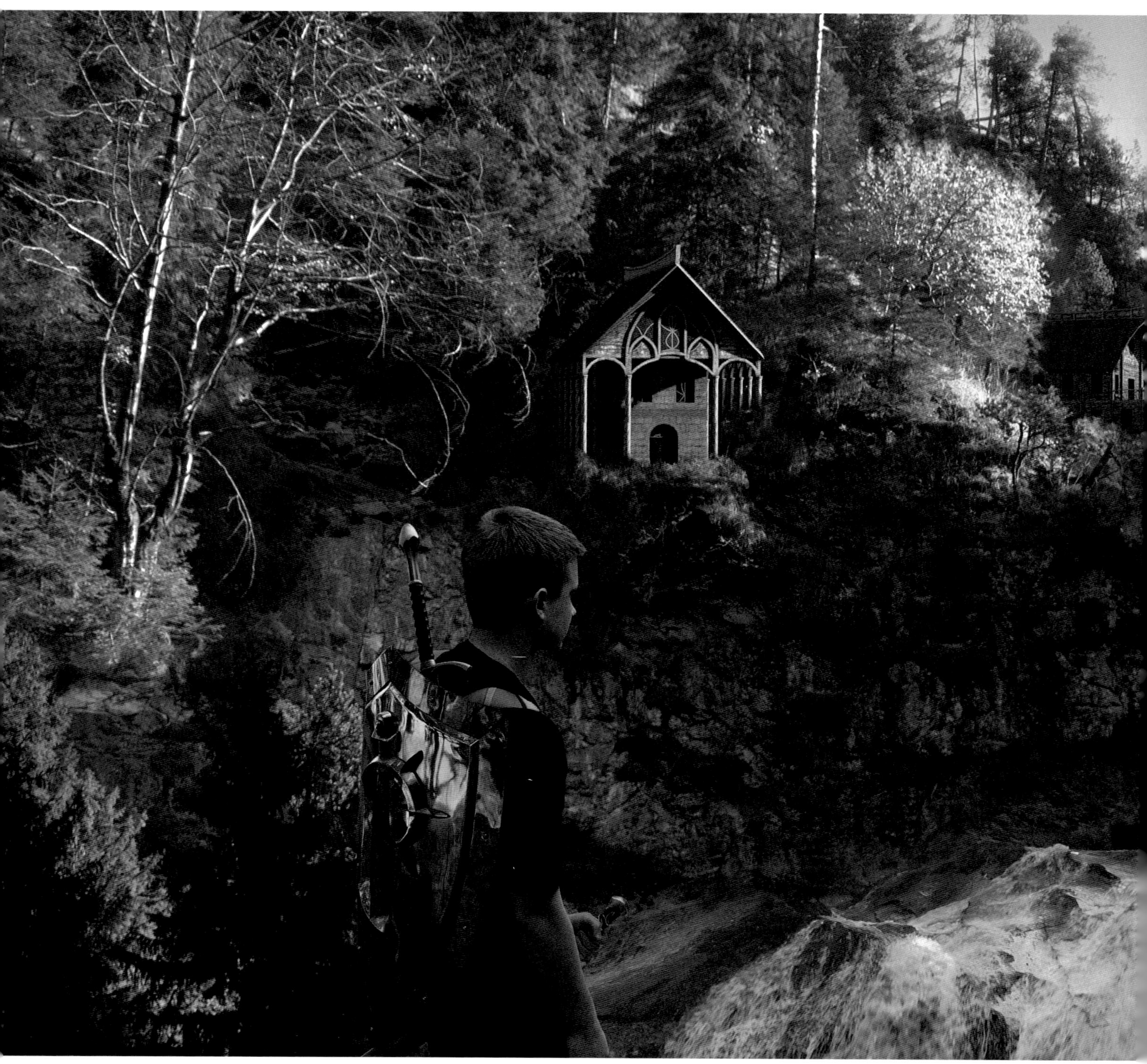

37. The final image of the Ivory Castle with everything together. I do some final color correction for that warm afternoon palette feeling and some cloning and patch-up work to improve the image. Subtle light rays were painted in for some additional atmosphere.

TUTORIAL 2: Skyward Life

I want to present a simple matte painting for this tutorial and focus on sky creation. This is a variation on a previous work I did for a commercial. I was given a reference sky, and from there I created a focal point in the center of the image (the tree). I stick mostly to Photoshop in this tutorial, but during the project that inspired this tutorial I also used CINEMA 4 to light and render the tree.

The inspiration for this image is the time 30 minutes or so before the sun sets – the 'golden hour', when the sky is awash with wildly saturated colors of golden-yellows, oranges, reds, pinks, blues and purples. I want this to be a majestic sky produced from a fantastical color palette, with cumulus thunderclouds clearing after a storm that drenched the young tree that is reaching up to the sky.

The tree will be framed on top of a grassy hill and, in time, more trees will grow to accompany it on its journey. I want this piece to symbolize life yearning for its potential – to always be growing to achieve that potential using the best things available to it.

Software used: Photoshop CS6, CINEMA 4D R14

1. I start out with the reference photo, something that inspires me and can guide me. This image has the horizon I want but the sun is obscured (the sun had already set). I want to have the sun off-screen left, and the image bathed in the last hour of light with puffy rain clouds and a ground plane and support for the tree (the focal point). My aim is 1080 pixels HD resolution, so the base plate, photo elements and the final matte painting will be at least double this resolution (approximately 4K pixels wide).

2. Here is the base plate with the horizon drawn out. I'm going to remove much of the background tree line and just keep what's below the horizon line.

3. Using the Lasso tool, I manually extract the back line of the tree. After extracting all around it, I feather the mask by .25 pixels by right clicking on the mask and then choosing Feather. I click on the Layer Mask to mask this portion out.

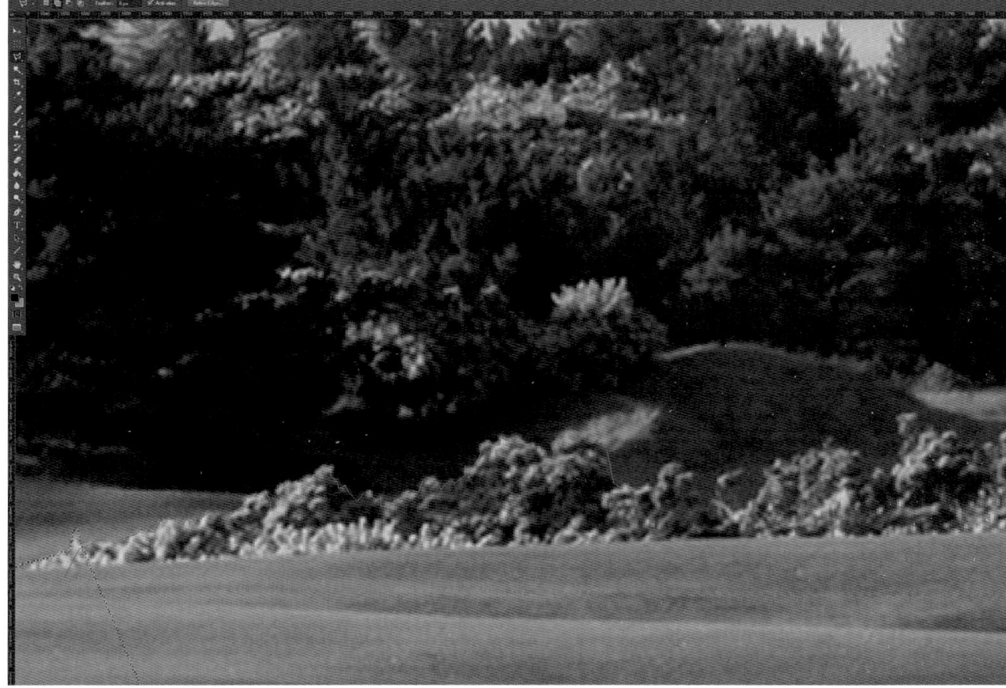

4. Here is what the masked-out hill is on top of black; it has clean edges and represents out-lighting for everything else.

5. This is my reference for the sky. The gradient goes from orange to yellow, to a pinkish color, then to teal and blue. This is the basic color palette I'm going to use for my clouds and the sky.

6. I've placed the sky behind the foreground plate and brightened it up a bit. It works well with the foreground. When choosing a time of day to match, stick to within a few hours of that time. The sky gradient in this piece is after sunset but I can cheat a bit and it'll still work for this pre-sunset time.

7. I shot this from my backyard of some clouds after a storm. It was about an hour before sunset – exactly the time I need. It's important to keep a huge library of many types of textures and photos to use in your matte paintings. Here I match up the horizon line and the approximate position of the sun.

8. I use the Eraser tool to mask out the areas I want to keep (the areas I don't want are blackened).

9. With the sky extracted, next I find some middle and right elements to support my sky.

10. This is another photo I shot in the same sky but at a different angle, so the lighting and clouds work well as they're consistent. The sun position doesn't match, but I'm cheating a bit and just using the right side of this photo for some texture.

11. Here it is extracted, and what's left now is the middle part of the sky. I want something that will frame the tree in the middle.

12. I found this photo with very 'golden hour' colors. I'll be extracting certain areas of the cloud using a soft Brush tool, and then color correcting it into the existing sky.

13. The middle sky has a nice framing element to it as it curves up to the right.

14. The middle sky patch is color corrected in with some erasing of parts to blend them in.

15. I add in another patch of sky on the right to soften the busy look on that side of the image.

16. Here is the sky extracted and color corrected to fit my palette.

17. I add in another cloud patch to the right to reinforce the puffy framing clouds.

18. The clouds extracted and color corrected.

19. Here is another photo to use, cheating on the lighting. I'm going to use these sloping clouds for some texture on the left side of my sky.

20. The clouds color corrected in and extracted for additional detail.

21. This patch will be used as a bridge between the left, middle and right side clouds, reinforcing the lighting.

22. The cloud patched in and color corrected. Notice how previously this cloud was more straight-edged, now it is puffier.

23. I mirror the previous photo to get some lower hitting, closer-in perspective clouds for the top right of the sky.

24. The patch color corrected and extracted.

25. The top right of the sky was looking too teal and too busy, so I tone it down a bit using a blue color on a layer on top of everything in Normal Blend mode.

26. In this step I extract some mountain shapes and paint in silhouettes of mountains on the horizon to give the piece a greater sense of scale and distance. I give it a gradient from a more orange light color to a cooler, purple tone in the distance, representing atmospheric perspective and the sun's rays glaring through the moisture-laden air.

27. I do overall contrast and color corrections to the sky to bring everything together.

28. Now that I have my sky colors finalized, I color correct the ground. The ground gives me a general horizon and lighting while the sky gives me the colors – now I need to match them together. I lift the shadows a bit and give them a slight purple/blue tone, while giving the key light a little more of a red tone using Curves.

29. I paint in some subtle light rays emitting from the sun, which is out of frame left. I use a brighter yellow in the sky near the light source as my color for the light rays. Then I paint radially outwards, contouring the shapes of the clouds as if the clouds are shadowing the light. This gives the middle patch of clouds more reason to be hit with light that's been traveling from the sun, unfettered, through the sky.

30. Now I save out a .tif file of the sky and bring it into C4D as a background image plane so I can set up a tree I've chosen from the XfrogPlants model pack. To simulate an environment light, I light the tree with two lights – a warm spotlight key and a cooler soft box on the right-hand side.

31. I render it out and paint in the final details, as well as color correct it to match the colors of the ground and sky – red/orange key light and cooler blue/purple shadow environment light.

32. I paint in a dirt patch at the base of my tree to 'seat it in'. It is more gravely than some older dirt, which gives it a little more attention due to its brighter tone.

33. Because I don't need to model the ground to match it in 3D, I choose the faster route by duplicating the tree and replacing it with a solid color that represents the shadow color in the existing scene. Here I sample the shadow tone from the hills.

34. I transform the tree, angle it, and squish it to fit the ground plane and light angle direction. Because I sampled the colors correctly for the shadow, they meld together with the existing shadows.

35. Because the contour of the ground isn't flat, I use the Puppet Warp Transform tool and add joints to the shadow layer. Then I move them around to match the bumps and undulations of the ground.

36. The final image with additional black level tweaks, matte adjustments, and the adding in of some tree roots to 'ground' the tree some more. That completes my Skyward Life tutorial matte painting, with an epic sky, a tree focal point, and a fantastical color palette of the 'golden hour'.

TUTORIAL 3: Monolith City

This tutorial is the most extensive in terms of use of software, knowledge, and the time it takes to execute. It is generated from a guerrilla/indie-style approach, which involved going out with my own camera, shooting a live action plate and doing everything from match-moving it, matte painting in Photoshop, creating 3D elements, lighting, rendering and rotoscoping, to projecting the images on to cards and then doing the final compositing.

I went to shoot some videos on my Nikon D800E as well as on my iPhone 5, but in the end the right moment was caught on my camera phone and so I use that as my base plate footage (it's still full HD at 1080 pixels). I support the base plate later with my D800E, with high-resolution 36-megapixel stills shot back on location, which I use as textures for this matte painting. There were some blurry artifacts and rolling shutter problems on the camera phone so I rotoscoped Xena the dog completely and replaced her with an integrated matte painting environment.

I want this matte painting to encompass not just a regular still, illustrative 2D painting, but a fully moving live-action matte painting with animated CG elements and camera move. So, throughout the tutorial keep in mind that this is for an animated shot.

Many matte paintings feature people in the shots. In general, I think we could use animals more in visual effects, and I wanted to do one starring my beloved dog, Xena. She will be at the front of the frame, looking out to discover a futuristic alien city ruled over by a circular city high in the sky. The circular city-ship orbits a monolithic mountain that pierces up through the horizon, drawing on an unknown energy. The aliens seem to have populated their own city, perhaps by experimenting with how humans live and then cultivating it in a remote area of this deserted planet. Xena observes from a safe distance, but some drones fly by her; luckily she goes unnoticed!

I want to generate an alien-looking landscape but also integrate it into the plate so the original still has some resemblance in the final. The cityscape and the circle city present a great opportunity to use Greyscalegorilla's City Kit to produce the final look.

Software used: Photoshop CS6, CINEMA 4D R14, NUKEX 7.0

1. To shoot my live-action plate, I walked around with my dog, Xena, and found a field with nice dried grass. I let her wander around on her own and took multiple takes with the camera on my iPhone 5, panning from the ground up to the desired final resting framing. The camera does auto-exposure and auto-focus, so be sure to lock the exposure and focus on your camera. I locked onto the background for both exposure and focus. I did about four or five takes before I stopped and called it a wrap.

I tried to get things in frame that were stable and not moving, so I could get a proper track and get some walking in, which gives the camera XY translation and lets the software calculate parallax correctly. Objects that won't help me in the shot are trees (with moving leaves) and the sky. So I didn't rely on these, but rather on the rocks and parts of the ground that weren't moving, as well as the cars in the background. Due to the camera being a CMOS-type sensor camera, it was prone to rolling shutter, which can give the image a jello-like movement, shearing left and right any vertical lines that are off-center in the frame. It gets worse the more you use a non-stable, hand-held movement, and I had lots of this in my videos. The videos also had some blurriness on the right-hand side of the frame.

So, there are already two problems with shooting this on my camera phone. The idea was to isolate Xena and her shadow completely with rotoscoping, and then come back later and shoot the ground plates again with my high-resolution D800E camera to replace the ground with a matte painted version of it. Some programs such as After Effects and NUKEX have rolling shutter correction plug-ins, but I am going to replace the background entirely anyway and the track is still okay with this amount of rolling shutter.

Note that the video from the iPhone 5 is 1920 x 1080 pixels full HD, which is great but it's also at 30 frames per second. I want it to be filmic, so later I'll re-time this to 24 fps, which is less work in the end but still produces great results.

2. The movie file comes in as inverted in NUKE, so I use the Mirror node to flip it horizontally and vertically to get it looking right. I then write out the native quicktime .mov file to individual 16-bit .exr files. I use 16-bit half with zip (1 scanline) compression for the .exr files. I can read this file sequence as 24 fps (which would give a slight slow-motion effect from 30 fps – totally fine for this project). Individual files will yield better match-moving in programs and better overall file management between programs.

3. After reviewing the video further, I decide to take just 48 frames (2 seconds) of the 285 frames. I edit the rest out. I then do some dirty garbage mattes of Xena and of the ground up through to the sky. I don't want Xena to be included in the track since she's moving, and I don't want the moving leaves and sky in there either, so they also get rotoscoped out. This matte I generated from the rotoscope gets shuffle-copied back into the node stream for the CameraTracker to use.

4. The default setting for the CameraTracker is pretty good already, but I go to the Input Mask menu and change that from none to Source Alpha, which was the garbage matte I created in the last step. Then I go to the Tracking tab and click on Preview Features to see what will be tracked. I set the Number of Features to a healthy 200. The Detection Threshold defaults at .1 but I set it to .7 to remove less solid track features. I bumped up Feature Separation from 12 to 15.

5. After doing this, I can see the trackers with their motion vectors. I go to the Solver tab and input my camera data there. In the Lens tab I leave it on Unknown as it's a camera phone, and then I click Undistort Input at the bottom. I want it undistorted for a 3D scene later on. I click Solve Camera in the CameraTracker tab and the good tracks show up as green, with orange tracks (unsolved) and red tracks (bad tracks). I delete the unsolved tracks. (You can also manually select the tracks in the viewer and delete them, too.) I go to the Refine tab and look at the Solve Error Rate, which is at 3.129 (I want it under .5), so this is no good.

6. I further refine my track by selecting the Error attributes. I adjust the min length (frame count) – the longer the better. Some tracks turn red, and I delete them and then Recalculate Solve and see my Solve Error go down. I do this for Max Track Error and Max Error, and I go as low as I can while still keeping at least 30 tracks on screen. The contact point will be right where Xena is so it's important to keep most of the tracks near her and not worry too much about the farther tracks or tracks in the corner that might get deleted. After adjustments I get the Solve Error down to .369, which is below the magic number of .5. Now I can continue past the Tracker node.

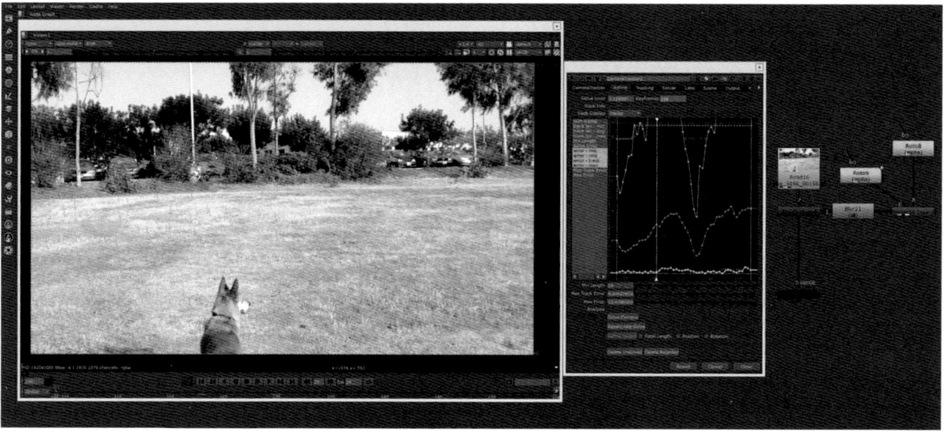

7. Now I want to set the ground plane flat. If I don't do this, the world will be in a strange orientation, which will make it difficult when I want to add 3D objects (which default to the 0,0 origin). I select some of the good points near my live-action object.

8. I double-click on the Scene mode and Camera node, and see that the points are in a weird orientation before I set the ground plane. It is upside down and diagonal! I set the ground plane correctly.

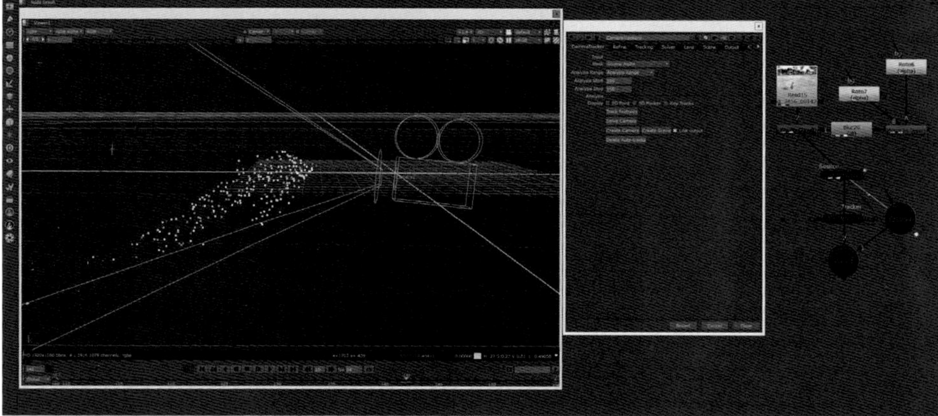

9. I go back to the 3D viewer and see that it's now flat on the 'ground', with the camera upright. Sometimes it bugs out and the camera is upside down, and you have to go back to the previous step and re-set the ground plane.

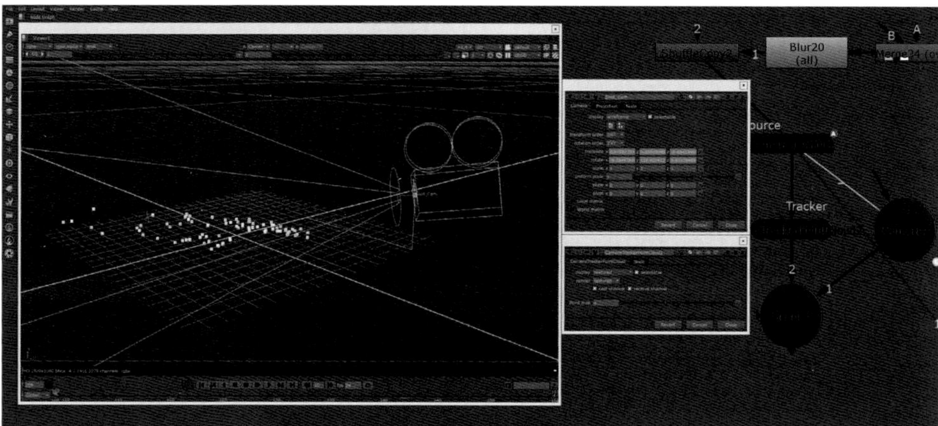

10. I start creating proxy geometry, or test geometry, in my scene, then I create a Checker node to attach to the proxy geometry I created (the proxy geometry could be something simple such as Card or Sphere node). I plug all of this into the Scene node to see where it is in 3D space in relation to my tracked points. I then scrub back and forth in the time line to test it out, to see if the track is accurate. I then plug the background input of my Scanline Render into the CameraTracker node to provide the background. This will allow me to see the proxy geometry I created with the footage I shot to see if it lined up in the track. When I switch back to my 2D viewer I can see the proxy geo with the background. I do a test play in the viewer to see if the track 'sticks' with not much sliding. Remember I got my solver to be under .5 in Error so I don't see much slippage.

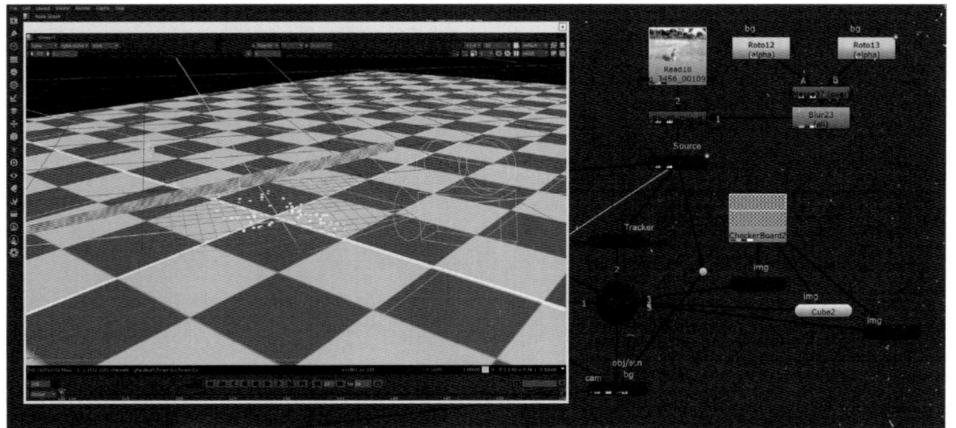

11. Now that my track is solid with proxy geo tested, I do a write-out of the undistorted image into a file sequence. I choose .tif sequence with a _#### file number padding, which C4D likes; 8-bit is fine. I also do a WriteGeo of the scene by connecting it to the Scene node of this tree and write-out an .FBX scene so I can import this into C4D for 3D creation. I export geo/cameras/axes/point clouds.

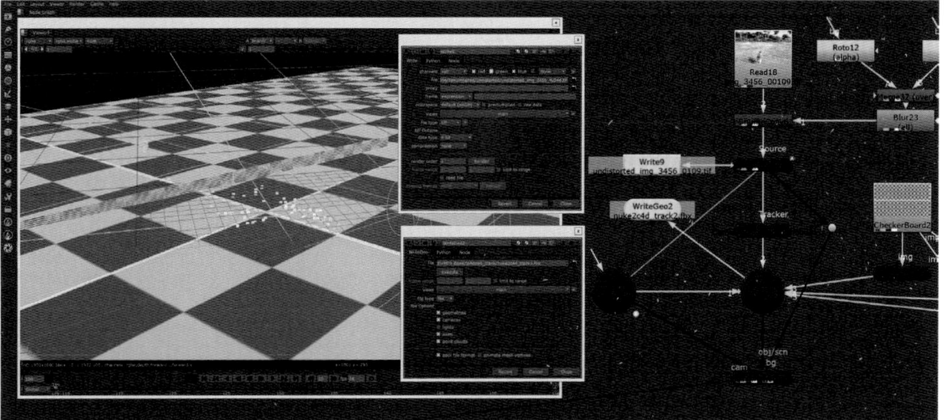

12. Now I will delve into the C4D portion of this tutorial. I open up the .FBX file I saved with the NUKE scene in C4D. I can see all of the point cloud, proxy geo and camera. I go to Cameras and view through the camera of this FBX to see the track. I play it a bit. It looks right, so I move on.

13. I need to make sure my render window and my viewport settings in the scene are set up correctly. I do this by going into the Render Settings and changing the output width/height to 1920 x 1080 pixels, and then making sure I have the Lock Ratio checked so the dimensions stay this way even if I need to render at a different resolution (say for testing at a smaller resolution or at a higher resolution for final printing). This sets my film aspect automatically. I set fps again to 24 and frame range to just Current Frame so I can do test renders. This is a digital progressive video source so Fields are set to none. At this stage I also want to group all of my elements in the FBX file into one group, and then scale them 10 times the amount. NUKE works in centimeters but C4D likes to default to meters – that's why I need to increase the amount by 10 times to fit C4D's default sizes.

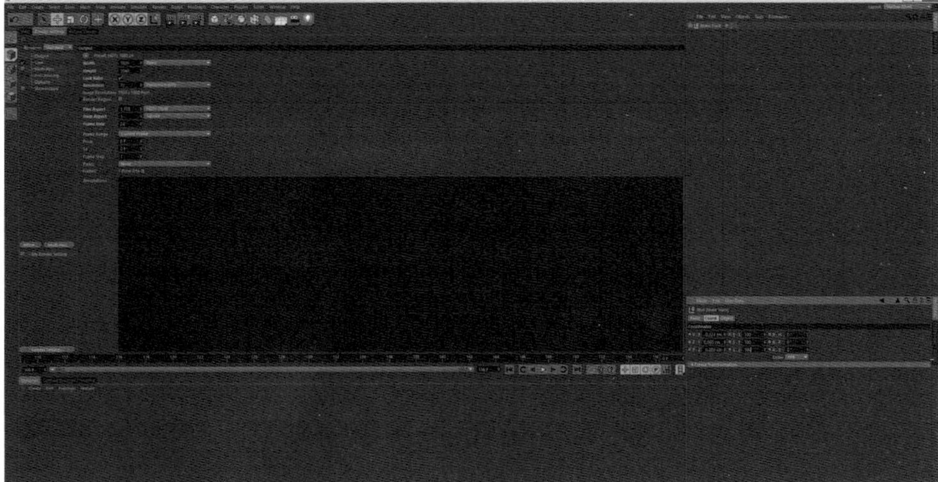

14. I also need to set up the Project Settings correctly or the track will be incorrect. This is an important step. I change the fps to 24 (the same fps as my footage). I change the min/preview time to my start frame (109) and max time/preview max time to 156. I change View Clipping to Medium, otherwise it will start clipping unnaturally.

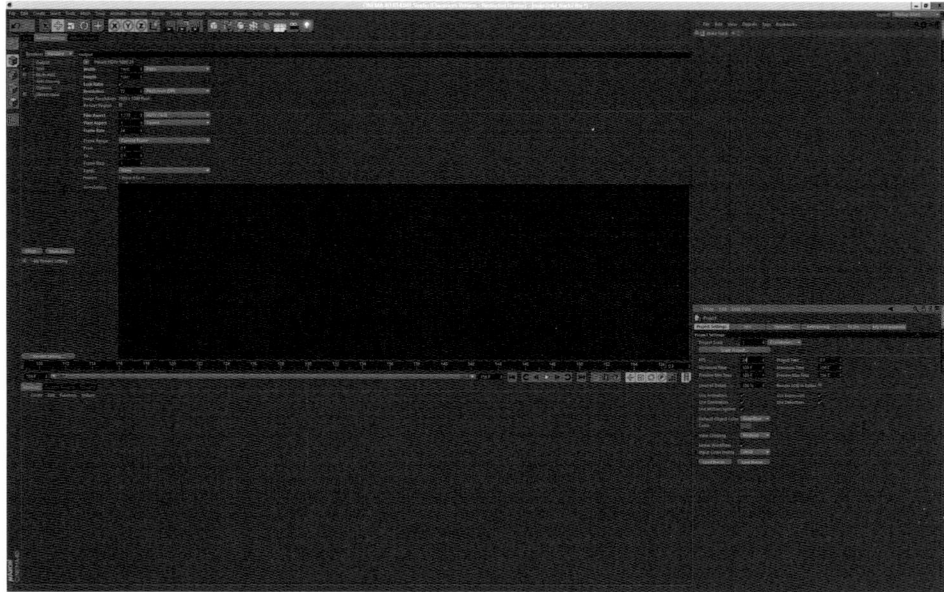

15. To create an image plane as a reference, I make a Background Element. Then I create a new material and uncheck everything but Color. In the Texture Arrow I browse to the undistorted image I wrote out previously with the FBX node creation.

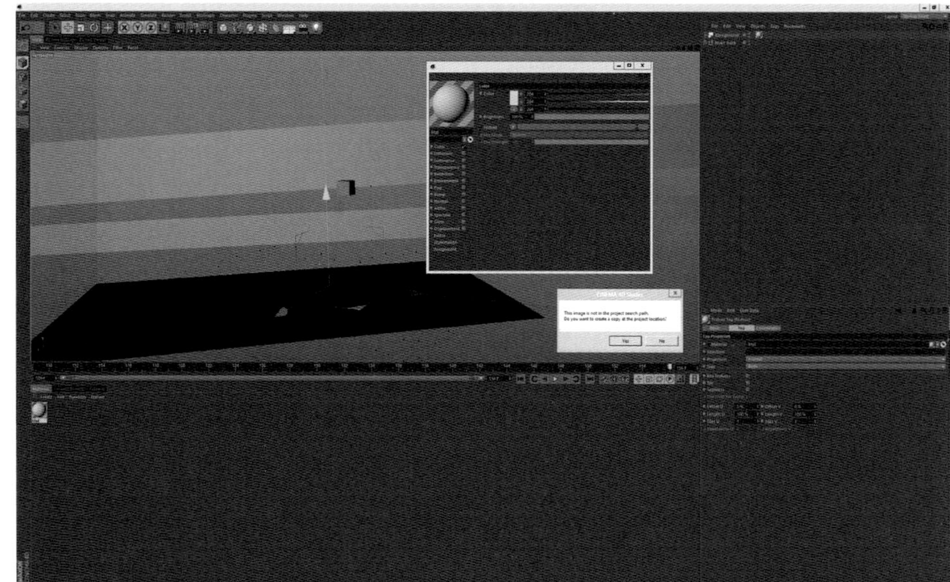

16. With my image plane in the material, I drag the material into the Background Element and then go to my shot camera and view it through. I can see the tracked elements with the Background Elements. I need to line it up exactly by setting up the resolution, fps, and the material correctly as the last step. I want some more options for this texture. For Timing, I use Exact Frame and for Movie Start I change to 0. Starting at 1 actually shifts it one frame ahead, which I don't want. End Frame is 156 as it is normally. The fps is 24. There was no need to calculate anymore with these manual settings. Under Material in the Editor tab, I check Animate Texture. That should do it for this match-move; it should be a solid transfer from NUKE to C4D now.

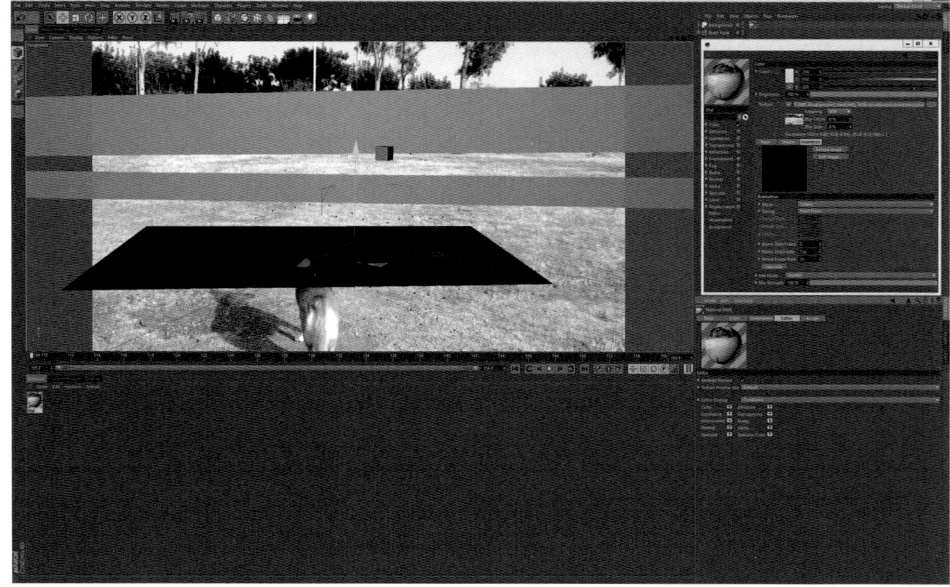

17. Now it is time for 3D asset creation. The Background image plane with the tracked images show me the horizon line and grid. I create a cityscape using Greyscalegorilla's City Kit plug-in. I create a circular layout with a hole in the middle so I can add in my custom building. I place the city far enough in depth from the camera so it will move correctly as the camera moves. I place it pretty far according to the distance I have in mind.

18. I use some stock models of futuristic sci-fi buildings, which I clone, duplicate and place in layout. These two buildings will serve as the main focus of the cityscape – the heart of the aliens' new civilization.

19. I continue to use City Kit and customize my layout. I create another building patch with higher elevation so it's not a flat, boring city just at ground level. I place it to the left of the two main towers for the sake of good composition. The plan is to make a few more of these to add interest and balance to my city.

20. I duplicate a few more buildings and move them here and there – one on the far left but scaled down a little, and a couple more on the right to balance the city's composition. To make them seem different to each other, they are all rotated and scaled separately, giving the illusion of a whole new batch of buildings, which is what I want. My viewport is refreshing very slowly now due to the high amount of geometry in the scene, especially as this city makes intense use of Xpresso. So to help this, I turn off the viewport visibility.

21. Using another of Greyscalegorilla's tools, I light the 3D scene with the Daylight (Afternoon) light kit. I edit the sky gradient to be a little more gray/blue on the left-hand side, which represents the ground of my alien landscape. I then bring down the blues and light blues more to the left from default. I adjust the sky color, intensity and the brightness. Then I rotate the sky to be where the sun position would be in the scene. I want to get the color, intensity and light positions as close as possible to the original lighting in the plate, but I can adjust the colors a bit in the compositing.

22. I render the viewport along with the background to see if my lighting matches. The textures on the models are a little plain, but I can texture-up the buildings in Photoshop later. The plan now is to render out a single frame in the highest possible quality and then reproject it back onto simple geometry (most likely a sphere) in NUKE. This will save me lots of time as opposed to rendering it from 3D. It will also give me more control – I will be able to make it look better in Photoshop for the final. This is the advantage of digital matte painting versus full 3D environment.

23. Now I move onto the circle city. I create a customized torus-type City Kit model and place it in 3D space above the city that works best with the angle and perspective of this camera angle. The circle city is centered around the ground city right now, but as a matte painting it will circle the large monolithic mountain. This will still work spatially in Photoshop, even if it doesn't work in reality for 3D.

24. Here is a close-up of the circle city. It is pretty simple with lots of repeated models and flat structures, but as a faraway object it works well for my purposes. By flattening the downtown area of the City Kit I can get a flatter and more uniform surface on this torus, which is what I want.

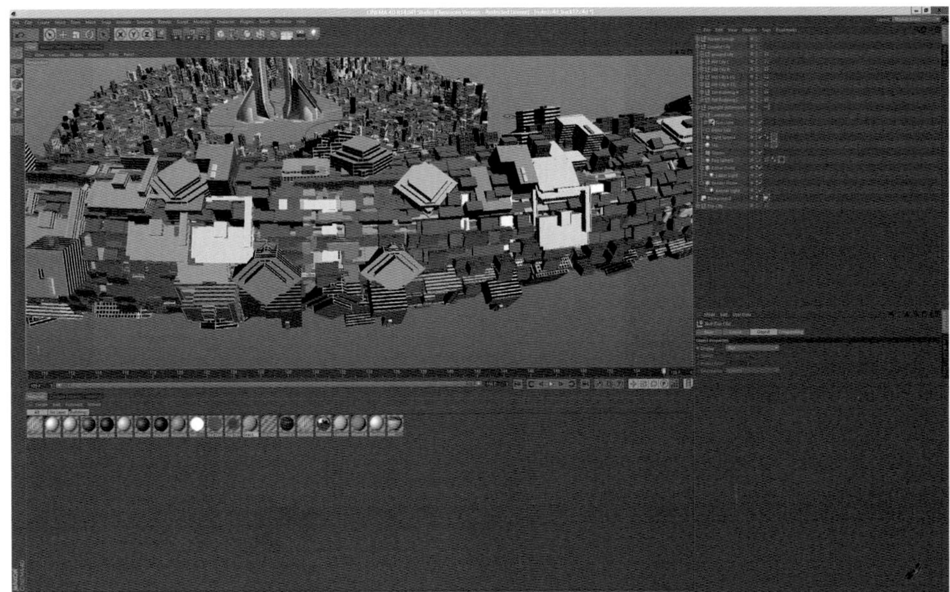

25. I test render with everything to see if it works with lighting versus the plate. My lighting for the most part works here, so I can move on. I want to render out the bottom city separately from the top city so they can be tweaked independently.

26. Here is a closer view of the render of the cityscape. I wanted to do my tests on low anti-alias settings, with no ambient occlusion or global illumination. These are off so I get faster iterations; they will be turned on later.

27. After getting some decent renders from C4D, I turn on full high-quality settings and ambient occlusion with global illumination, which takes a little longer to render but it's only for one frame. I want the best quality as a base to paint on. Here, I re-render everything on high quality to be checked in NUKE as two separate layers – the circle city and the ground city. This way I can treat them separately.

28. I render out my passes with the Position Camera effect in a multilayered .EXR file. This enables me to put in a depth pass from the camera's position to simulate atmospheric perspective. I shuffle my P pass into all greens (which is where the depth pass from the camera is located). I use a Grade node and adjust the black and white points. The black point represents where I want the atmosphere to start, usually right in front of the camera. But here I'm choosing to go with the front of the city. The white point is where the atmosphere will be at its strongest. I invert my image to get it looking right. I render this black-and-white image out of Photoshop as a .tif file after adjusting it with a Grade node. I'll later use this to adjust the atmosphere in Photoshop.

29. To get a projection looking decent in the composition, I need to make my Photoshop canvas area large enough to accommodate the camera move from beginning, to middle, to end. I analyse the video footage and find where the biggest swings are. I write out an image at those locations. I find four spots where the image and camera swing the most. I bring these into Photoshop and try to line them up on the closest object that would be giving parallax, in this case my dog Xena. I expand the canvas to cover this image area. I bring in the 3D elements and place them according to where I modeled and rendered from (from frame 156, the end frame). It isn't exact but this technique gives me a good starting point.

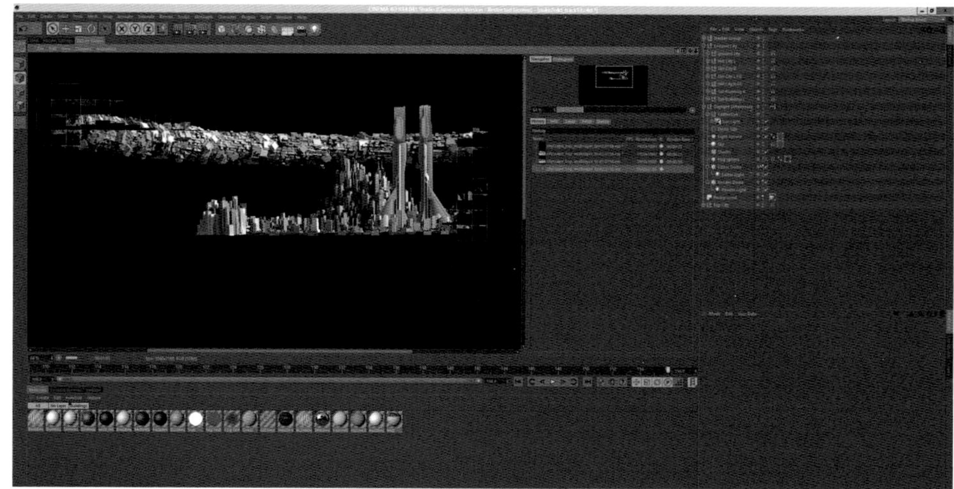

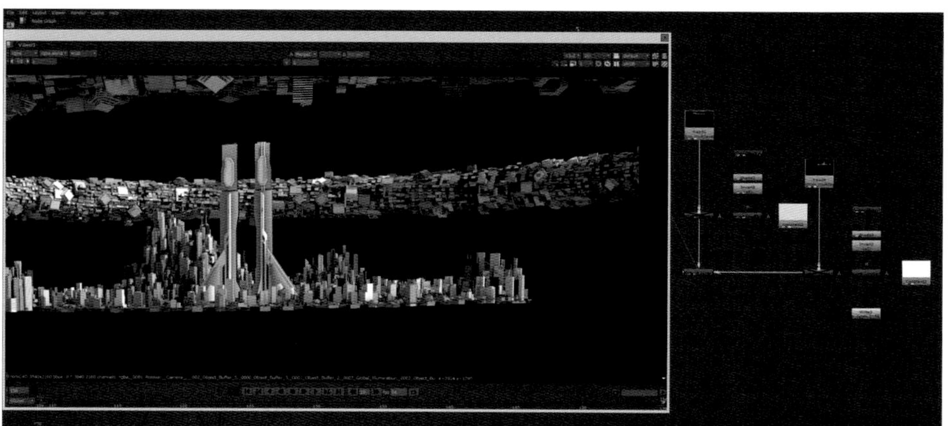

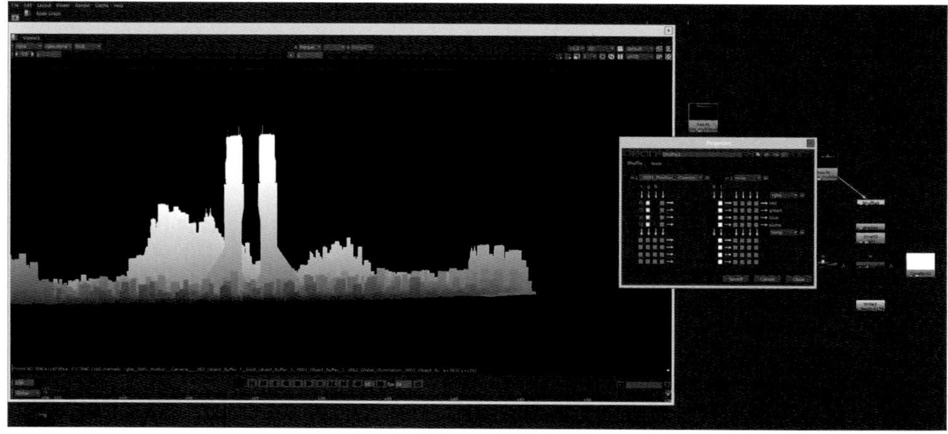

30. Now I can start on my rough matte painting. I turn off the frame check layers and keep just one layer visible along with a quick garbage mask to see how my live action plate might fit into the scene. I can later refine this live action plate. I want it to be an alien environment, so there needs to be lots of interesting rocks and mountains and a rocky, dark-gray ground. It'll be sort of a desert matte painting.

31. I clean up some edges and play with a road that winds into the city. I'm making progress with the ground, with a full mask and a more final position for Xena, who is looking out towards the city. The monolithic mountain is now coming into play also.

32. Now that I'm in a good spot for the matte painting, I'm going to head back to NUKE to do some projection tests. Using one of the older versions of my matte painting as a test, I project the image using the shot camera onto a huge sphere, way beyond the tracked points in the 3D scene.

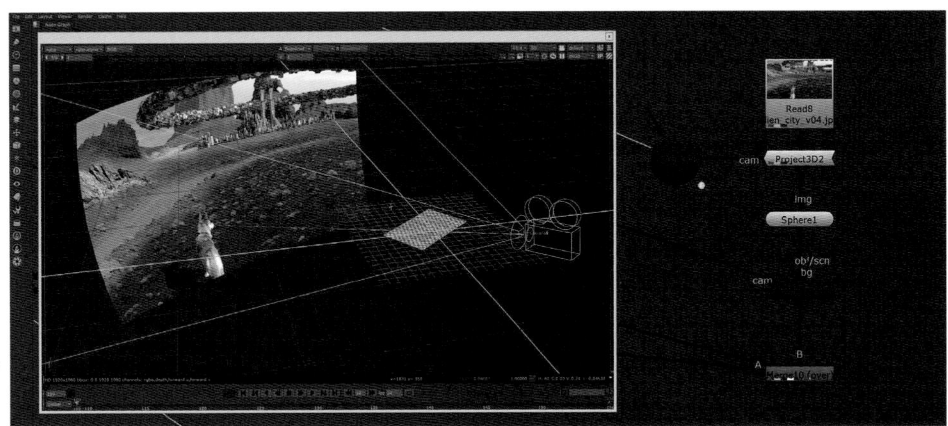

33. I choose the ending frame of the shot to be my projection frame. I'm going to duplicate the shot camera and then delete the transform animations in the camera, which will serve as my projection camera.

34. As I scrub the sequence around I notice there are a lot of black areas in the image. Mostly the blacks occur in the beginning of the image and in the middle, so I need to adjust my projection camera to accommodate this.

35. Because I have so much room for a bigger matte painting, I can take the projection camera and move it around, mostly pulling it out, so I can cover these black areas. I want to pull back just enough so I can remove the black areas but not so much that it causes too much stretching of the projected image. I scrub back and forth and test the projection to see if it works with no more black spots.

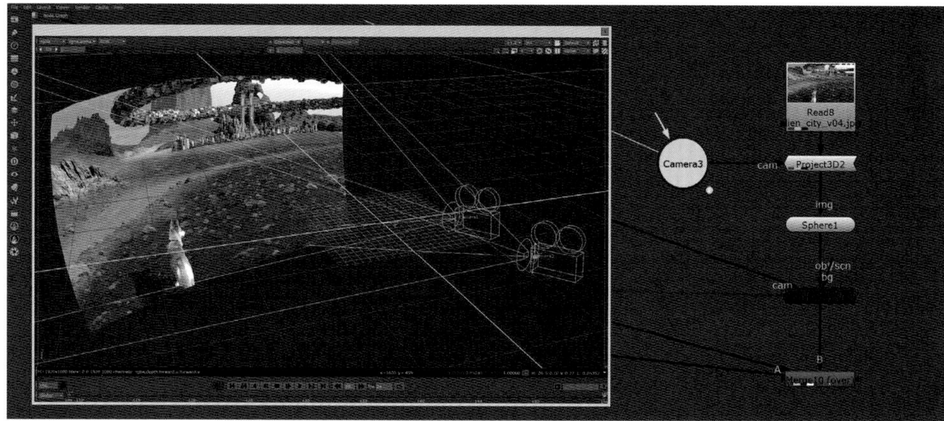

36. The road isn't working so I decide to do away with it and keep the ground cleaner. I will later take the high-res photos of the ground I have from my location and integrate them into my painting. Now I have the final composition of the monolithic mountain, though I'm still tweaking the other elements. I stretch out a sky gradient from a photo, which will cause the grain to enlarge and stretch, which I don't want. So I will create a whole new sky in Photoshop.

… I do some more tweaking, and make the curved mountain on the left smaller. I also add the Position Camera pass into my painting. I add a Layer Mask of just a solid color, sampled from the sky, and use that as my atmospheric color for the city depth pass. I paint in further atmosphere for the Background Elements and the monolithic mountain. I sample the lower part of the sky and paint with a soft brush on the horizon to match the sky gradient. This will act as a low-lying 'dust' haze in the sky. The monolithic mountain is so big it rises above the dirty haze.

37. I need to add some more depth between the ground and the cityscape, so I put in little ridges in the front of the city, which give it more scale.

38. I adjust color and black levels, and paint out areas I don't need. I also add further atmosphere on the big circle city.

39. Here is the high-res photo of the ground plate I took after I shot the video. It's a lot cleaner and of higher quality than the video version. The lighting matches perfectly to the video because it was shot on the same location at about the same time. Now the element standing out most is Xena. I color correct her to sit into the matte painting more correctly as far as saturation, brightness and colors go.

40. I do a rough integration pass of the grassy ground using a soft brush. I have yet to color correct the grass so it's a little off.

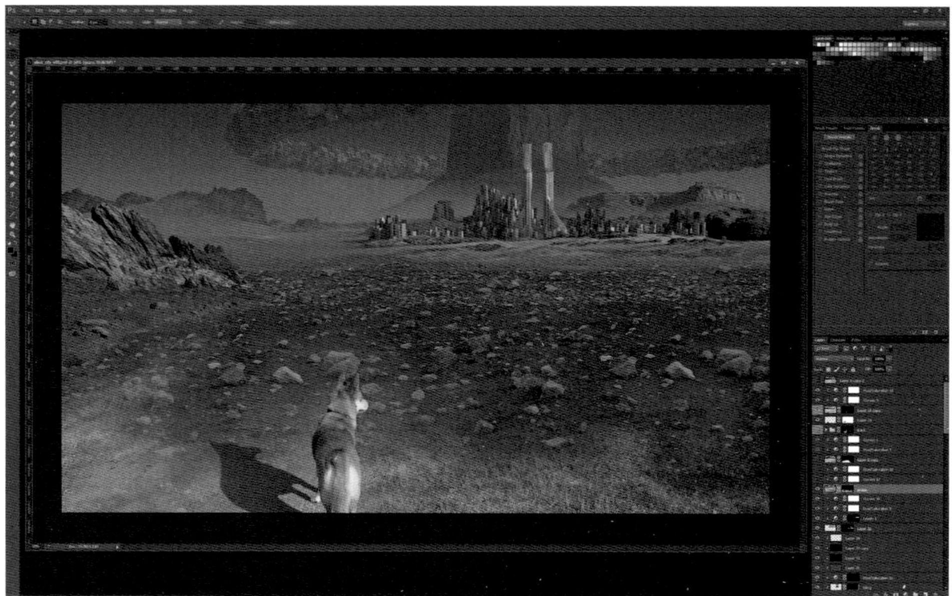

41. Now it is fully integrated, color corrected and painted where I want it. I also change more of the background, making the curved mountain more in the background and smaller.

42. My attention now turns to the cityscape and texturing it further. It's pretty plain so I get some building photos that have an interesting texture of repeated patterns and that are not too wildly different in perspective.

43. I mask in the texture photo and duplicate it as much as needed to cover the rest of the city. I use various Blend modes – Screen, Linear Add and Overlay.

44. I can further paint on my buildings and color correct them to get them looking the way I want. They are shiny and have more detail than before. Later on, I'll add a subtle lens flare to the buildings to look as though the the sun is glaring off them at the right angle.

45. The right side of the painting is looking a little unbalanced and plain with just the ground and some rocks. So I get some obsidian/volcanic texture and match up the horizon line to add some interest to this side of the painting.

46. After painting in some areas to integrate into the ground, and doing some color correcting, a nice curved path is created from the foreground to the midground and out to the cityscape.

47. My painting is looking a little dark so I use a Curves to give it an exposure and contrast boost. I also go to the background and remove the original grainy photo and create a new gradient using the Gradient tool, with colors based on the original sky. It's now much clearer. I can later add subtle grain to everything to make it all sit together well in the composite.

48. I find some real-life lens flare elements and duplicate them once to be used on a lower part of the two cityscape towers. Because the original lens flares are on black, I can use it on top in Screen Layer mode and it should pop through pretty well.

49. Here are the lens flares after some color correction, transforming and painting – I was able to get them sitting nicely with some red and violet tones to complement the blues in the scene.

50. Here is an almost final version of my matte painting, with another exposure boost and a slight darkened vignette on the top of the frame.

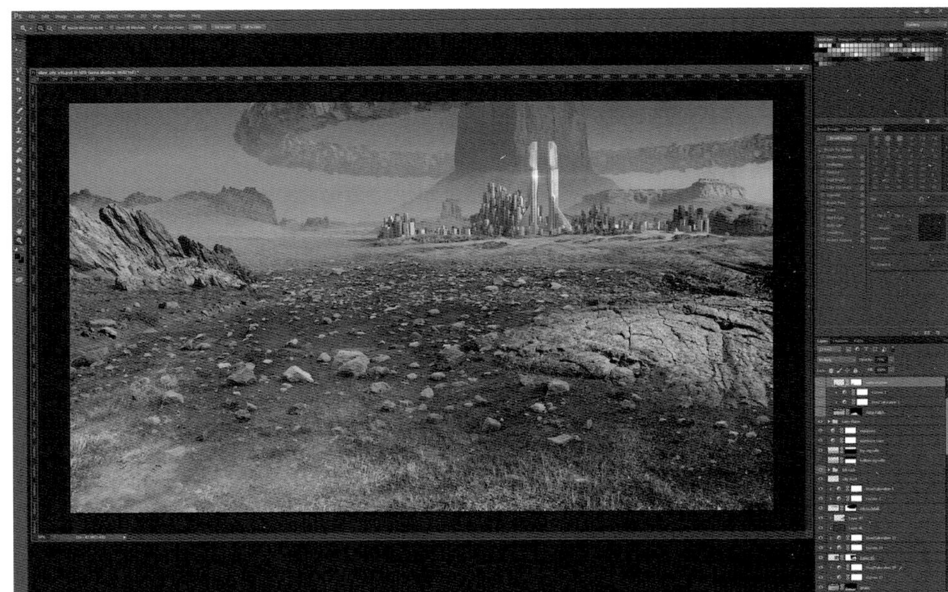

51. I add Xena back in to see how she sits, and see that she needs some color correction and desaturation. I also paint out the rock right above her head so it doesn't interfere with her silhouette. I'm now ready to set this up to project in NUKE.

52. I create a ground plane and a card for the left-hand side rock in the midground. The rest of the background will be on a sphere. I need to consolidate all of the layers and color corrects into three layers only. The first one is the background with a soft mask right before the cityscape. That will be projected onto the background sphere. Then I need a ground plane without the left side of rock, so that will be projected on a card as the ground. Finally, I need the left side rock to be on its own layer to be projected on simple geometry for some parallax.

53. Now I jump back into NUKE for some final projection testing. I've brought back in the proxy geometry so I know where everything is in relation to Xena. I now have three projection cameras – one for the ground, one for the left rock, and one for the background sphere. I need to do some tweaking to get the cameras to line up, and to remove further black areas after the projection is in. (This is due to the ground being closer than in the previous sphere projection test, so it'll have more parallax and relative camera move.)

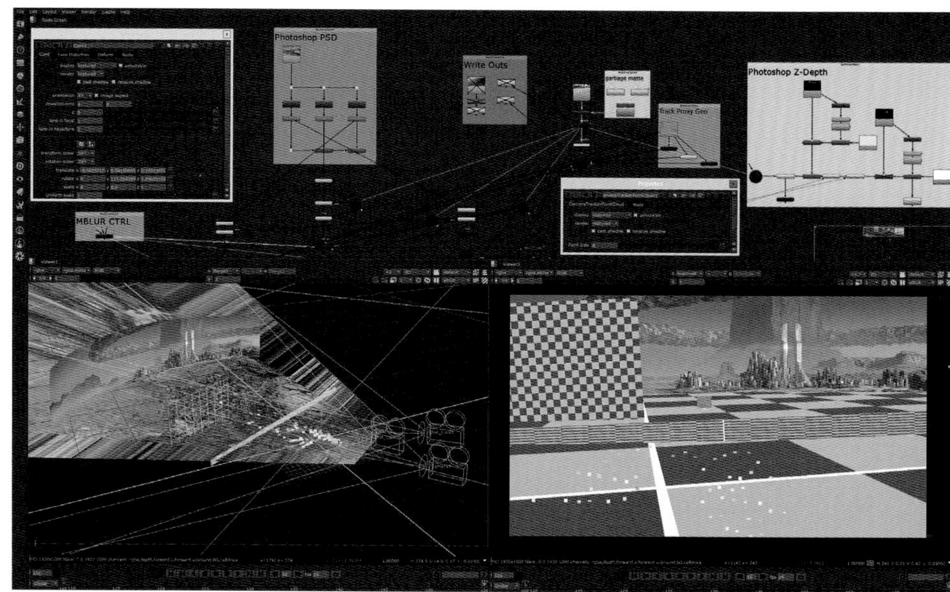

54. I play with it to get it looking right and come up with this final projection in NUKE, with the simple geometry and the three cameras in the side view. If I wanted to make the geometry more complicated for a further parallaxing look, I can do so here in NUKE or back in C4D.

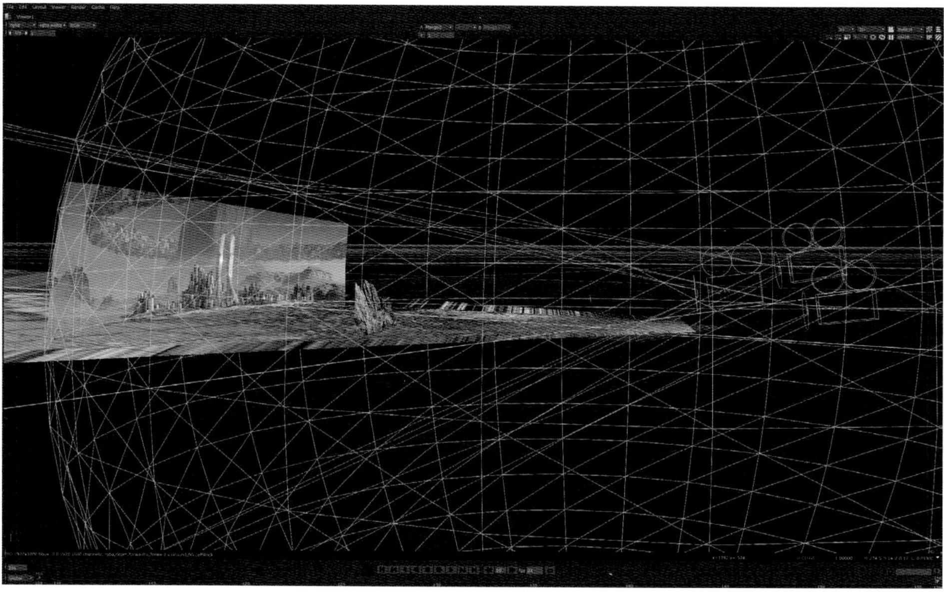

55. Now I add an additional element to my painting – some spaceship drones animated from behind camera flying towards the city. This will give the painting some more life. I go back to C4D to do this. I have some stock 3D spaceship models here that I animate, light and render. I use the same C4D file as the cityscape file, so there is not much set-up I need to do.

56. I animate the drone along a path, and switch the type of path from Spline to Linear so the spaceships don't start accelerating and then decelerate towards the end. I want it to be traveling at full-speed throughout. Having two windows open – the first being the shot camera and the second being the perspective animation window – really helps.

57. I add even more fun by duplicating the spaceships to three. Now I can have a better composition with three spaceships coming from the top left, middle and right. I time it so that the spaceships fly past the camera with a little shake, as if the camera man was startled by the fly-by.

58. I need to add some shadows from the spaceships to the ground. I've put in a ground plane here. After getting it in the right perspective for the shadows, I render out just the ground with shadows and turn off camera visibility on the spaceships.

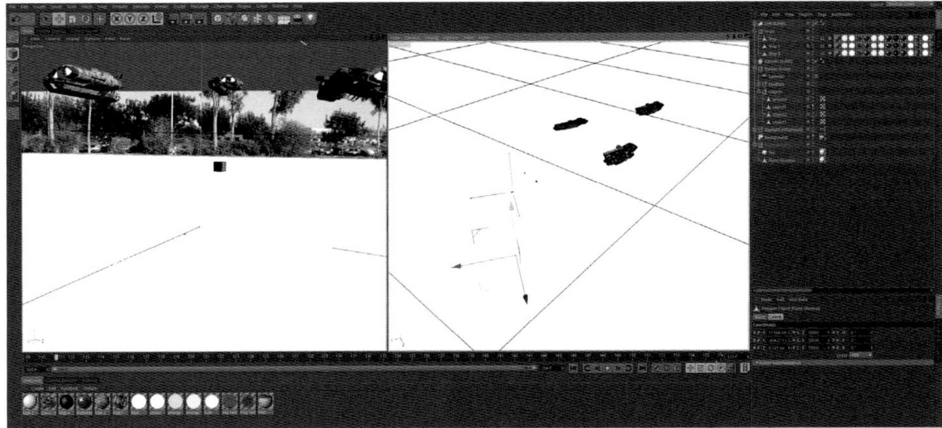

59. Because I want to have Xena in the video with a completely matte painted ground for replacement, I need to rotoscope her out. I rotoscope at key frames where she's moving the most first, then I go into the middle of the previous key frame and adjust it. Rotoscoping every frame causes lots of unwanted jittering to the mask. I also create multiple shapes that cover logical and manageable areas, like her head, neck, body, behind and feet.

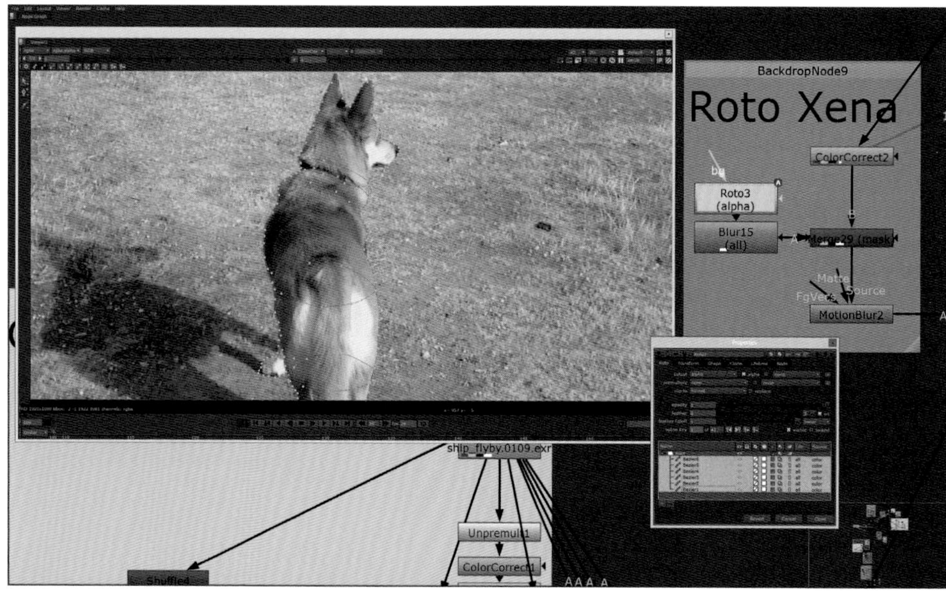

60. Now I need to roto Xena's shadow. Because the shadow is hard to see clearly on the grassy ground of the original footage, I use the Spline tool in C4D and mask out one frame in the beginning of the image sequence and then flatten those splines down into the ground, which is lined up with the match-moved camera ground plane. This allows that spline I just made in C4D to stick. I can then just fill in the spline with a Loft Nurbs by placing the spline into it and then rendering it out. Because Xena doesn't move much, having a still-frame shadow is fine here as a cheat.

61. After lighting and rendering the spaceships, I place them back into NUKE for compositing. Full 3D motion blur was too slow, so I rendered them out with vector motion blur, which is a 2D post-process in C4D. It's not as accurate but it's much faster and for our purposes here it works well. I also render out a P Camera pass so I can add some atmosphere depth in NUKE.

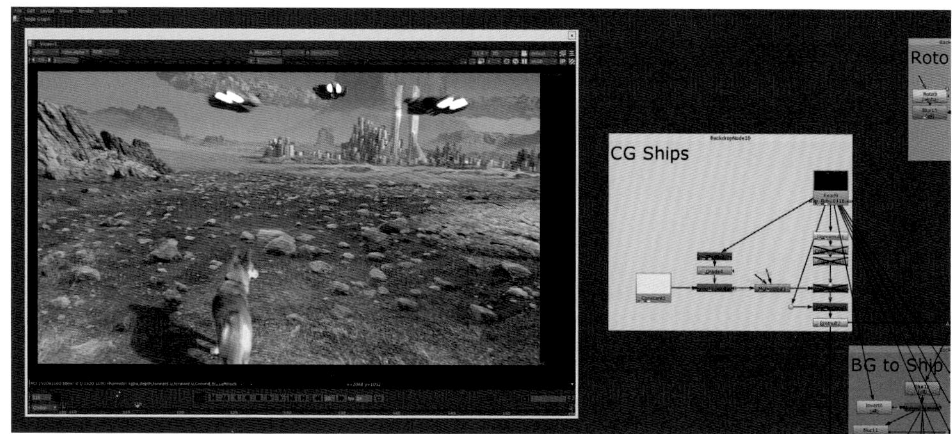

62. Here are the spaceships in the composite with some color corrects and atmosphere added in. I also do a light wrap technique from the background onto the ship. This will blend the spaceships into the sky nicely.

63. I add some glows and light flares coming from the spaceships' engines. I did a Luma Key on the spaceships, with the brightest parts showing through as the mask, then graded an orange color and pre-multiplied it to get that white heat spot in the engines. I blur that element a small amount and screen it back on top of everything. I do this a few more times, each time making it more blurry. For example, I start out with a 5 pixel blur, then go to 15, then 30, 60, etc. (approximately doubling the blur each time). This gives me a nice logarithmic-looking glow.

64. I do some overall color correcting, vignetting, and add grain and motion blur on the projected matte painting elements. Here is the final frame.

Dust: Station Exit
Maya, mental ray, Photoshop
Client: Ember Lab
Szabolcs Joseph Menyhei, GREAT BRITAIN

David: I really like the misty atmosphere in the mountains and the overall nature-enveloped set. It feels like a very humid, unkempt village in the middle of the mountainside with the occasional tourist coming through to see the locals. I would take a train here to explore the lands here if I could; it has some great character to it, especially the overgrown moss and vegetation on the power lines.

Bucolic Temple
Photoshop
Client: The Aaron Sims Company
Francesco Corvino, USA
[far left]

David: The lighting in this works quite well with the warm key light coming in from off-screen right. The lighting on the temple accents the part of it that gives it shape, while keeping the other parts in shadow. The rock textures in the foreground reflect the warm sunlight and bounce light, while the shadows have a cool environment color to them.

Multiversum Memoria
Photoshop
Client: Arnoldo Mondadori Editore SpA
Roberto Oleotto, ITALY
[left]

David: This is a very fantastical image with a striking composition. We follow the gaze of the woman on the cliff to the massive city in the distance. This piece has a nicely laid-out sky and cloud composition, with a hint of a planet in the background and the waterfalls in the foreground. The last glint of sunlight on the water is perfect and gives the whole scene a breathtaking quality.

Surf Fishing at Sunset
Photoshop
Dylan Cole, USA
[left]

David: This matte painting by Dylan is quite marvelous. His use of curved buildings on a beach shore environment matches perfectly in color, tone and atmosphere. I love the windows in the buildings as well as all the little details in the darker windows. The composition is exquisite, from the three suns in the sky, the cloud's vanishing point, to the waves, the buildings, and the people playing on the shore. I also love the specular hits and reflections from the sky and people onto the water surface. Having the people in there enjoying the environment, such as the boy learning how to fish and the puppy running joyfully around in the waves, reminds me of the idyllic paintings of the great Hudson River School artists. This piece of art is just as masterful as those for our contemporary age. A truly inspirational painting.

Across the Park
Photoshop, Maya
Jadrien Cousens, USA
[bottom left]

David: Here's a park I would love to visit sometime as it's clean, peaceful and full of futuristic buildings on the skyline with nice, curved walkways across the grass. Showing people just enjoying the sunshine and hanging about in the grass really sells this as a nicely designed environment that could one day come true.

Aladoria
Photoshop
Anthony Scime, USA
[below]

David: I think the exposure of this painting is pretty cool. There's some highly contrasting values in the foreground buildings, with neon lights and holograms atop the roofs. Your eye goes out to the right where the sun catches the building tops, then into the foggy distance where you see further elements reinforcing this as a sci-fi cityscape. Exposing for the sky, and with the right kind of atmospheric perspective, this piece works well.

Manhattan Future
Photoshop, 3ds Max
Igor Staritsin, RUSSIA
[above]

David: Having been atop the Empire State Building myself and seen such a vista, I think this is a great vision of what it could look like in a few hundred years, with a new, taller skyline and some flying vehicles in and around the city. Igor really has some great colors of a cool overall atmosphere contrasting with the warm sunlight catching the top halves of the tall buildings. Having a couple of planets in the background gives it an extra sci-fi element, and the foreground buildings frame the image well.

Downtown
Maya, Photoshop
Jadrien Cousens, USA
[above]

David: I can imagine this matte painting being in the same world as Jadrien's previous piece 'Across the Park'. Both have grass and people integrated into a sci-fi environment to make it instantly relateable. This area shows a much higher terrace in the middle of a busy metropolis, where flying cars are zipping up and down on an aerial freeway. The lighting frames the focus point of the right-hand side pretty well, and vignettes the bottom and left side of the frame naturally.

A Long Journey
Photoshop
Jadrien Cousens, USA
[left]

David: In the middle of a desert, a family finds refuge in a distant city. I hope this wealthy and technologically advanced city accepts this nomadic family. The monotone lighting on this is slightly offset by the turquoise lighting inside the middle of the main tower and reflects some complementary colors. I can really feel this city offering new hope to the traveling family. The bounce light and reflection on the shadow side of the building is particularly interesting.

David: I love the silhouette and back-lighting the artist has created in this painting. It's a very realistic palette and tone for a hazy sunset in the desert sky, with distant clouds and an atmosphere that makes this city feel massive in an expansive golden desert. The palm trees on the left-hand side frame the image well and the light wrap in the palm tree just in front of the sun gives this piece a great glow of realism.

Desert City
Photoshop, Maya
Jadrien Cousens, USA

David: Here Stefan mixes curved sci-fi buildings with a natural landscape, and does it beautifully. I love the tall, vertical canvas here, with the taller buildings with a hint of gold that complements the bluer tones in the sky and surrounding environment. The circle- and saucer-shaped ground environment has a great design, with each terrace having its own little forest of trees. Here's living in the future and still being green about it – very cool!

The 12th Colony
3ds Max, Photoshop
Stefan Morrell, NEW ZEALAND
[above]

City Desires
Photoshop
Igor Staritsin, RUSSIA
[above]

David: An ancient city environment slowly adapting to new technologies, with flying balloons on the horizon. The blend of waterfalls and the lush forest in the misty mountains gives this piece a magical, adventurous feel. I can see the tiny birds in the sky, which gives some nice scale to this image. The transition from the dark foreground into the hazy background shows Igor has a good understanding of atmospheric perspective.

The Balcony
Photoshop
João Marcos Britto da Costa, BRAZIL
[right]

David: An exotic woman enjoying the last rays of the sun in what looks like a great place to relax away from everyday life. The sky reflects the right amount of color into all of the elements here, and the sun gives off the warm glow this woman can bask in until it fully sets. The shadows cast from the balcony add a nice compositional element to the piece.

Brave New World
Maya, 3ds Max, Photoshop, V-Ray
Ashish Dani, CANADA
[right]

David: This is a massive city that harkens to the great *Star Wars* episodes 1–3 matte paintings by the masters at ILM. It's wonderfully executed with the lower city blocks complex enough to sell that it's a part of a bigger city, while the taller buildings support the overall composition well. Having the vanishing points all going towards the curvacious building on the top right third is great. I love Ashish's use of 'golden hour' lighting here as the sunlight really shines on the bottom right first, and then slowly we look around and our eyes settle onto the big building. The sky and haze is integrated very nicely, and some distant taller buildings show this cityscape has a huge life to it.

Fury: The Tales of Ronan Fierce (city high view)
Photoshop
Client: OcularStorm Productions LLC
Gia Nguyen Hoang, VIETNAM
[above]

David: The city lights, moon, and their reflections in the water are very realistic here. The moon is small and casts a dim glow, as if it has been shot by a big, wide-angle lens. The city glows with life from our vantage point, which is darker, as if we have stopped at a distance to enjoy the view of the city at night. Gia does a great job with the freeway that curves into and through the city and then leads you up to the night sky with the correct exposure.

Desert Journey
Photoshop
Usama Jameel, INDIA
[above]

David: The people in the foreground walking up to the city gates really show how massive this city is. I think the dust kicked up from the ground gives it some life and a great atmosphere, as well as a touch of mysticism. The city's main building is like the Hagia Sophia in Istanbul but in a different time period and environment – a desert far, far away. Usama handled the black values well with the huge rock piece on the left, then going to a lighter shade for the midground rock (right), and then into the city's atmosphere haze.

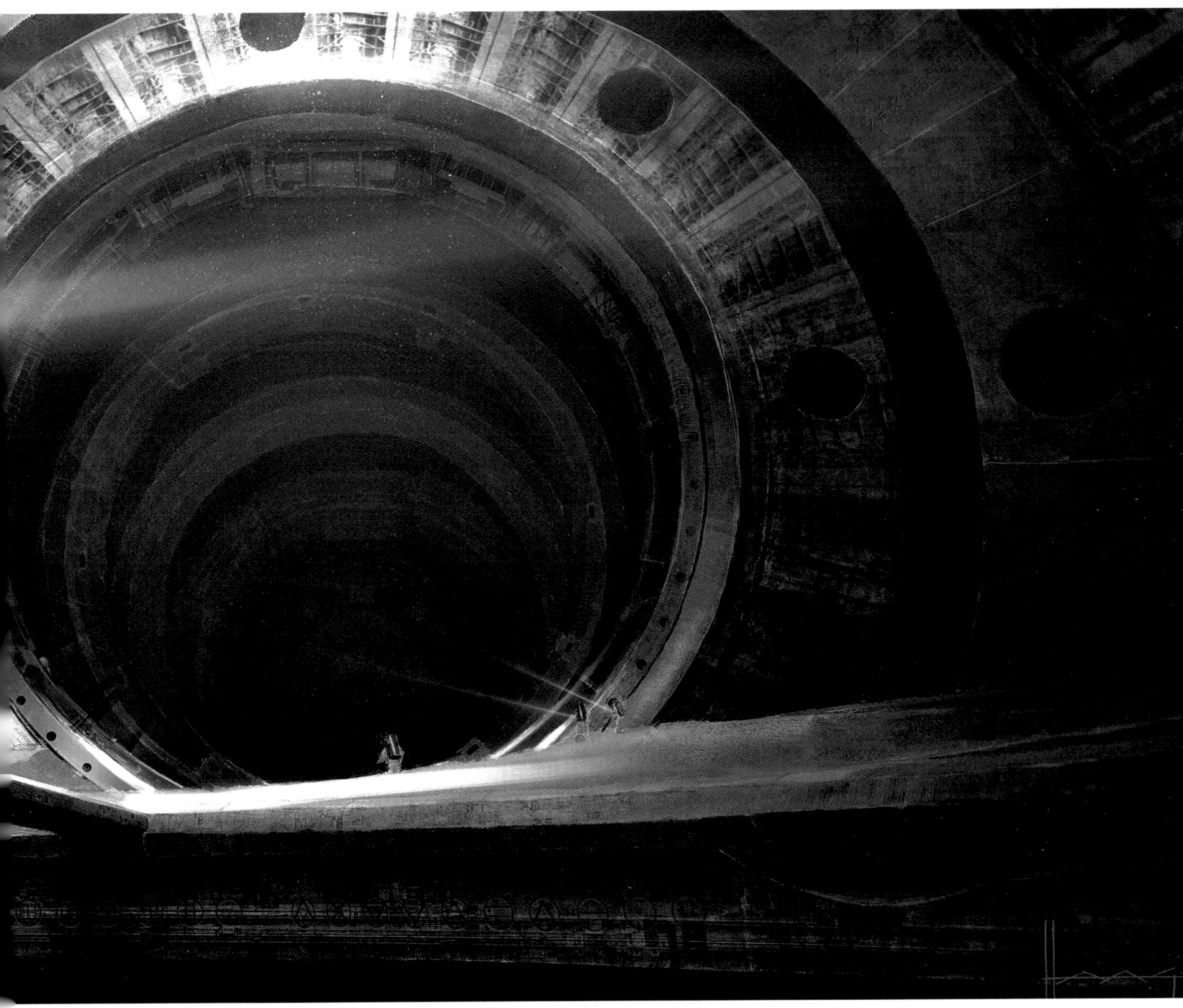

Discovery
Photoshop
Wayne Haag, AUSTRALIA
[above]

David: Some astronauts exploring the inside of a massive metal tunnel, presumably from an alien race far beyond their technological understanding. The lighting and atmosphere in this image is wonderful, especially the glints of light coming off the top of the tunnel, and below it. The flashlights have a believable beam and glow around them, and suggest a damp environment.

Downtown
Photoshop, Vue Infinite
Dave Tipper, NEW ZEALAND
[left]

David: This piece is a very European-inspired town with a strongly desaturated palette, yet it still has some hints of color so it's not entirely monotone; for example, the cyan rooftops and the muted-orange rooftop on the right. The overcast sky with a slight accent of intense light on the left-hand-side building really makes this a strong subject matter. The shadow on the left, as well as the strongly silhouetted tree, keeps your eye contained on the right-hand side of this image.

The Ocean's Return
Photoshop
Steve Horsfall, GREAT BRITAIN
[top]

David: The sky in a strong blue in an otherwise dirty and orange-lit environment gives this piece some nice contrasting colors and makes this image sing. The idea of the ocean overtaking the once dried-up land shows a true cycle of life, even if this cycle takes hundreds or thousands of years. Once there was no hope in this land, now the water has returned to bring back what was once there. The boats in the foreground show us that there once was life. The waterfalls flowing down the cliffs give a nice snapshot of the environment that is returning.

Parisian Mass Housing
Photoshop, formZ, Maxwell Render
Derek Jackson, GREAT BRITAIN
[above]

David: Here is an alternative housing and energy efficient city that I can see working well in this minimalistic piece. Although the focus lands right in the center, it is asymmetrical in that the right-hand side has a block of clean apartments, which look great reflecting the environment around it. The trees on top of the apartment block are a great design. The left building has another take on the condo life with trees on the corner balconies. All are supporting the middle structure where we see giant wind turbines generating a good deal of this city's energy. Derek has balanced the green with the future well here.

Frozen Dawn
Maya, Photoshop
Adam Kuczek, CHINA
[top]

David: This is such a cold-looking land with a frozen-over mountainscape where the pale-yellow sunlight provides a little warmth and hope in the distant sky. I think Adam has created a nice tone with this piece of an icy terrain along with some structures suggesting some kind of civilization that has tamed this rough environment. Its inhabitants can enjoy the slight warmth of the sun for now, which will be soon enveloped in the looming clouds on the horizon.

The Valley
Photoshop
Rasmus Berggreen, DENMARK
[above]

David: This alien landscape has some great designs in the circular buildings and the dock port on the right. It's as if the inhabitants have built their civilization hundreds of years ago and nature has started to grow back over its structures, while the aliens have gone on with life unharmed as their colony has peacefully expanded. I like the lush environments in this piece, and the great rock structures remind me of the Huangshan mountains in China.

Old Western Town
Photoshop
Simone De Salvatore, GERMANY
[left]

David: It is a rare sight to see a Western, realistic-type matte painting these days. This piece has a great environment of a town that's been long forsaken, or perhaps the town's inhabitants were counting the days until the volcano would once again erupt in the distance and they would have to flee for their lives. The combination of the volcano and the dilapidated houses really make this piece an eerie reminder that not all places are liveable against the forces of nature. The color palette of this piece is very striking and drearily realistic.

Jungle Palace
Photoshop
Pablo Palomeque, ARGENTINA
[bottom]

David: Here is an old temple with a striking perspective angle to it. I love how Pablo has handled the extra vegetation growing on the unkempt palace, which sits well in the nice green environment. The palace may be abandoned, perhaps to be wrapped up in the beauty of nature. The designs of the palace's dome and bridgeways are nicely executed.

Cluster City
Photoshop
Maxime-Raphaël Cyr, CANADA
[facing page bottom]

David: This is sort of a dystopian society matte painting, showing how a poorer population has slowly taken over large and great structures built by the wealthy overseers of this city. I can really feel the dense, smoggy air in this land, which has led to people building their houses as high above the ground (and smog) as they can. Maxime really did a nice job executing this idea. The little neon signs with their soft glow show that there is still life down in the city below.

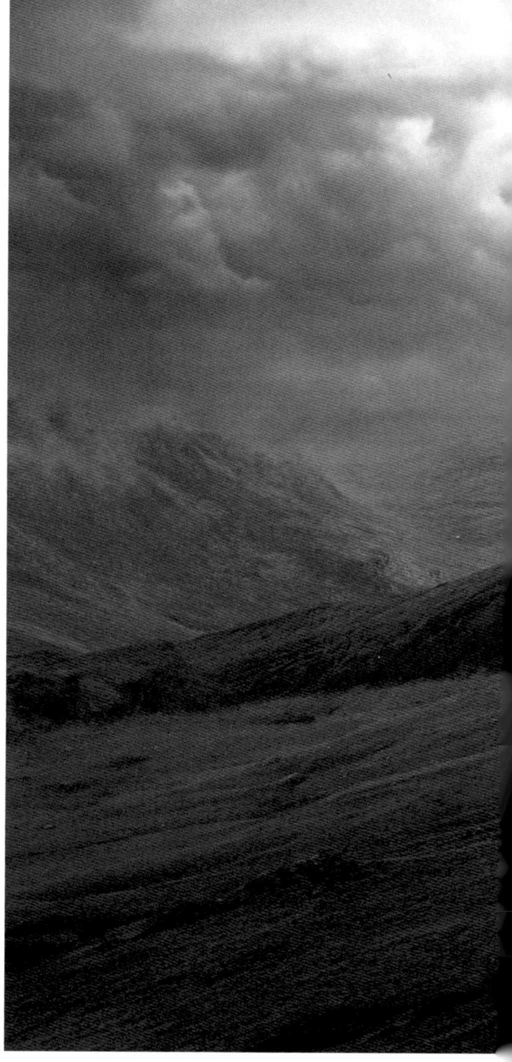

Dust: City of Kabe
Maya, mental ray, V-Ray, Photoshop
Client: Ember Lab
Nick Giassullo, giassullofx, USA
[top]

David: This war-ravaged city shows the aftermath of a war, with its broken bridges and smoking ruins. The rising sun provides a ray of hope, suggesting that the city will rise once again. The exposure and color values are pretty nicely done in this piece, with hints of light beams cutting through the buildings. The water was handled very well with its color and reflections.

New World
Photoshop
Fabio Barretta Zungrone, USA
[above]

David: I really like Fabio's use of strong, saturated 'golden hour' light, with great storm clouds juxtaposed with the cooler, misty landscape on the right side of the frame. This reveals a theme of light against dark, hope against confusion and despair. The way Fabio layered in the mist and the atmosphere was very well done. The bits of sunlight striking the left sides of the mountain here and there are really interesting, rather than having the sunlight all blasted in one place, as might be the case in the hands of a less-skilled matte painter. The middle mountain peak has some huge scale to it and draws attention to the lively waterfalls and rivers cutting across the image in the foreground.

New Day
Photoshop
Fabio Barretta Zungrone, USA
[facing page top]

David: My favorite part of this image is the sky and the bright sun showering the landscape with inviting, warm light. I can imagine myself atop a high cliff overlooking this great view of the peaks and their snow-capped ridges on the left and the more hospitable sight of green rolling hills and forest to the right, topped off with a river running through the middle, glinting in the sun. I think this is a beautifully done matte painting by Fabio that encompasses a very serene and enjoyable landscape for any audience.

David: Here we have a lone hut sitting on top of a rural green landscape, untouched by industrialized civilization. The land is still ripe with life of all kinds. The single piece of land being used to the right pales in comparison with what is left for nature to rule over (left of canvas). The atmospheric perspective is pretty great, from the strong blacks in the front to the background shrouded in a great, grey mist. The sky reflects all of this, with its strong rain clouds moving in from the horizon to shed their weight upon the land. The curved arc in the sky gives the piece a nice composition that pairs well with the peak of land jutting out from the ground (which is on the same level of the hut so your eye is immediately drawn there after the hut).

Les Territoires du Nord
Photoshop
Seema Schere, CANADA
[above]

The Village
Photoshop, Vue Esprit
Anthony Eftekhari, USA
[above]

David: Everything is sharp and highly detailed in this matte painting, yet it still has a soft feel to it due to the great atmosphere and layering of elements that Anthony has expertly done. The right side of the image has powerful silhouettes of trees and ferns near the water that frame the image nicely, while the building scape steps back into the distance to where we see a gathering of some sort in the main building (middle). The subdued orange light radiating from the house lights is a great complement to the blue overtones in this mysterious piece. I think the reflections on the water surface are superbly handled in terms of displacement and perspective.

Dredd: Mega City
Photoshop, CINEMA 4D, Maya
Client: Prime Focus World/DNA Films/Reliance
Neil Miller, GREAT BRITAIN
[right]

David: Having seen this movie a while back, I remember saying how cleanly monolithic the matte paintings were, while still managing to have very oppressive designs due to their being more straight-edged than other futuristic cityscapes I've seen. This piece is no exception, and Neil's great design brings a dreadful feeling to the viewer. These huge buildings have been built atop the original city, where districts grow with little planning and overseeing from the government. Seeing these monoliths going from overtaking the foreground frame to getting progressively smaller really sells the large scale of this piece. Neil did a great job with the overcast lighting of the cityscape, with hints of color in the neon signs.

David: This matte painting has a great mist-veiled forest, which is layered in such a way that the trees don't get lost in the forest. Usama took some inspirations from *Avatar* it seems, and that's a great inspiration to pull from. The dense forest below with the waterfalls in the distance, coupled with the high mountain peaks covered in vegetation at all angles, make this piece look as though any creature could be living below the tree canopy. The angled rock peaks on the right side direct your eye to the left of the composition, and the birds and thin strips of clouds floating around the tops of the distant mountains give a nice scale to this world. The sky is integrated well into the environment, and the piece's color, lighting and the planet (right) contribute well to the overall look.

Alien Landscape
Photoshop
Usama Jameel, INDIA
[below]

Cypress
Photoshop
Matthew Rodgers, NEW ZEALAND
[top]

David: This is a great panoramic by Matthew of people enjoying the landscape, and rightly so. The backdrop to their playful sport is a gorgeous mountain that is the centerpiece of this matte painting. The golden hues of the sunlight catching the tips of the trees during the last hour of the day really make this piece powerful. The blue/violet shadows against the creamy orange sunlight works quite well. The little wispy clouds near the top of the mountain range depict how massive and distant the peaks are. I'm jealous of the people snowboarding and skiing to be able to behold such a view!

Tropical Shore
Photoshop
Einar Martinsen, NORWAY
[above]

David: Einar takes us back in time in this matte painting. The little boat pointing right at the distant pirate ship is great composition. The palm trees on the left- and the right-hand-side vegetation reinforce the composition well in angles and in black values framing the shot. The overall texture and detail of the water and its reflection of the environment, as well as the realistic details of the sky, show that care was taken to make this piece feel as integrated as possible. This tropical paradise would be a great location to explore.

Island City
Photoshop
Lisa Ayla, GREAT BRITAIN
[above]

David: This image of an amazing beach with nice palm trees and a great view to a futuristic city on the horizon is pretty great in my books, and this matte painting renders this idea nicely. The blue sky in a daytime-lit shot shows that relaxing is the main objective, and this goes well with the small waves breaking onto the sand in front of us. The light intensity and colors of the clouds are really well integrated into the overall environment. Having distant cityscapes flanking the main ones show how big this city is. Great care was taken in showcasing the middle cityscape with some nice flares of light on the shiny windows and tall, thin silhouettes demonstrating an advanced building technology.

Sky Freight
Photoshop, Maya, mental ray
Matthew Rodgers, NEW ZEALAND
[above]

David: This retro-looking painting reminds me of the Art Deco style of the early 1900s seen in buildings and metropolises. The squarish buildings and rounded top with the panelled turning of the edges harken to the days when people were still exploring the potential of skyscrapers and minimalistic designs using height and diagonal lines. The retro sci-fi feel of this piece is also felt in the floating freighters that are a combination of old and new technology. Great saturated tones of sunlight and the cyan sky encapsulate the essence of colored posters in the booming days of having the best skyscrapers in the world.

DAMIEN MACÉ

Damien Macé is a digital matte painter whose work for the film and TV industries has spanned a decade. Throughout his career he has been based in various locations across Europe. Within the visual effects industry Damien is widely known for his conceptual artistry, and has contributed significantly to many blockbuster movies such as *Avatar, Sherlock Holmes* and *Harry Potter*, and the major hit series *Game of Thrones.* Having won a VES Award and received an Emmy nomination for his work on *Game of Thrones*, Damien is undeniably an accomplished and experienced member of the matte painting world.

This is a concept I did for one of my film projects, with my co-director Alexis Wajsbrot. The story takes place in London after a few years without human activity. This image is made up of a number of different locations blended together.

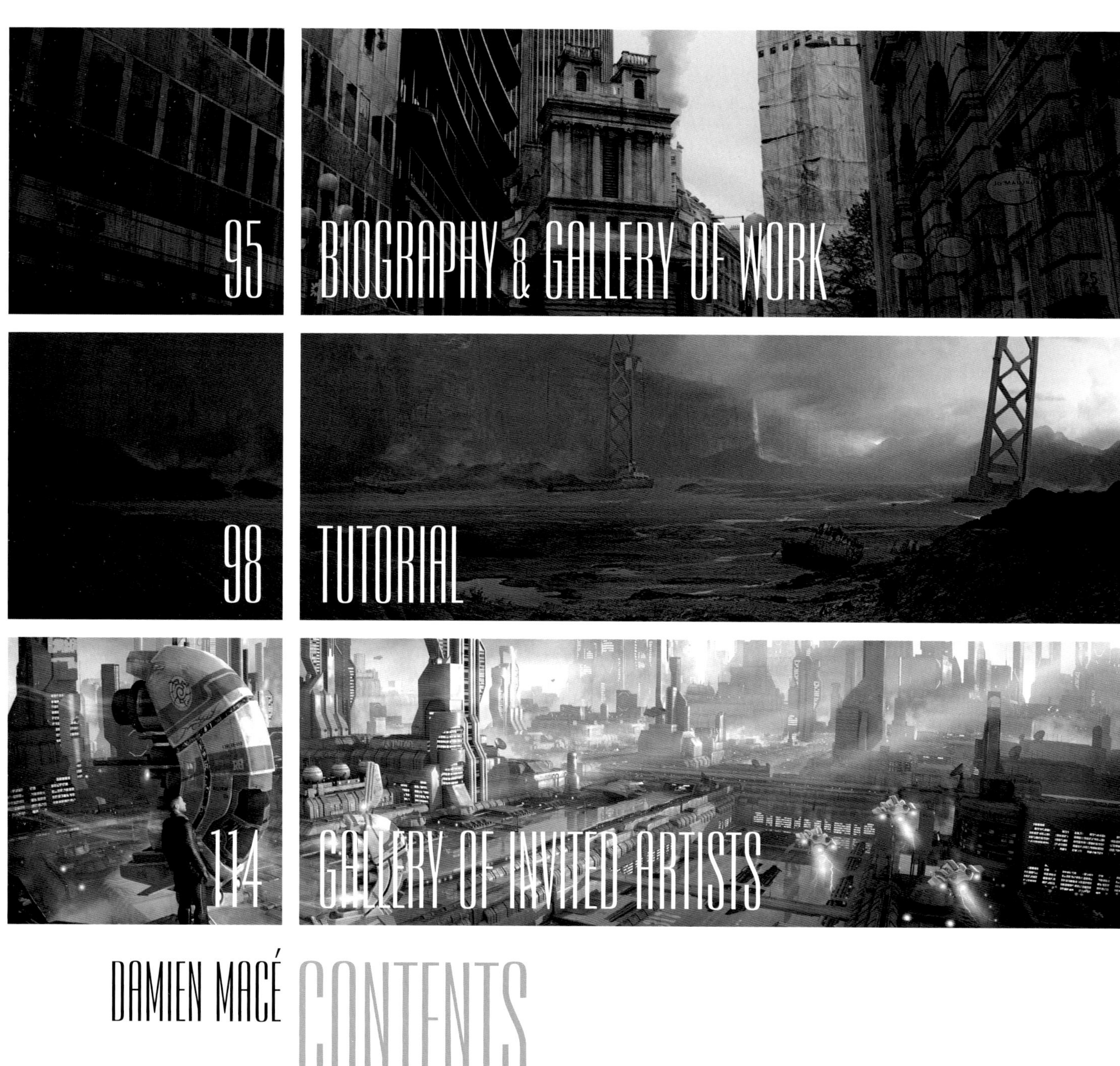

DAMIEN MACÉ

CONTENTS

DAMIEN MACÉ BIOGRAPHY

MY EARLY YEARS

I grew up in a small town in France. When I was younger I was a complete geek and spent a lot of time playing role-playing games and losing myself in imaginary worlds. I played *Dungeons and Dragons* and also lots of miniature war games. This is how I got my inspiration and motivation to move in an artistic direction as I got older.

In my final year of high school I studied how to build factories for processed foods – nothing to do with art at all! I have been good at drawing since I was a child but I was a very average student. After high school, I followed my passion and spent three years at art school. After I discovered my passion, I was no longer an average student.

I learned classical drawing and arts at École Pivaut, a great art school in Nantes, France. It was like I discovered another world. And the teachers there were amazing.

MY EARLY CAREER

I really wanted to do character design, as I loved doing animation, so I applied, unsuccessfully, to Walt Disney Studios, who still existed then in Paris. Instead I joined SIP Animation and helped with character design for background characters. I then worked as an assistant director for a few weeks on a Canadian cartoon, re-touching storyboards. It was one of my first jobs in the industry.

Around that time, the whole animation industry in France was pretty much shutting down, with Walt Disney Studios closing its doors also. I spent six months in a 3D school and was hired by BUF Compagnie, who had done VFX for *The Matrix Reloaded* and *Fight Club*. They had a reputation as a very demanding company and we all worked really long hours. I remember once finishing around 1.30 am and getting ready to go home when my lead called me as I was the only one in the office. He said, "We need to finish a test." I finally got to bed at 8 am. At 9.30 am they called me in again because they wanted to redo it.

During my years at BUF Compagnie, I spent a long time enhancing my painting skills. I had done a few matte paintings for some low-budget films – enough for me to have a small portfolio – and I moved to England in 2006 to join MPC London as a matte painter on *Sweeney Todd*.

STUDIOS AND PROJECTS

In my second year at MPC I started to do concepts as well because I had a background as an illustrator. My versatility was very helpful for them. I moved between the Painting and Art departments most of the time. I did some concepts for *Harry Potter and the Half-Blood Prince* that was picked up by the client. What ended up on film is pretty close to what I had painted, which was the first time that one of my concepts had actually gone forward and been produced.

I moved from MPC to Framestore in London, working on *Australia, Where the Wild Things Are, Prince of Persia, The Chronicles of Narnia: The Voyage of the Dawn Treader,* and *Avatar.*

From 2010–2011 I worked as Lead Matte Painter at BlueBolt on projects like *Snow White and the Huntsman, Great Expectations, Sherlock Holmes 2,* and *Game of Thrones Season 1.* I moved from there to Pixomondo, working on *Game of Thrones Season 3* and *Star Trek 2.* That was very cool. *Star Trek* is one of those

cool sci-fi movies that everyone wants to work on.

GAME OF THRONES

In 2010 Chas Jarrett, who I'd known since moving to London, asked me to join a company he'd created called BlueBolt. He wanted me to come on board as his Lead Environment Matte Painter on *Game of Thrones*. Being a geek, I knew what that meant – it was as big as *The Lord of the Rings*! I knew the scale of the project and what opportunities it presented for a matte painter.

The Art Department at BlueBolt worked ahead of our team, and we did the environments, technical concepts and mood boards, as well as put everything into the plate. We had very strong input as a team; even though I was the only concept artist there, it was really an amazing group effort. We were all very excited to work on *Game of Thrones*; at the time we thought we were the only ones who knew how huge it would be.

FAVORITE PROJECTS

The one that really stands out is the Wall from *Game of Thrones* – it's my baby. It is such an iconic element from the book. I designed it, and there are about 30 versions of it. I really put my heart and soul into it. The writer, George RR Martin, had such a great imagination and brought so much design to it, I could picture it so clearly in my head. I had read the book years before, and to get the opportunity to actually work on it was a dream come true.

I was also so happy that I got the chance to work on *Avatar*. When we got word it was coming to Framestore, where I was working, I practically begged my boss and everybody around me for the opportunity. Even though we mainly did enhancements, there was a little background that was fully matte painted. It was such a great experience and there was a huge buzz around it.

When *Avatar* was awarded they invited all of the London artists to Warner's private cinema in Soho Square about eight months before the release. Nobody had seen anything of it up to that point. They showed us 56 minutes of the movie in stereoscopic final and everybody was just shocked. We were just not prepared for it – it was amazing.

Sherlock Holmes was also a very challenging show as it had the kind of shots where the plate that is in the film had nothing to do with the location. We just got the geometry of the site and the camera projection, and had to start painting. I remember my first shot was of Piccadilly Circus, and I had 15 camera projections! I took me nearly three months.

ADVICE

I still do some traditional drawings and paintings. It is so important to do this kind of work as it adds a lot to your skills as a matte painter. You should never stop learning.

I remember at art school being shown the chromatic color circle for the first time – it was a revelation to discover how colors went together. To be a matte painter, you need a good knowledge of color and how light reacts on objects, how the light fades, how to depict distance, and how it affects your black levels and your white levels. It is more than just getting your perspective correct, it's about getting the right tone and the right light, as well as creating a composition that allows the viewer to read it properly in

Space Wolf
This is a concept I drew while reading *Space Wolf*, a novel by William King set in a distant future on an icy planet. I liked the mood of the book and its location, and I was inspired to create this quick concept of armored warriors fighting in the snow.
[left]

the picture. Traditional drawing, illustrating and painting really helps me a lot with all of these things.

You also need to be very willing to learn. If your supervisor tells you to pay attention to something, you really should concentrate hard on learning it. I try to always have open conversations with my team. Regardless of my position as a senior, I believe the work is better when everybody on the team can talk freely. VFX is teamwork, and matte painting is just one part of it.

I would say that being humble is one of the most desirable traits in a team member. One of my bosses at Framestore was Jason Horley, who always brought such a nice mood to his team. It was such a pleasure to go to work, and we had a blast for the six months duration of the *Sherlock Holmes* project. Jason was so open with us, inviting us every day to comment on his work, and he had so many more years experience than us. That really affected me, and that is something I really try to bring with me to the teams I work with. It is not always easy to open up your work to other people's comments, but it's so valuable to be willing to listen to other people's opinions. Regardless of the area you are working in, whether you are an artist or not, it is about bringing a kind of maturity to where you are working.

The challenge now is to keep up-to-date with new technology and tools so I don't fall behind technically yet still manage to incorporate these technologies and tools into what I already know. We are now working in a very technically aggressive environment. You have to be crafty and find your own solutions a lot of the time. It is often down to the experience of the matte painter or the supervisor to bring forward methodologies and techniques to get the job done. There is something very artisan about it still. We do not paint on glass anymore, but we still have an artisan-like approach.

Speaking directly about matte painting, I always try to spend a lot of time researching, getting the right images, and building a library – a very big library – of good-quality images. It is better to spend your time looking for good images for two days and work for one day than the other way around. It's all down to getting the right image – the right light, right everything. Sometimes it is not possible but you try to get as close as you can.

THE FUTURE

I love the matte painting side of things because it's very rewarding spending time getting an image correct. I have really enjoyed my experiences so far. Also, you know everybody in this industry has a passion for VFX, and it is very motivating.

I often have strong ideas about the direction of the pieces I work on, so in the coming years I would love to be involved as a matte painting supervisor or art director, where I can really drive the direction of the show artistically, or work directly with clients in pushing ideas forward.

WOULD YOU RATHER

Slay the dragon, or rescue the princess?
Slay the dragon. There is a bit of hero wannabe in all of us.

TUTORIAL 1: Aftermath

For this tutorial, I intend to develop a matte painting that entices the viewer with a landscape with a long history – a post-apocalyptic world. As I planned this concept, I decided that I wanted to use a combination of my own photos, and then introduce various other elements and a lot of hand-painting in Photoshop over the top.

I went on a holiday to Egypt with my partner in 2012 and had some good images to select from when I started this tutorial. I began my concept with the intention of creating a post-apocalyptic landscape captured in a moment of early morning stillness. It is perhaps 50 years after a cataclysmic event that has changed the face of the world.

Across the landscape you would be able to see the effects of a monumental change – with remnants of human activity here and there, like cars and boats, a ruined city, and a partly demolished bridge. Also, there are small bushes and trees around the place to illustrate that life goes on.

I am going to go through how I managed to achieve this matte painting, from beginning to end, step by step – from my initial concept to my final matte painting. So let us start with a look at my concept of the proposed matte painting.

1. First I painted a very quick, rough concept in Photoshop. My aim for the concept was to block in the story I wanted to tell. Halfway through the concept, I could see the need to add some modern structures, so I added the ruin of the bridge. My final image will be of a dilapidated modern city that has been changed forever by this apocalyptic event. The ground has shifted, the water has disappeared, and the shape of the world has changed.

2. This is a picture from my trip to Egypt in 2012. This photo was taken early on a very clear day in the middle of the desert. This is the base image from which I will create my landscape matte painting, and the setting for the story I have in mind.

3. I add a Hue/Saturation Adjustment Layer as it's easier to match my black and white levels. I do this so that when I get into Saturation mode I know the black and white levels are correct – then I just have to worry about color. I don't need to get a perfect match yet.

4. On another layer, I sketch in some guides (in red) for myself, and these indicate the line of massive cliffs that I want to build. Also, you can notice that there are a lot of color artifacts left from when I stitched the original photographs together. I want to keep them because I find them quite interesting. They look a bit like sunrays coming over the distant hills.

5. I start to extend and restore the rock bank in the left foreground, as I need to cover the black areas that were left behind after stitching the images together.

6. I continue patching over the recent human-made elements in the original shots using sections of images I find online. I use about three or four different images. At this stage, I don't need my red guides. I take care to use Layer Masks for these so I can make further adjustments easily.

7. I use CGTextures a lot – it is a great resource if you want to get into matte painting. Here is an example of how I begin to extract parts of a new image for use on my cliff wall. I try to blend information I have from both the imported photo and my original plate.

8. I start to grade the new background wall. I place the new chunk of rock on top of the mountains in the photograph, and try to match the color, blending it all nicely.

9. I want the focus of my finished piece to be in the top right-hand corner (the setting sun). The left-hand side of the frame will not be so interesting as it will be in shadow.

10. I continue building up the main part of the massive cliffs, being careful to match the color and tone to the original hills.

11. Whenever I am blending images I take great care to keep consistency between them, and also to be mindful of their varying perspectives.

12–13. In the two images directly above, you can see that the light on the big chunk of rock in the middle is inconsistent with the sun being low in the sky; the sunlight in my final piece won't be hitting that part of the rock like that. So I take some time to adjust the highlights on the cliff face.

14. I add some atmosphere by doing some grading – trying to establish the feeling of the new landscape. I want to change it from a warm, sunny day in the Egyptian desert and start to create an atmosphere that is evocative of a post-apocalyptic landscape.

15. I remove the last of the modern elements from the original picture. I continue to adjust the light on the left to help create drama. I want to guide the viewer's eye diagonally across the image toward the sunrise.

16. In this image you can see that I have added clouds onto the horizon. I want them to lick the edge of the mountains, not cover them. I try to match the sky to the original horizon as much as possible because a sky doesn't look right if it's not sitting on the new horizon correctly.

17. I continue to work on the sky, using Color Balance and Hue/Saturation, changing the sky's color to match the mood of the rest of the painting.

18. I also change the color in the midground, but here I try to keep some color from the original image as I like the passage of light and the shift of color, and I want to replicate it. I add the waterfall to show that life carries on.

19. You can see a subtle color shift in the foreground here. I want to guide the viewer's eye to the hint of light on the horizon, slightly to the right of the waterfall cascading down the cliff.

20–21. I found an image of a bridge from an internet search. The image was the wrong perspective but I liked the structure and shape of the bridge and its pillars. When I put it into my image it wasn't the right height so I repositioned and modified it to fit. A friend helped me get the base CG from my original concept of the bridge, and match the geometry and the perspective.

22. I didn't end up with as much of the bridge as what I had in my concept, but building more of it helped me to get the correct geometry. I was just taking the idea on board and using it for positioning purposes. Here you can see that I add the picture of the first pillar and start to reconstruct it.

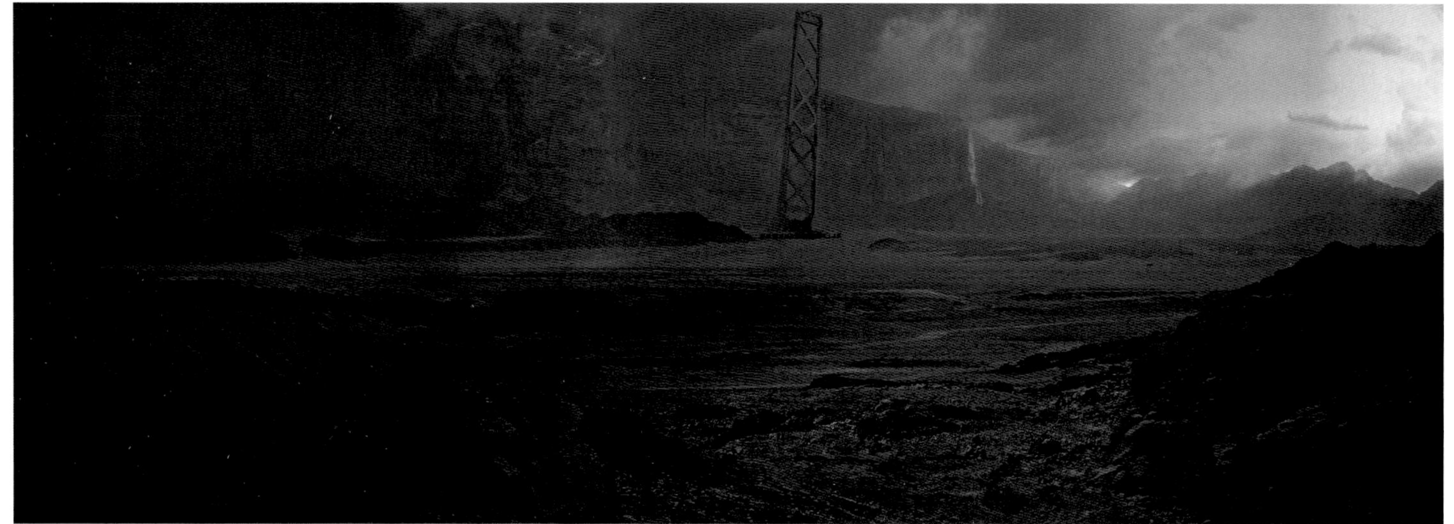

23. I don't want to put anything in between the two pillars, as it is starting to look a bit heavy in terms of composition. Also, I want the waterfall to help lead the eye through the landscape and this would be obstructed by extra pillars. I continue to match the colors with the atmosphere of the overall painting.

24. Here is a detail of the broken part of the bridge. You can see I have extended the bridge to meet the cliff and added support cables and broken pieces of concrete.

25. I repeat all the same techniques with this second pillar.

26–27. Now I need to insert some boats, which is fun to do. I take my first picture of a boat and position it where I want it, then I balance the colors so the boat's color is more in the tone of my image. I look at the black and white levels and try to find a better balance. I add shadow so the boat sits better in its new environment.

28. I am careful to balance my black and my white levels because I want to keep some of the original purply-blue color from the original image.

29–31. I follow the same principle with the second and third boats. I use the Transform tool to make sure they fit the landscape with the proper perspective. I again use Color Balance and Hue/Saturation Adjustment Layers to ensure the boats conform to the new atmosphere of my matte painting.

32. I pick one of the colors from the lower rocky outcrop and apply it to the boats using a partly transparent layer. This creates a haze on the boats and helps them sit a bit better into the background. I also add a bit of shadow contact. Three boats is enough – I could have put in 20 or more boats but it's not going to sell the point that this used to be a waterway any better than only three boats.

33. I add a puddle of water in the midground. I managed to find a puddle with good resolution and nice vegetation around the edges, and then I work to balance its color with my painting. I deliberately leave the vegetation around the puddle to help illustrate that life continues.

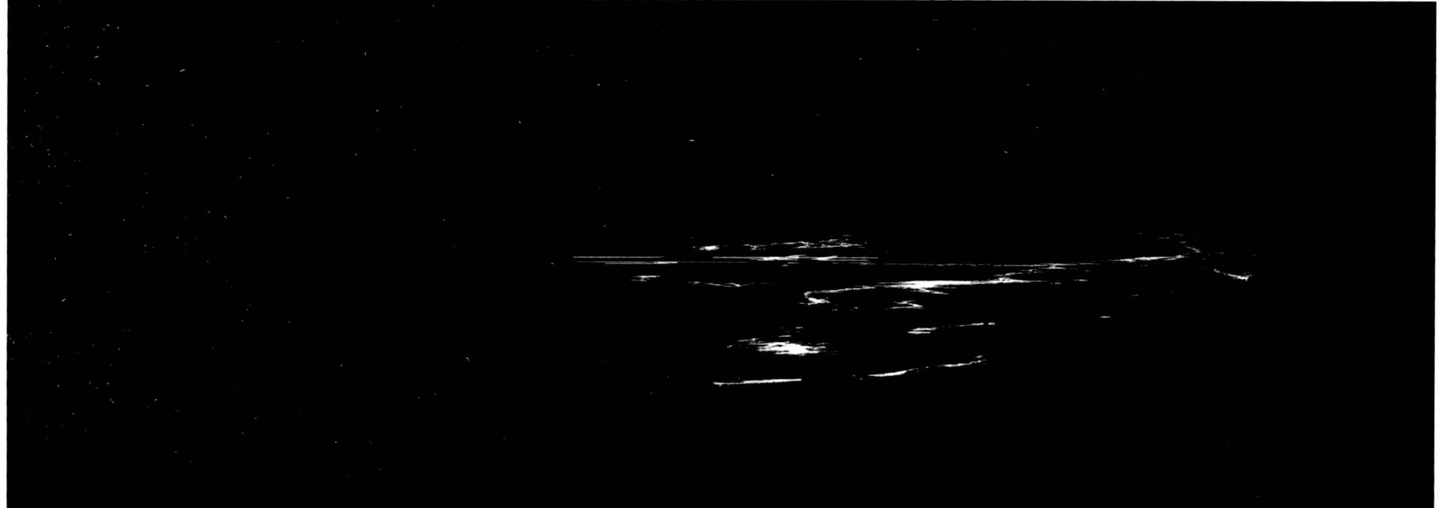

34. I add some more pools of water in the middle – these look like they are meandering out from the base of the waterfall. To do this, I duplicate the sky layer and invert it to create correct corresponding reflections.

35. I take a brush and try to work out where the water might be as it runs down the valley from the waterfall. I make sure that color from the sky is reflected in the puddle. I do this by creating a Layer Mask, and with the sky color, I start to paint with a brush, choosing where the water goes, telling my own story.

36. I make some adjustments that darken the water, add some more reflections around the edges of the puddles, and some more shadows. These extra little details all help to make a matte painting more believable. It also helps to make my painting a bit less flat.

37. Now for some focus on the waterfall. I got this image of a waterfall in the Pyrenees from an online search. In the original image of the waterfall, there is a break in the fall of the water where it goes over an obstacle, which matches the obstacle in my image, so it fits very nicely.

This kind of element in a matte painting will be there just as a place-holder on the film, and another department will generate some noise or do a simulation on top of it to create the impression of movement.

38. It's a bit easier to see in the enlargement that I've also added the kind of water spray you would expect from a large waterfall, and some smoke or mist rising from the base of the cliffs. In theory this would be done in Comp with some live-action element. Along the top of the cliff you can see the ruins of a city, which completes the illusion

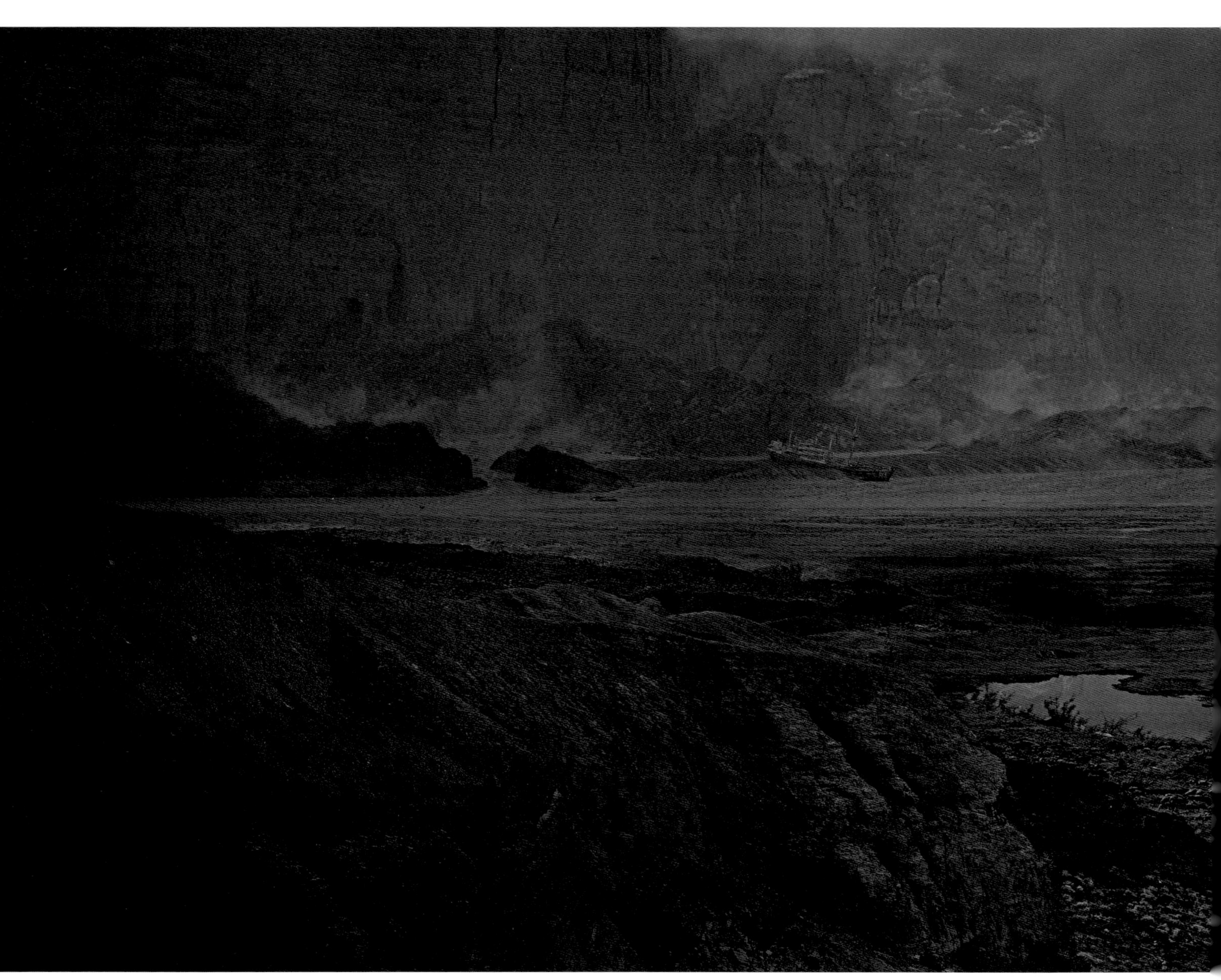

39. The final matte painting.

Damien: This piece from Jadrien is one of my favorites. It has great a story happening. It's like an old painting with a romantic feel, but of a futuristic city. It has great atmosphere and is a great concept.

Along the Penobscot
Maya, Photoshop
Jadrien Cousens, USA

SuperCity
3ds Max, Photoshop, finalRender
Stefan Morrell, NEW ZEALAND
[above]

Damien: One of my favorites. I like the composition and the atmosphere – it could easily be a concept from a high-end Hollywood film. It's always good to see a great idea finished off with a great execution.

SciFi Cityscape 2
3ds Max, Photoshop, After Effects
Stefan Morrell, NEW ZEALAND
[right]

Damien: Similar to the image above, this has a nice shape and great depth. I also like the tone. Both of these concepts are telling a strong story, and that's what you are looking for.

Thailand Trading
Photoshop
Jason Horley, GREAT BRITAIN
[above]

Damien: Great artwork, and a great color palette. This concept is at film standard. There is a great story happening here. The different layers are clear and well defined, and it is rich in color.

Room With A View
Vue Esprit, Photoshop
Christian Hecker, GERMANY
[right]

Damien: I really like the mood of this one. The colors, composition and execution are very good. I like the contrast between the warm atmosphere of the apartment and the colder colors outside. It looks like a nice place to live.

The World of a Huge Mountain
Photoshop
Igor Staritsin, RUSSIA
[facing page bottom]

Damien: Igor has really managed to create a great sense of depth in this image. I particularly like the use of color opposites – a warm light in opposition to a very cold shadow. It is a textbook concept that brings a lot of drama.

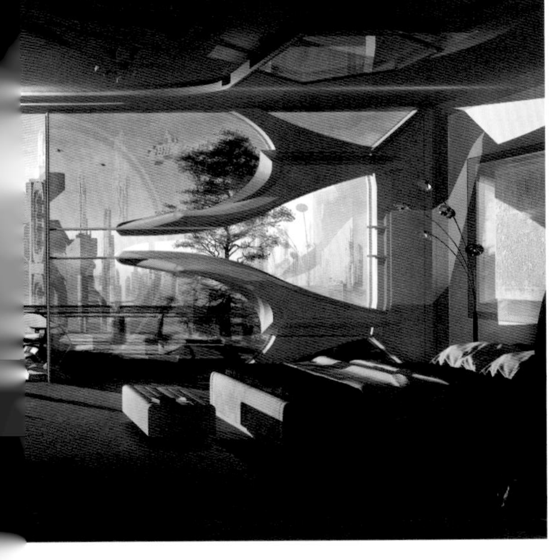

Damien: This painting has a great sense of atmosphere. It's got great depth and is a really nice concept. I really like the mood of it.

Assassin's Creed: City of Acres
Photoshop
Client: Ubisoft Entertainment
Benoit Ladouceur, Ubisoft Entertainment, CANADA

Dust: Chiiori Village
Photoshop
Client: Ember Lab
Igor Staritsin, RUSSIA
[right]

Damien: This one is very nicely executed. The misty aspect of the image is really well done. I really like the dominant green of this image – the moss on the roofs really helps to blend those buildings into the forest.

Discovery
Photoshop
Raine Kuusi, Fake Graphics, FINLAND
[above]

Damien: Very nice atmosphere. The artist really brings to life the element of this wild scene by playing with the density of its different layers and the fog generated by the waterfall. It has a very strong composition.

Town
Photoshop
Usama Jameel, INDIA
[right]

Damien: Usama has worked this landscape with very realistic tones, keeping the cold-colored greys and blues dominant. The results feel very realistic, though some more work on the perspective and white values would elevate the whole piece even more.

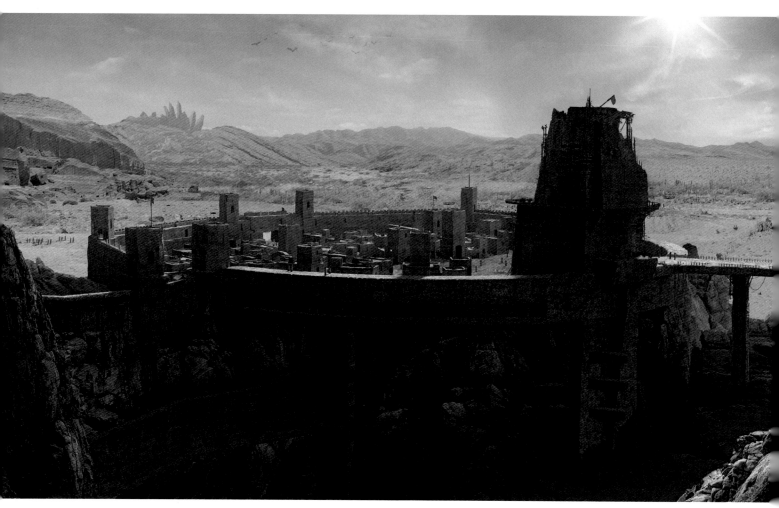

Thyn
Maya, Photoshop
Adam Kuczek, CHINA
[top]

Damien: This piece has a nice atmosphere, and an original shape. The background is not as strong as the foreground, but I think that overall it is a strong original idea and a nice concept. It has a very 'film' look to it.

Continuum: Downtown Vancouver 2077
Photoshop
Client: Artifex Studios
Gordon Oscar, CANADA
[above]

Damien: Great futuristic city. The depth of this image is very interesting. Gordon uses highlights to create the volume of the buildings in the distance, but keeps the foreground very dark. We then read the image from its light and outline rather than from the texture and details of the building. A very nice photographic exercise.

Grand Tower
Photoshop
Duc Truong Huyen, VIETNAM
[top]

Damien: I have always liked a great sci-fi landscape, and this concept is a great example. Duc Truong has played with the light to guide our focus to the building in the center of the image, while keeping an overall consistent mood.

Coming Soon
Photoshop, 3ds Max
Igor Staritsin, RUSSIA
[above]

Damien: I have a particular affection for this image. I really like the pink tone contrasting with the grey-blue shadows. It has a very *Star Wars* feel to it. The distant shape of the massive building towering above the city adds a lot of scale to the concept.

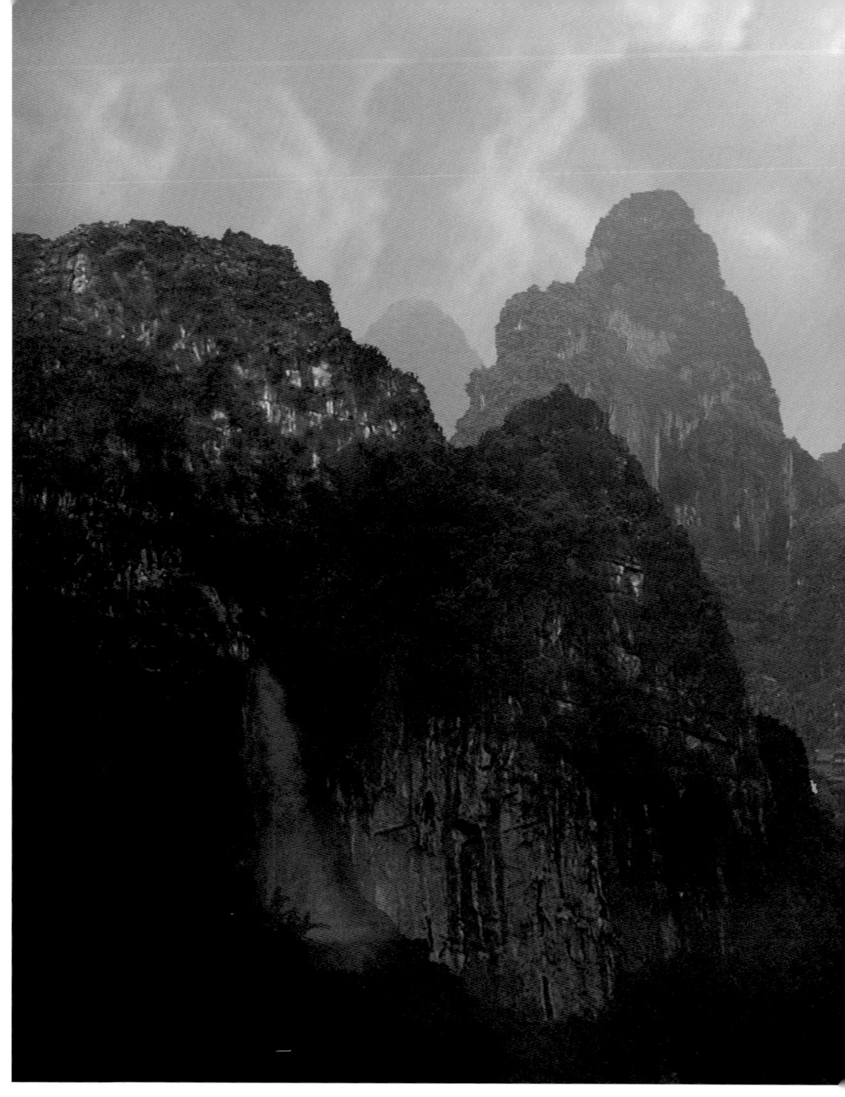

Misty Valley
Photoshop, Maya
Adam Kuczek, CHINA
[right]

Damien: I like this one a lot. I am always more sensitive to a storyline in a concept. This one conveys a great sense of traveling and discovering a new landscape. The technique isn't the strongest part of this work, but Adam has created a great atmosphere.

Eternal Tales: Legend of the Janovi Gem (Futuristic Fortress)
Photoshop
Client: Marcos Brumfield
Sourav Dhar, INDIA
[left]

Damien: Sourav is trying to direct/assist our focus point by playing with contrast. Our eyes are attracted to the areas of greatest contrast; where black meets white and dark meets bright. In this case, we see the spacecraft first as it stands out the most, then our eye is directed to where the spacecraft is heading, which reveals the futuristic station. Even though the station is much bigger than the spacecraft, it isn't what stands out the most, because it is hidden in the depth of the image. This is a clever narrative trick.

City High View
Photoshop
Client: OcularStorm Productions LLC
Gia Nguyen Hoang, VIETNAM
[above]

Damien: I chose this image not so much for its originality but for its mood. I like the heavy, dense, polluted feel of this city. There is something special about it. It has a good mix of very modern buildings with old-school American-style signage on top of them. These elements work nicely together to create a strong atmosphere.

Tethered Islands: Aerial
Photoshop, Maya
Client: The Aaron Sims Company
Francesco Corvino, USA
[left]

Damien: Francesco has created a really interesting concept with this piece. I really like the angle of view of the image. Also, the very subtle integration of the structure into the landscape in the concept is very well done. I think it could have been weathered a bit more for integration purposes, but the overall feeling is very realistic.

Lampisia
Maya, V-Ray, Photoshop
Francesco Corvino, ITALY
[facing page bottom]

Damien: I really like the art direction of this piece. The arches are very original and give a strong identity to the picture. It has great lighting, and uses color opposites to help in the reading of the structure.

Jade Castle
Photoshop
Adam Kuczek, CHINA
[bottom]

Damien: Adam has generated very beautiful scenery for this piece. It is reminiscent of a great medieval saga. I chose this image for its color palette and its strong mood. Once again, Adam uses contrast as a storytelling device to help us see the castle in the midground as the dominant feature instead of the giant statue in the foreground.

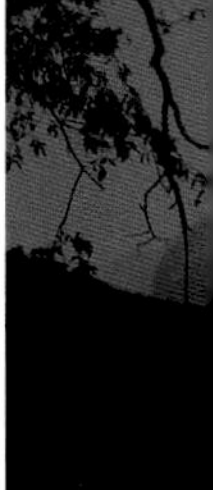

The Eyrie
Photoshop
Guillem H Pongiluppi, SPAIN
[top]

Damien: I really like Guillem's matte painting. If you look at the image from near to far, you can see a lot of narrative elements – the waterfall, the castle in the midground, and the castle on the top of the mountain in the background. These elements help direct our eye through the piece. I really like the quiet and peaceful atmosphere. Very nice work.

LiveCity
Photoshop
Igor Staritsin, RUSSIA
[above]

Damien: We all love a good apocalyptic concept, and this is a perfect example of the genre. It has good mood, and makes good use of the hot-orangey color to break up the grey and gloomy atmosphere.

Landscape
Photoshop, NUKE
Lubos dE Gerardo Surzin, SINGAPORE
[top right]

Damien: The artist has managed to bring a lot of character to this concept by playing off the strong contrasts between light and shadow. There is a very confident color palette and a nice integration of the background with the sky.

Village in the Fog
Photoshop
Simone De Salvatore, GERMANY
[above]

Damien: Simone has created a great work here. It's a nice concept. I really like the subtle light behind those buildings in the background. He has developed a strong sense of atmosphere, and the portrayal of depth is very well done.

Winter Landscape
Photoshop
Igor Staritsin, RUSSIA
[top]

Damien: This is the best matte painting of my selection. I love the way Igor has developed the light and the overall balance of color.

The Valley of a Huge Mountain
Photoshop
Igor Staritsin, RUSSIA
[left]

Damien: I like this one a lot also – it is a good concept. There isn't much in it to see, but the little you get is telling you a great story. It has nice depth and a strong use of the sun.

Over the Cold Mountain
Photoshop
Bastien Grivet, FRANCE
[facing page bottom]

Damien: This is a really nice concept with a very strong atmospheric feel. All of the image is shrouded in mist, but Bastien really manages to use it to draw out the different layers of his vision. By using a vignette effect on the bottom of the image, he helps us in our reading of the different layers as well as focuses our attention on the center of the frame.

The Bright Darkness: Shepherd's Bush establishing shot 1
For comment, please see page 157.

MILAN SCHERE

Milan Schere is a leading matte painter for the feature film industry. He studied visual effects at the Vancouver Institute of Media Arts and graduated from Bournemouth University with a Master's degree in digital effects. A defining moment in his early career was creating the matte paintings for Sony's *MotorStorm: Pacific Rift* trailer. That lead him to Prime Focus London as Lead Digital Matte Painter where he worked on TV documentaries, and was heavily involved in their successful pitch for the movie *Dredd*. In 2010 he joined Mr. X Inc. in Toronto as Senior Matte Painter, working on numerous titles such as *Tron: Legacy*, and taking responsibility for the technical aspects of the studio's matte painting pipeline.

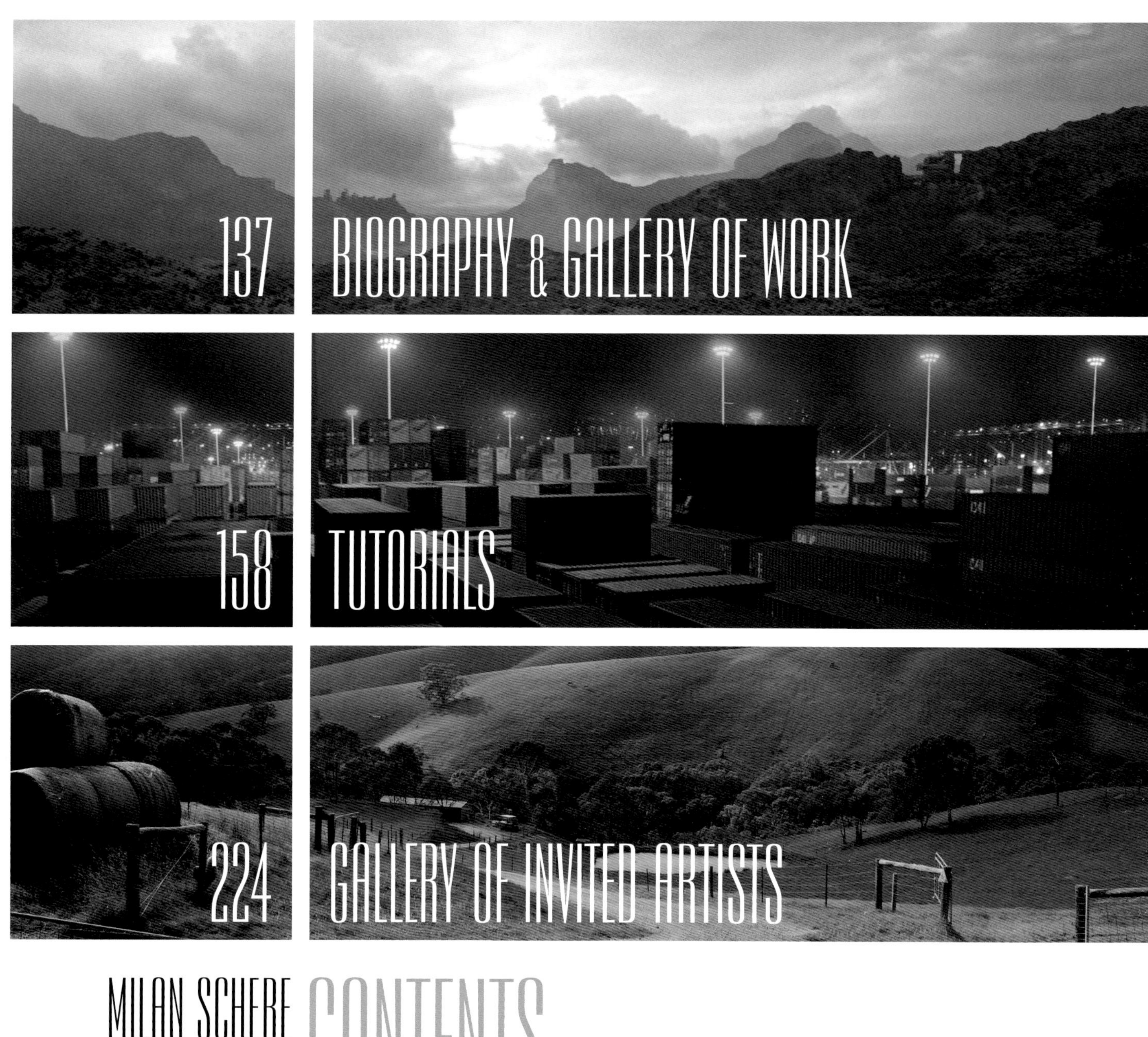

MILAN SCHERE

CONTENTS

MILAN SCHERE BIOGRAPHY

DEFINING MOMENT

I grew up with a passion for drawing and painting, and visual arts has always been the path I have followed. One of my first film inspirations occurred after watching the classic *Indiana Jones* movies at a very young age, and after that I became increasingly fascinated with the world of filmmaking. Later, I found out that almost all of my favorite movie shots were not only hand-painted but were created by the same person, Michael Pangrazio. I became a huge fan. I even learned airbrushing because of a story I heard about how Michael got into the industry. *Glim the Glorious* and *The Art of Star Wars* books, which have illustrations by Michael in them, are on my bookshelf today.

For me, everything in life always has to have a purpose. Especially art. I have always been drawing and painting, but I grew up in Germany where you have to get a 'real' job. I was told that the only work I could get was as a fine art teacher. However, after I saw *The Lord of the Rings: The Fellowship of the Ring* and, more importantly, read *The Art of the Fellowship of the Ring* book, I realized I could utilize my artistic skills within the realm of filmmaking. Visual storytelling has been the one constant in my life.

Unable to find a suitable film-related art degree in Germany, I decided to study visual effects in Vancouver, Canada. I later graduated with a Master's degree from Bournemouth University in England. Towards the end of my studies, it dawned on me that the professional matte painters I'd been looking up to were the same people I would be competing against to get a matte painting job. This gave me the necessary motivation to work even harder on my demo reel, and I began getting small jobs as a matte painter and concept artist.

FIRST INDUSTRY JOB

The first real step in my professional career came when I was given the chance to work on the trailer of *MotorStorm: Pacific Rift*. The visual effects producer took a risk hiring me despite my lack of experience, but it was exactly the opportunity I needed. I put in a lot of hard work and in the end the effort paid off, and I started to gain a reputation in London as a matte painter. The way you perform under maximum pressure is how people are going to remember you. I had a very memorable time in London, especially while working as Lead Digital Matte Painter at Prime Focus, alongside my wife, who is also a matte painter in the entertainment industry. After working on a few documentaries for broadcast television, I became involved with a pitch for the feature film *Dredd*, working as Environment Lead. I truly enjoy these types of hands-on projects because of the creative freedom involved.

Moving to Toronto, after being offered a chance to work on *Tron: Legacy*, was another life-changing experience. I joined the talented team at Mr. X Inc. as Senior Matte Painter and have been contributing to various projects since. It's important for me to be in a progressive workplace that encourages individual creativity, which allows artists to stay innovative and as involved as possible. I find that Mr. X. Inc is a unique place to work, and I'm able to constantly expand my skills through new experiences.

TOOLS

Over the years your tool set will change, so you need to adapt to what is available and

Vikings: A King's Ransom – King Ælle's castle: This painting is my favorite from all the shots I did within the King Ælle setting. The low camera angle and the composition very much appeal to me, and I was glad to be able to work with such a great plate. I find the strong natural atmospheric depth perspective and the color tone extremely harmonious and calming. As a matte painter in a professional environment, you do not usually get to suggest color corrections to the original plate; therefore, having a well-shot base to match to is something I value a lot.

what new techniques you learn. Right now, I use Photoshop, Maya, MARI and NUKE, but knowing software is not really at the core of what I do. Ultimately a matte painter must train their eyes for realism and a sense of lighting. Most of my shots are based on film footage or 3D renders. I get almost no locked-off shots assigned to my task list these days. It is important to familiarize yourself with the plate or pre-viz and all the surrounding shots within the sequence before you start.

Until recently, I used to solve all large-scale environment shots with multiple projection set-ups and layered shaders, but since MARI came along and NUKE has been getting more powerful, I've been incorporating them far more significantly into my matte painting workflow. The techniques themselves are very simple. I still do the majority of my work in Photoshop. It is important to judge, depending on the necessities of the shot, what approach would be most efficient within the given time frame.

On that note, it is also very important to understand that NUKE projections are often more than sufficient, and you don't have to run everything through a full 3D package like Maya. I like Maya, and it is my primary 3D application. It has been absolutely essential to me, especially when I was using Shake before NUKE came along, but more and more I find using Maya for matte painting shots is simply overkill.

ROUTINE

My daily routine begins with checking renders or messages and submitting either a styleframe or pre-comp to morning dailies. (Dailies are regular meetings with supervisors where artists can present their progress on individual tasks.) After morning dailies I have to address the notes I received and put my updates into afternoon dailies for the supervisor to look at. Matte paintings go through a lot of revisions and can change drastically from one version to another.

In the afternoon, I usually take care of another round of notes and, depending on the shot, I fire off some renders or get my still paintings ready to have another look at first thing next morning when I have a fresh pair of eyes.

TRADITIONAL

Outside of the office, I try to stay away from computers. I enjoy gouache and watercolor painting, and had one of my best moments in life the other day while watching my two-year-old son paint. He ran out of purple, which is currently his favorite color. So he promptly picked up red in one hand, blue in the other and started pouring both onto his sketch pad. Once he was done mixing them, he turned to me and exclaimed, "I mix purple!"

INFLUENCES

Other than my son's work, I enjoy the personal art of Erik Tiemens. He has a very unique technique that allows him to quickly capture an impression of a landscape. I have been inspired by his work for some time now. When I was a student, I constantly returned to Christian Lorenz Scheurer's work for inspiration and guidance. I am especially fond of his *Entropia* book and the fantastically detailed world he created within.

London's National Gallery was a great resource for me, and I spent hours staring at Romantic paintings trying to understand the magnificent way those artists painted with light. I'm also a real traditional matte painting enthusiast. I have books such as *Ellenshaw Under Glass* and *The Invisible Art*, and often get lost flipping through them.

In the digital realm, I have great respect for matte painters who understand how little is required to make a matte painting work. As

Vikings: Burial of the Dead – King Ælle's castle: King Ælle was the king of Northumbria during the time of Vikings, and is an important character in the saga of Ragnarssona Báttr. I created a series of seven matte paintings with the royal villa setting for episodes 6 and 7. The varying camera angles kept this environment interesting throughout all seven shots for me. To get the feel of my paintings right, I played a lot with the atmospheric haze and the wet look of this fairly overcast, after-the-storm type of scene.

far as digital matte painters go, I've always enjoyed Dimitri Delacovias's professional work. Finding the right balance of real paint strokes and photo elements is the key to making a matte painting come alive.

As much of an inspiration as a matte painting might be, it is important to understand that none of it should be used as reference for one's own work. It is much more advisable to take cues from photographic reference instead. As matte painters it's our responsibility to recreate reality, not a perception of it. Preferably, try to take your own photos and keep building your image library. Especially when traveling, take advantage of such opportunities as helicopter or boat rides to enhance your body of reference images.

As a matte painter it is important to keep in mind that the environments are there to complement the story and should not be distracting in any way.

ADVICE FOR BEGINNERS

Unfortunately, there's no formula for breaking into the industry. As with most things in life, I believe persistence is the most important attribute. The more you practise a skill, the better you will be at it. I recommend developing a professional demeanor by working on projects together with other people, rather than locking yourself up at home. Even an unpaid opportunity will help you gather a certain level of experience.

Matte painting is a very specialized artform, and in the end the tools you use don't matter as much as developing artistic skills like 'seeing light'. Don't rush your education either, but rather build a strong foundation by doing a BA in fine arts and an MA in visual effects in order to obtain a full understanding of the industry's requirements.

With a certain maturity and level of experience you learn to let go and delegate work rather than trying to get it all done yourself. There's a difference between perfection and realism. And it is important not to fall in love with your work – especially matte painting. Over the years I have learned that you should not get too attached to your art, or else you won't get anything done in a professional environment.

NEW CHALLENGES

Matte painting is the original visual effect and the techniques are older than the motion picture camera. I think the future of matte painting goes hand in hand with the future of filmmaking. I hope that Japanese animation becomes a major influence in global cinema; the worlds being created in anime have virtually no boundaries. Creatively, those are the types of environments that I enjoy the most. From a technical point of view, digital matte painting is going through an exciting time with many new technical innovations. Software is becoming more artist-friendly, enabling matte painters better control over technical aspects of their workflow.

I will continue to evolve as a matte painter, but I'm a filmmaker at heart and am planning to realize one of my own stories soon. In my future career, I hope to be able to art direct more and further expand the visual influence I'm having on the projects I'm involved with.

WOULD YOU RATHER

Slay the dragon, or rescue the princess?
That's easy. Slay the dragon.

Vikings: Wrath of Northmen – Lindisfarne
The monastery of Lindisfarne lies just off the north-east coast of England. It was featured in five shots and we knew the producers were planning to display it prominently in the promotional campaign for the series. The challenge I faced was that the given lighting scenario from the plate dominated my matte painting. I had to integrate my buildings properly, while respecting detailed notes about specific materials, such as the thatched rooftops. It took a lot of attention to detail to achieve believable photo-realism. After the Photoshop part, I projected the matte painting onto some simple geometry and passed on a pre-comp with a working NUKE projection set-up to the compositor.
[above]

Hanna – Hamburg container park 2
I painted multiple mattes for the *Hanna* container park chase. This particular one functioned as styleframe guide for all the shots, and helped the compositors to keep the look of the sequence consistent. It was especially important to match the overhead lighting in different views because this was the original styleframe we presented to the director and which we received approval for.
[above]

The Three Musketeers – airship u-turn
This is another one of my plate-based Louvre shots where I had to turn Würzburg into Paris. Everything other than the main building is part of my matte painting, including the ground and the garden with the gate on screen right. To keep visual interest I tried to contrast the symmetry in the foreground by breaking up the shapes in the background beyond the tree line. I also added some 'life' to the large number of trees by varying their shades of green. The final image received additional touch-ups by Matt Schofield and the compositor integrated the airship and more soldiers to complete the shot.
[left]

The Three Musketeers – Paris airship approach
The Three Musketeers is an entertaining period adventure with a steampunk flair. This matte painting was created as a paint-over on top of a Modo render provided to me by fellow Mr. X matte painter, Mathew Borrett, and then reprojected onto the geo. It incorporates a fair amount of brushwork. I have about four to five regular brushes in my set but I mainly use the default soft round one with the pen pressure option turned on. Some other matte painters completely disregard this function and instead toggle the opacity with the number keys in order to apply paint in layers onto the canvas. For adding additional detail there was also some MARI work involved on this shot.
[above]

A Dangerous Method – New York skyline

The New York city approach in *A Dangerous Method* had to display a historically accurate 1909 skyline. The initial concept we presented to the director, David Cronenberg, was at first mocked up by Mathew Borrett. I based my matte painting on recorded footage off the Staten Island ferry and used Mathew's image as visual guide. Most of my time was spent with research because there was no color photography in 1909, and, interestingly, a lot of the landmark buildings' façades have changed drastically over the years. We had some difficulties with the track, as it drifted off towards the end, and I had to move my set-up from Maya to NUKE, enabling the compositor greater control. The reason I remember this shot so well is because my wife went into labor the night before we had to deliver the shot. In the end it felt like all the hard work really paid off when we received a Canadian Screen Award nomination for Best Achievement in Visual Effects.
[above and right]

The Mortal Instruments: City of Bones – Hotel Dumort interior
I painted this shot for the teaser of *The Mortal Instruments: City of Bones*. The director of photography, Geir Hartly Andreassen, did a wonderful job with the practical set, allowing me to complement and add to his work rather than reinvent the shot. The version for the full-length feature film received some touch-ups by Matt Schofield. The image displayed here is the teaser version.
[above]

Carrie – suburb flyover
The *Carrie* teaser consists of one continuous flyover. I started this shot by painting some conceptual sketches in Photoshop for layout purposes. The 3D Department then built a full digital set based on my concepts and rendered out specifically chosen frames for me to paint on. The final environment consisted of three matte paintings in order to cover the entire camera move. Due to time constraints, the entire Matte Painting Department became involved with this shot, utilizing the same MARI matte painting pipeline established on *Resident Evil: Retribution*. We photo-surveyed the location to be able to match our matte paintings to the live-action footage. Most successful environment shots of this scale are the result of a talented creative team, and as such we were proud to have completed this challenge within an aggressive schedule. One important factor was the very skillful visual effects supervision of Dennis Berardi at Mr. X Inc.
[right]

Complete list of digital artists: Michael C. Tang, Yuhay-Ray Ng, Alfredo Octavio Arango, Katsumi Suzuki, Rob Greb, Trey Harrell, Chris MacLean, Jason Edwardh, Matt Ralph, Farrukh Khan, Barry Lam, Ben Mossman, Scott Riopelle, Keith Acheson, JJ McCallum, Ken Mackenzie, Florent Revel, Sunkwan Lee, Dmitriy Kolesnik, Ian Spriggs, Ran Long Wen, Ray Faenza, Wang Yang, Igor Avdyushin, Tom Morrison, Wei Gao, Angel Meng Li, Sean Mills, Hernan Melzi, Cyril Frederick Chu, Mai-Ling Lee, Andy Chan, Eric Cowan, Shaun Galinak, Jim Maxwell, Tracey McLean, Matt Schofield and Milan Schere.

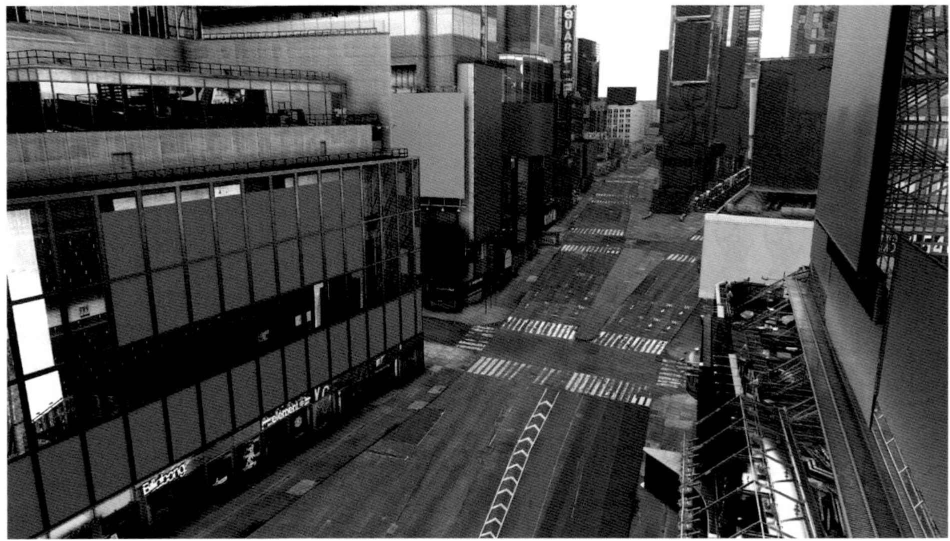

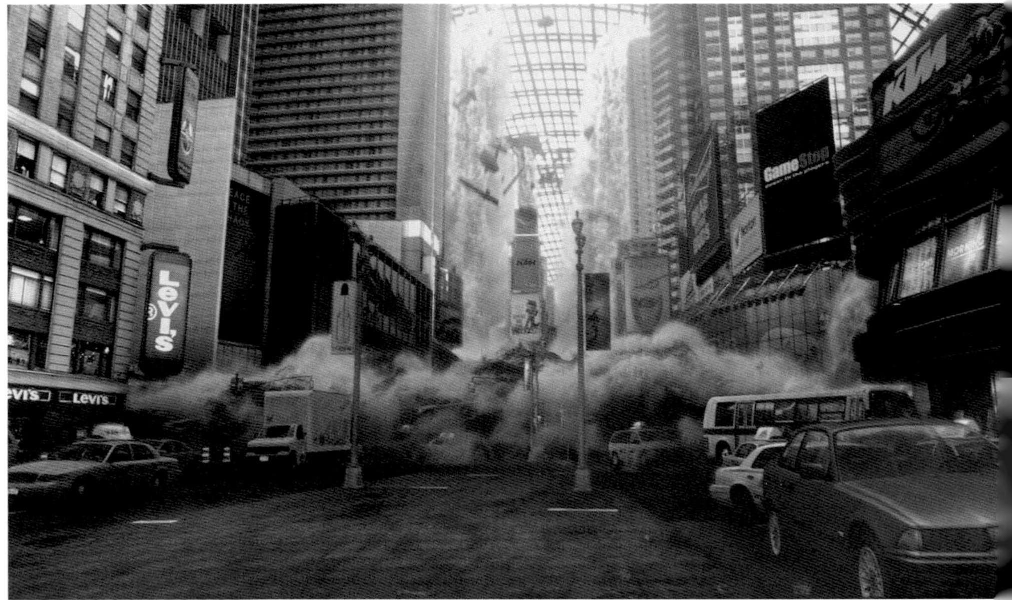

All images on pages 148–149 from "Resident Evil: Retribution": Image[s] from Resident Evil: Retribution, provided courtesy of © Constantin Film International GmbH and Davis Films/Impact Pictures (RE5) Inc.

Resident Evil: Retribution – Times Square 1
In *Resident Evil: Retribution*, besides Tokyo, Berlin, Moscow and Raccoon City, the Umbrella Corporation also built a simulation of downtown New York. For this Times Square matte painting I had to paint over 3D geometry and was able to save some time by utilizing the Texturing tool in MARI. It was quite interesting to paint an abandoned version of New York, as I believe this situation would never happen and it is definitely more cost-effective to create a digital version instead of having such a landmark spot cleared for a movie shoot.
[above right]

Resident Evil: Retribution – Times Square 2
I created another Times Square matte painting within the same sequence prior to tackling this shot, and I was able to re-use most of the first painting. For this I first set up my projection camera that had to cover the entire stereo area of the widest frame. Then I was able to bring this camera into my main Times Square shot and render a frame to paint on. As a benefit in doing so, I merely had to matte paint the two foreground buildings and do some MARI touch-ups on one other structure. Overall this represents a really time-efficient procedure used by most matte painters nowadays.
[right and below]

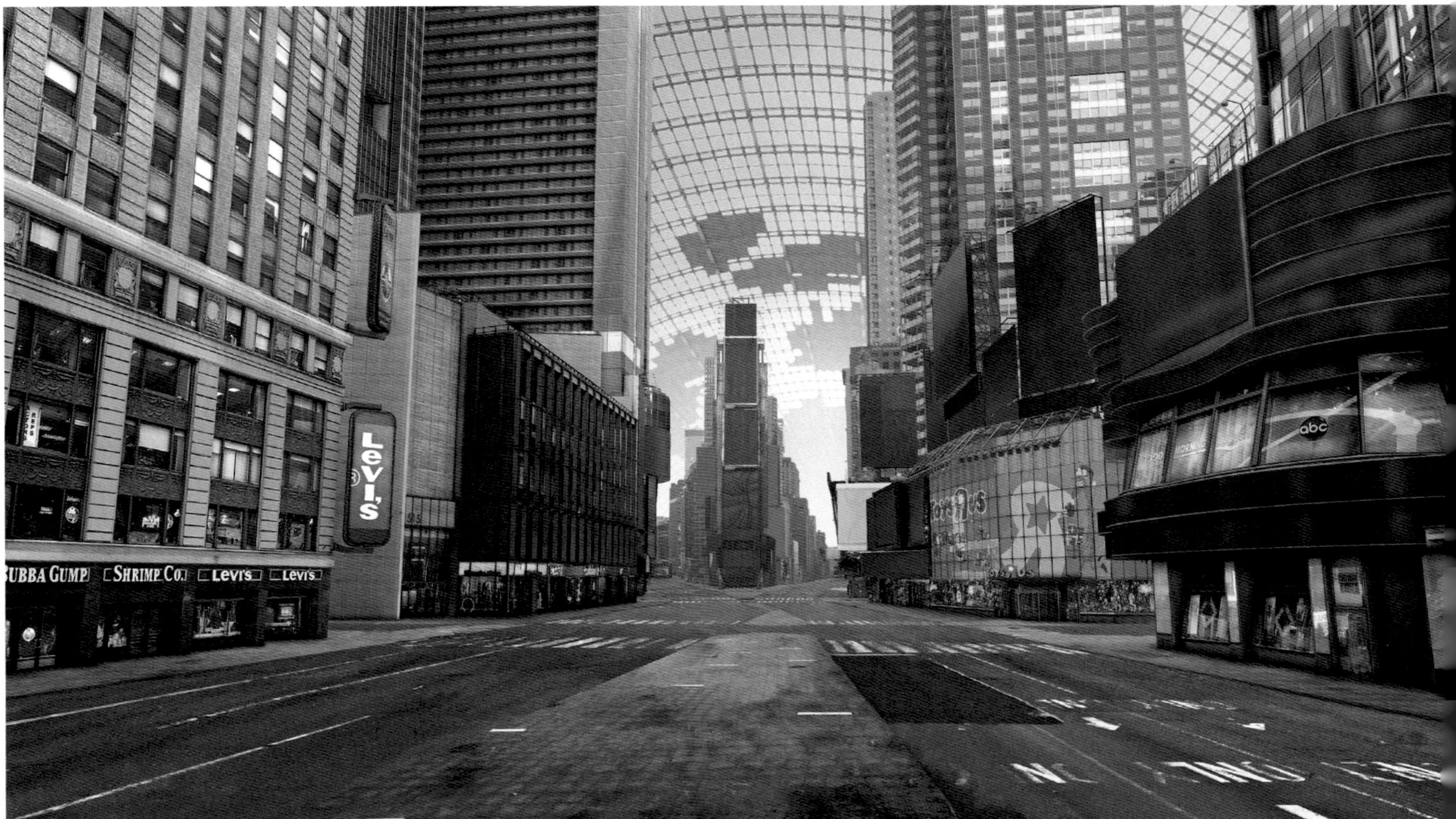

Resident Evil: Retribution – GUM store back
The GUM is the main state department store located in the Kitai-gorod part of Moscow. While its façade is facing Red Square, this matte painting shows the back of the building where an Überlicker attacks the heroes of the movie. Part of the storefront is a physical set, the rest is my matte painting. The sequence incorporates a few more different angles of the same environment which were all based on my original matte painting in order to match continuity.
[top]

Resident Evil: Retribution – GUM storefront façade
This matte painting depicts the front of the GUM store in Red Square. I matte painted everything beyond the two main window displays in the middle with the actors in it. For this matte painting I had to create a clean plate of the foreground cobblestone surface because the camera was mounted on a rig that was running on tracks in order to dolly in during the action. After finishing the still-frame matte painting I reprojected it onto 3D geometry to be able to match the recorded live-action camera move.
[above]

Hanna – CIA headquarters

The CIA's headquarters are located in Langley, Virginia, a few miles west of Washington, D.C. As the filmmakers were unable to shoot there, this plate was recorded somewhere in Germany. As the matte painting progressed, everything other than the main structure was replaced and upgraded. This matte painting was originally started by Mathew Borrett but I took it over from him as he had to move onto another shot. It went through a number of versions with a lot of changes along the way. The final shot *[main image]* includes animated flags, flashing red light on the antennas, cloud movement in the sky, and corresponding shadows (especially on the foreground grass).

Images from Hanna®, provided courtesy of Focus Features, Inc.

Kreola After Earth: Phantom Memories
'Kreola After Earth' is my largest personal project, and also the one I am most attached to. Rather than being a single script, it is a world I am continuously building, with multiple stories taking place within the same realm, stretching over several generations and characters. This establishing shot is from the main story, set on Kreola. A human refinery becomes visible in the distance as we move in. I shot all the landscape reference from a helicopter, having this scene in mind. The matte painting incorporates more than 20 personal photographs and involved a lot of de-modernization paint-out work. I especially enjoyed art directing the mood during the visual development of this environment.

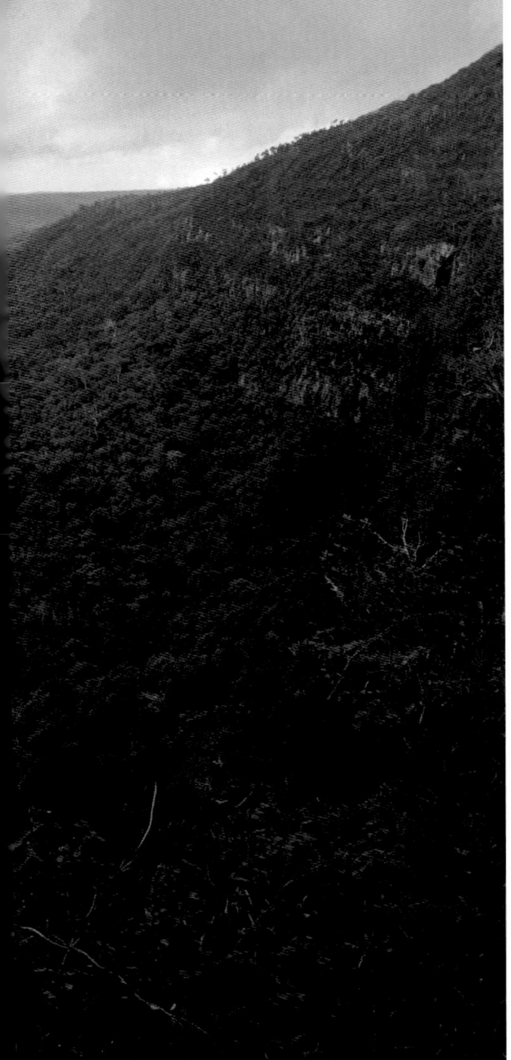

Kreola After Earth – Yuki's POV
In my personal film project 'Kreola After Earth' the heroin lives in a treehouse-like adobe overlooking a valley. This is Yuki's view in the morning when she leaves home and sets out for the day. A human outpost is visible in the distance, quickly establishing in which territory she resides. I tend to create very strong depth perspective and dial it back if necessary. In production, I would provide the compositor with separate haze passes to be able to tune the atmosphere later or, alternatively, match my proposed styleframe. Compositionally, I placed everything on thirds and tried to mimic an extremely wide focal length with a slight curvature of the horizon. In order to make it obvious that this is supposed to be a POV shot, I implemented some foreground elements, which simultaneously offered me an easy opportunity to color balance my painting with some warm tones. My overall intention for this image is for the viewer to take a quick glance at it; it is not a lingering establishing shot.
[left]

Kreola After Earth – K'harg radar station
'Kreola After Earth' is a steampunk science fiction tale revolving around a human girl on an alien planet who is caught between the lines at the brink of a war. As the external story arch develops, we gradually discover more about her past, ultimately placing her in a key position within the upcoming revolution. This flyover shot displays a K'harg station in the distance, as we approach. The K'harg are one of the three main groups in the story's outer conflict. I tried to portray a very humid environment with a high photon count in the atmosphere. Consequently, I decided to make the metal structures more corroded. Due to the characteristics of this race, I also avoided paint and any unnecessary color or gimmicks that I would usually add as fine detail or 3D elements.
[above]

Six Days: A Neo-Tokyo Love Story
'Six Days' is a personal project I'm hoping to realize as a short movie within the next five years. This production art piece is inspired by the works of my favorite filmmaker, Makoto Shinkai. I have been a huge fan of his vision and storytelling for years and welcomed the opportunity to follow Shinkai-san's art direction indirectly by referencing from his book, *The Sky of the Longing for Memories*. I started to build my Tokyo image library during my early career when I worked remotely for a studio based in Japan, and it has been growing ever since. I'm generally fascinated with Japanese culture, especially if there's a science fiction twist to it. If you're unfamiliar with Shinkai's movies, I recommend watching *Cosmonaut* from his *Byôsoku Go Senchimētoru* collection.
[above]

Return of the Dragon Queen: Wing and Fire
'Return of the Dragon Queen' is a short story about the metamorphosis of dragons through their interaction with humans. I have been working on this project since I was a student, and I am still creating production design styleframes for it. A styleframe is like a Joseph Mallord William Turner painting in that it captures a moment. I'm a huge fan of Romanticism and especially admire the works of Bierstadt and Constable. Similarly, styleframes are production art pieces that visualize the essence of a shot or an entire sequence. Their primary purpose is visual communication between artists and clients or the different areas of production. Although styleframes have to be of a photo-real matte painting quality, they often go beyond the purpose of a matte painting and include a still of a moving element such as a character, or, in this case, a ship. The 3D boat model is courtesy of Alfredo Octavio Arango. I composited it in, trying to retain as much of the big Obelix sail effect as possible. For all my matte paintings I always try to utilize my own images. Never having been to Scandinavia, I was kindly granted permission by Dominic Remane and Sean Mills to use some of their photographic reference work within this personal piece. The end result is this styleframe with the now standard 2.40 film-look crop. I generally start out my matte paintings with a 16:9 aspect ratio and use a bounding box to help me keep all the important information within the final output framing.
[left]

The Bright Darkness: Shepherd's Bush establishing shot 1
'The Bright Darkness' is a supernatural road movie taking place in 1899. I have been developing this project into a feature film pitch for two years now, trying to create a unique storytelling experience. I started this matte painting as a traditional sketch on paper and took it to Photoshop to finish it. I created the big negative space due to the story purpose of the shot. The natural limestone reference comes from my own photographs I took on the Jurassic Coast in Dorset a number of years ago. It was generally a very quick matte painting, once I had figured out the composition and lighting. Having a back story is one of the keys to understanding the needs of your shot.
[above]

TUTORIAL 1: Hanna – Hamburg Container Park

The container park chase sequence in the film *Hanna* was carefully choreographed by Jeff Imada, and created some very exciting action for the audience. It was my task to establish a vast environment without distracting from the performance. For night scenes, just as for interiors, you have a lot of creative freedom with the lighting because of the multiple light sources due to a lack of direct sunlight.

I enjoyed creating this shot a lot because it reminded me of my all-time favorite matte painting – Michael Pangrazio's *Raiders of the Lost Ark* warehouse set extension. Since sodium-vapor lights cause less light pollution than mercury vapor ones, I intended to take advantage of the practical set lighting to create a nice contrast between the cool and warm lamps.

The general brief was to make the container park seem to extend off into infinity. In the end, this shot turned out to be a true color space challenge. All footage is usually shot in logarithmic color space. Log scans are equivalent to film negative and have no clipping. The most common file type for this is DPX and you would read it as Cineon. What we're used to on the internet is sRGB video with a 2.2 gamma. The conversion for this would be 1 divided by 2.2, but sRGB is generally not used in our industry. The actual true-to-life color space with a gamma of 1 is 'Linear' and is foremost used for CG rendering with a bit depth of 32 float. Unfortunately, this creates a real pipeline headache from a matte painting point of view.

In this tutorial I will share some technical aspects of matte painting in addition to the actual painting process.

1. The plate

In the movie industry it is uncommon to start a shot from scratch or based on a stitch of location photographs. Usually footage has been shot during the time of production before the project moves into post-production. This is called a 'plate'. The plate for this matte painting has a moving camera that was mounted onto a crane rig on set. I analyzed the recorded footage first before deciding on a suitable frame on which to create my matte painting. Within a studio system where multiple artists from different departments share a shot like this, you have to double-check such things as the actual working frames or cut frames, the length of the camera track, and any lighting, effects or other information that might interact with your matte painting.

1. The plate
Continued ...

2. Digital noise vs film grain
When working with shot footage, you have to start by reducing the grain or noise from the plate. There's a significant difference between film grain and digital noise. Even though most productions are switching from film to digital these days, there are still some directors who will always choose real film over pixels. For the past few years, I've been getting great results reducing the noise with a Photoshop plug-in called Noise Ninja. Being more of a photography tool, it does a better job with digital imagery than scans; sometimes I still have to take a shot to NUKE to de-grain it based on multiple frames of the image sequence.

3. Identifying the roto-line

For this matte painting I was asked to retain as much of the original plate as possible. I therefore masked out a good area for the foreground where I could keep the plate in tact and start putting my painting behind the real location. It is important to keep everything well organized from the beginning with each element on its own layer. You should build your Photoshop file back-to-front from bottom-to-top in relevant distance to the shot camera, having the camera-move already in mind.

4. Background concept

Although I have never been to Hamburg, I had a specific look in mind from early on. I am a fan of science fiction illustration and wanted to incorporate a very industrial mood into this painting. To quickly establish a color palette I sketched up a very rough concept that, surprisingly, I never really needed to upgrade later on as it seemed to work right from the start. At first I went overboard with the color variety until I toned it down to suit the range of the foreground plate.

5. Shooting stills

The on-set crew shot a number of photographs that I was able to utilize. We always appreciate as much reference photography as possible back at the studio; it beats having to google for acceptable images.

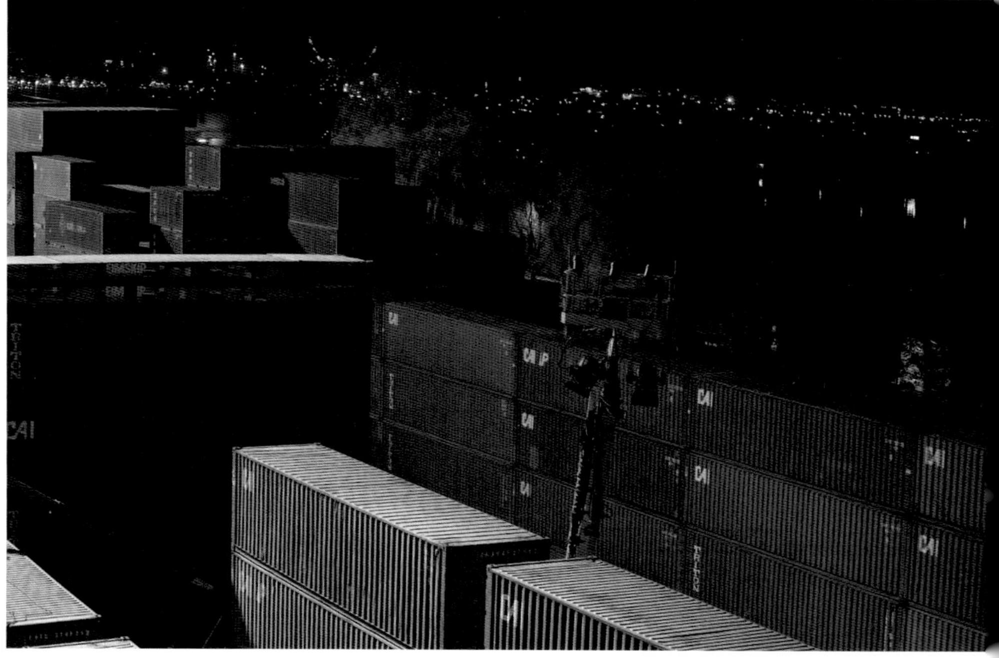

6. Preparing flat textures

I started by extracting the individual faces with the Polygonal Lasso tool and then flattening them out into a side view angle to be able to transform them properly within my matte painting.

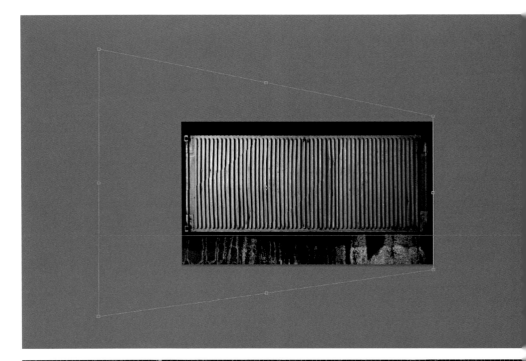

7. Perspective lines

I have many different ways of establishing my perspective grid but my favorite is still using the Line tool, as it is the fastest and simplest method. Knowing your perspective rules without having to actually think too much about it is essential and a key attribute of a matte painter. Alternatively, I could have taken it to Maya or NUKE, since there was an existing 3D track already, and duplicated a box in equal units along the same line. I found my 2D approach to be faster but possibly a little less accurate, which in my opinion gives it a more organic feel in the end.

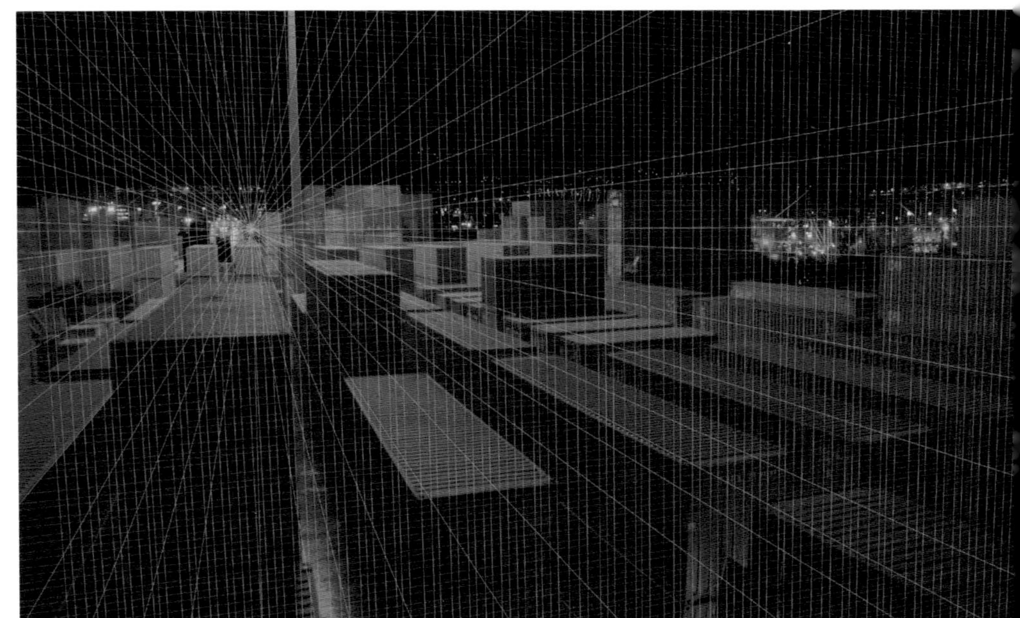

8. Set extension

Once I had the mood established, I was able to easily block in the set extension in the midground. Don't forget to layer individual elements properly in space to be able to save them out separately without overlapping faces and therefore allowing hidden parts of the painting to be revealed with the parallax when the camera is moving. This way you can avoid having to do a lot of patch work and texture fixing which would be a result of flattening your Photoshop file too much or building it inefficiently. I also painted additional haze and light spill on their own layers.

9. Color variation

Curves Adjustment Layers clip-masked to the individual containers give me the greatest flexibility and are usually sufficient to properly color correct photo references into my matte paintings. To quickly get some variation on the container stacks, I made a new layer and switched its Blend mode to Color before painting in some colors I picked off of the plate. This breaks up the painting aesthetically while limiting the color selection to those found on the plate.

10. Lighten the lights

To achieve the look of the matte painting, I used the Lighten Layer Blend mode as it performs a unique operation that creates a more favorable result than the Screen Blend mode. I also had to beat up my painted elements in order to match the live-action pixel artifacts in the plate.

11. Global color correction

At this point I decided to do a global color correction via a Curves Adjustment Layer on top of the entire file, before submitting the matte painting for dailies. Luckily my color correction was well received and I was able to continue using it.

12. Client notes

The feedback you receive can vary from vague individual words to elaborate verbal explanations with an included sketch or more. Here are the notes I was given with some very self-explanatory mark-ups.

13. Upgrades

I felt it necessary to introduce some more variations on the containers, and, especially after the notes I received, decided to replace the entire left side of the midground. I also brought back some of the industrial sci-fi background because I felt like it was starting to get lost a little bit back there.

14. Balancing

For the final matte painting I did an overall balancing pass and added some more depth perspective. This is a very important step to distinguish foreground, midground and background, but one must be careful not to wash out too much information as it is too easy to go overboard with adding haze and accidently making the final piece look unfinished.

15. Exporting layers

Next, I saved the matte painting out in layers with no overlap so that none of the elements were intersecting with one another. I usually keep my alphas separate because Maya sometimes has a hard time with embedded alphas and I don't really have time to deal with too many hiccups in the middle of production.

15. Exporting layers

Continued ...

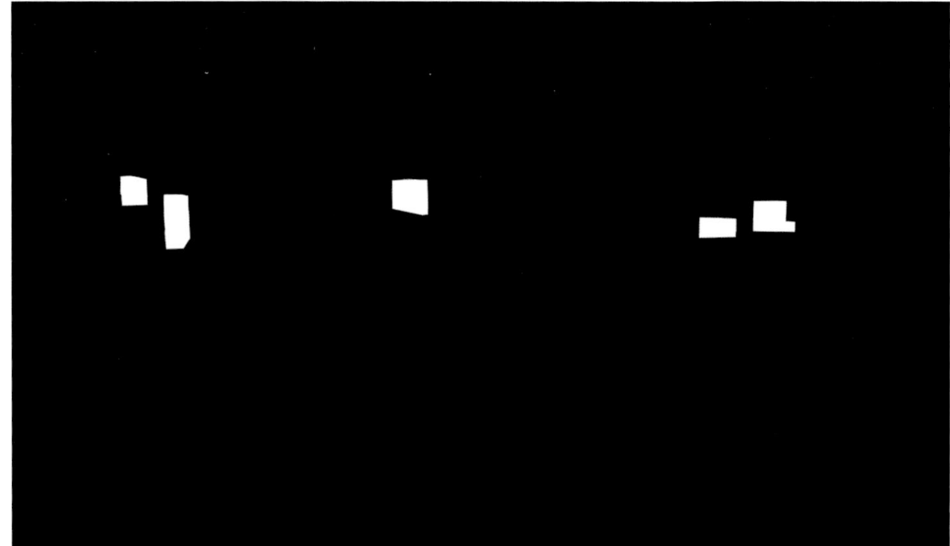

16. Modeling

To be able to project my flat layers in 3D space, I built geometry in Maya based on the tracking points cloud regarding the placement of my boxes. I created this shot in 2010 and nowadays there are easier ways of doing this step. As long as you understand what you're doing you can explore and find the most suitable approach to do anything.

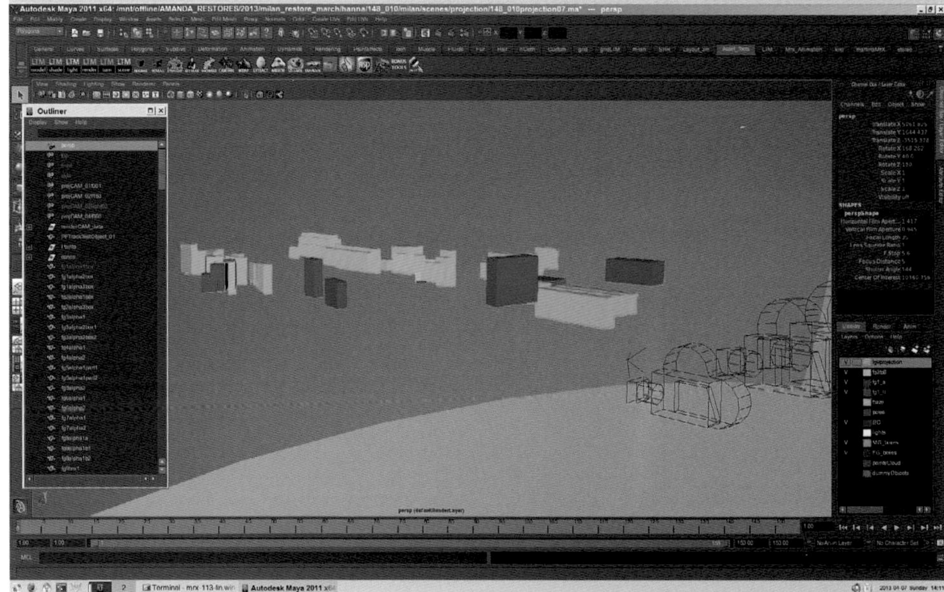

17. Maya shot camera view

When dealing with moving shots, you have to make sure your set-up works and your matte painting elements stick for the duration of the entire image sequence. This you have to test through the shot camera itself.

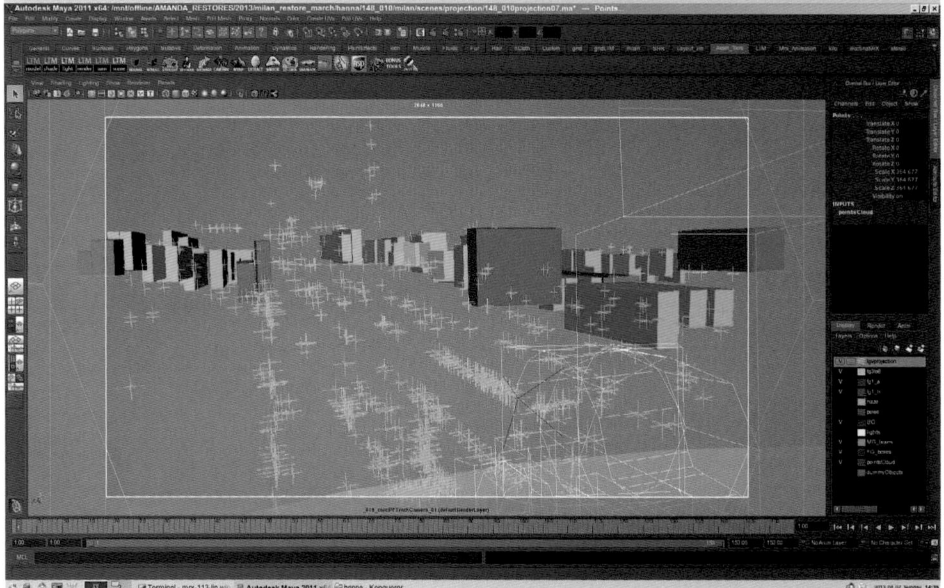

18. Maya light planes

Theoretically my light spill and lamp poles should be on the same plane. Practically, I had to keep the poles a bit further forward to avoid them occupying the same space as the light bleed and getting render artifacts as a result.

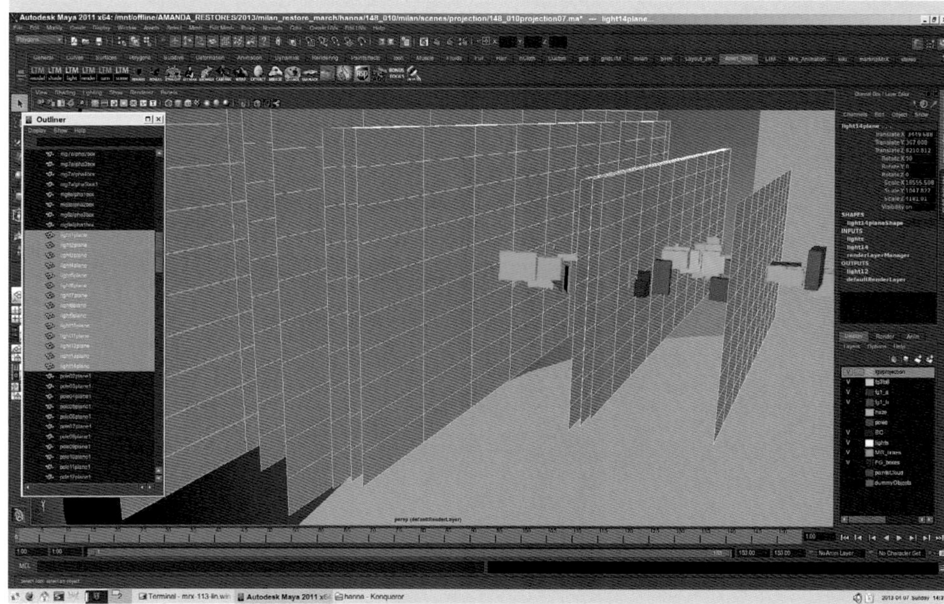

19. Maya to NUKE

The look I originally created in my styleframe was achieved by putting all the light spill into the Lighten Blend mode. Unfortunately, this operation is virtually impossible to recreate in another software and the results I was getting when trying to reassemble the rendered layers were not identical to the Photoshop file. It became obvious that Comp would eventually need more control and I decided to recreate the scene as a NUKE set-up. I exported the geometry as .obj files, although today you'd rather be using Alembic for this, and I brought over the cameras, including the shot camera as FBX with the animation baked in. At work, we have lots of custom tools but there are many useful scripts such as Chandump to get camera information out of Maya.

20. Light layers

Since the transparent pixels will be pulling in any background color from the image, I left my light layers as solids with a color behind the lights I sampled from the light spill itself. I have found this to be the most secure way to take any painted lights from Photoshop to another package. However, the industry has advanced since I created this piece and if you have access to a newer version of NUKE you can break out the layers from your carefully prepared Photoshop file instead of having to save them out separately.

21. Separate alphas

NUKE is a floating point platform. It linearizes all images when you file in. The Colorspace setting on the Read node is telling NUKE what to convert *from* to get the file's data into Linear light space, not what to convert it *to*. Due to the bit depth, conversion alphas have to be saved out of Photoshop as 8 bit to avoid mad-lines if you're keeping your masks separate as opposed to embedding them. Furthermore, you will have to specify them as Linear to keep the fall-off equivalent to what you painted in Photoshop. If your alpha is within your file, NUKE treats it as RAW and you should theoretically have no issues achieving the desired result.

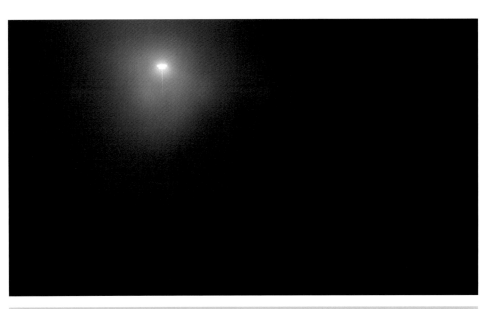

22. NUKE projection set-up

Once everything was properly prepared and ready, I simply imported the geometry, textures, projection camera and shot camera into NUKE, and plugged everything into a Scanline Render node.

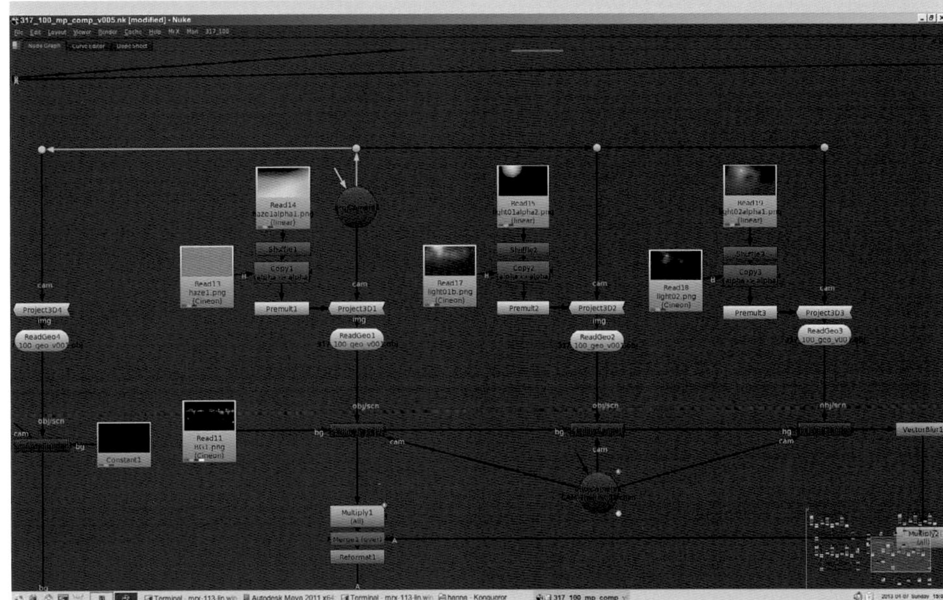

23. NUKE 3D view

NUKE is a very powerful application with great 3D projection capabilities as long as the geometry doesn't get too heavy. Cards and boxes are perfect.

24. NUKE Scanline Render

After some time of experimenting, pushing and pulling, the reassembled render out of NUKE was finally close enough to the original Photoshop matte painting, so I was able to pass over my pre-comp to the compositor without creating any headaches.

25. Final comp
For the final version, the shot received another color correction from the compositor before it was sent off to the client.

TUTORIAL 2: The Three Musketeers – airship landing at the Louvre

I very much enjoy being a matte painter. Art with a real purpose is extremely valuable to me and matte painting seems to precisely fit that bill. The main structure in this shot is from real footage filmed on location in Germany, while the wing extensions are full 3D assets. The rest of the environment, including the ground and the trees, is my matte painting.

The airship landing sequence is supposed to take place at the old Louvre residence of King Louis XIII of France. The former residence of the prince bishops in Würzburg functioned as a stand-in for the real Louvre baroque palace, and it was my job to sell the shot to the audience without anybody questioning the location.

Having visited Paris many times and also after lots of research during the conceptual stage of the project, I developed a very detailed picture about what the final matte painting should look like. This was the third shot I created for the airship landing sequence. While some of the buildings were a paint-over on top of 3D renders, areas like the far side across the Seine River, are a mixture of reference photography and digital brushstrokes.

I like to keep my matte paintings alive by implementing a fair amount of brushwork with the photo elements. For the buildings closer to camera, I used a matte painting technique called 're-skinning', which I will explain as part of the tutorial.

Matte painters have always been required to have the broadest skill set within this industry. Most traditional matte painters were also very well-rounded special effects artists. With the growing demands of filmmaking, stereoscopic imagery is currently one of the most popular features to entice moviegoers. I will guide you through some of its technical nuances within this tutorial.

1. Stereo footage

I started this matte painting by analyzing the right-eye centric stereo plate. Stereoscopic camera rigs give us the ability to adjust the position of one camera in order to vary the distance between both eyes and achieve the desired depth-of-field effect in stereo space. The fixed camera is generally what VFX artists work with. This is called the 'dominant eye'. All of the helicopter plates were shot with a RED camera, and on this project the right eye was dominant.

2. Projection set-up
In addition to the camera move, I also had to take the stereo aspect into account when setting up my projection camera. I generally work with the fixed eye but make sure to cover the area of the other eye with my matte painting. On this shot, I chose to create a unique projection camera between the widest frame of both eyes with enough over-scan to cover the visible area in stereo.

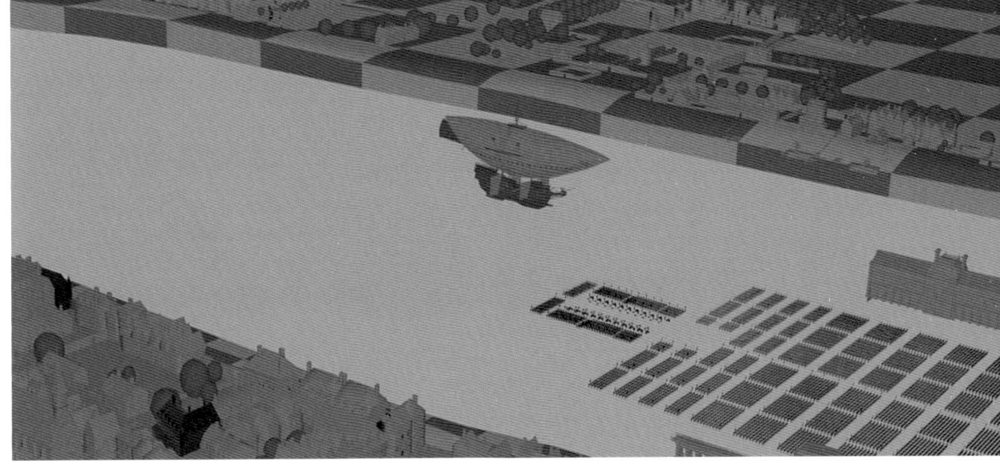

3. Layout over plate
This is the 3D layout combined with the original plate. The Animation Department was working on the approaching airship and the soldiers in the courtyard while I was painting up the environment. I used a checker pattern texture to help me with the perspective later. This is an inexpensive method that I use when working on 3D shots.

4. Modo render
After passing on my new projection camera, Mathew Borrett rendered me a frame of his Modo Paris set-up at 4k for me to paint on. Mathew also modeled and textured a few Tudor-style houses in Modo, which he then populated in several sections for us to use in our paintings. The way I start my paintings when they're plate-based is by enlarging the image to twice its size using Photoshop's Nearest Neighbor image resize function. Otherwise I take advantage of whichever bicubic option suits my needs most when scaling to odd sizes.

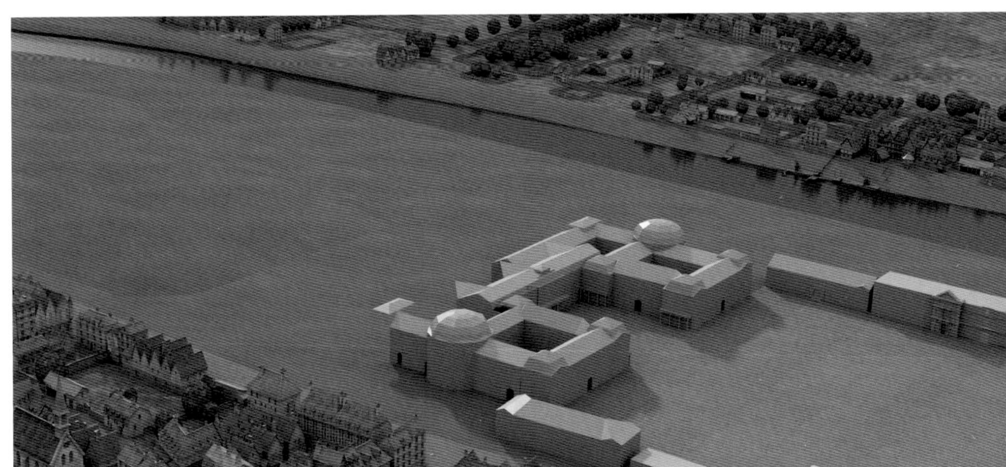

5. Ambient occlusion
The ambient occlusion is a tremendously helpful render pass that assists me with the self-shadowing within my paintings. It is non-directional and you can dial in its fall-off within the shader before rendering.

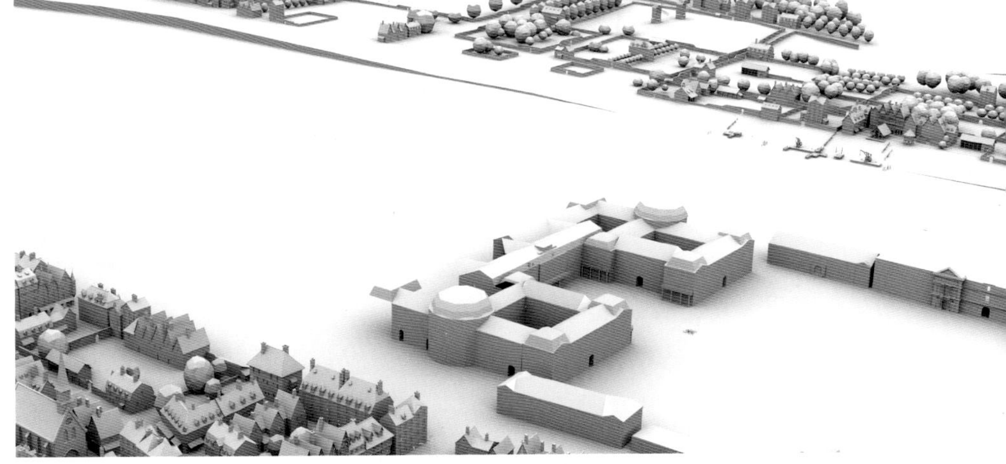

6. Z-Depth
With such a high amount of 3D, I like to take advantage of the depth pass. I used this pass to establish an initial atmospheric depth when I was assembling the render layers while creating a base to paint on top of.

7. Slap-comp mock-up
Here we're looking at the Modo pre-comp assembly with integrated plate. I assembled all render layers, catering their interaction to my taste. Then I placed the render in my shot to help me with the layout and to see what areas I needed to focus on first.

8. Clean plate extension
Next I had to paint out the trees as part of the clean plate extension. In some areas I painted in some additional trees to cover up modern structures from the plate. This is a task called 'de-modernization'.

9. Additional over-scan
Due to the helicopter's flight path, additional over-scan was required because the camera was rotating in a way that meant I needed enough over-scan to accommodate the camera move as well as the stereo offset. To determine the coverage area more precisely, I projected a frame onto the geo through the first and last frames of the left and right eye, and distributed this across various departments as the final projection camera for the shot.

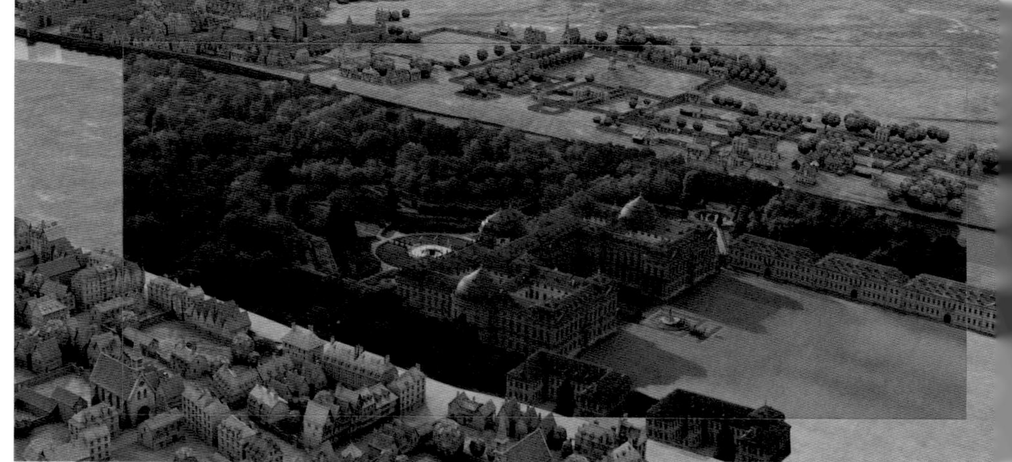

10. Concentrating on the coverage area
To be able to focus on the visible area only, I marked up a bounding box on a layer at the top of my Photoshop file. This would be the coverage area for the entire shot and I wouldn't have to worry about anything outside of this border.

11. Object ID
A pass like the Object ID speeds up my painting process by eliminating the need to Lasso each building individually. The solid colors can be extracted and selected by clicking the Channels in Photoshop.

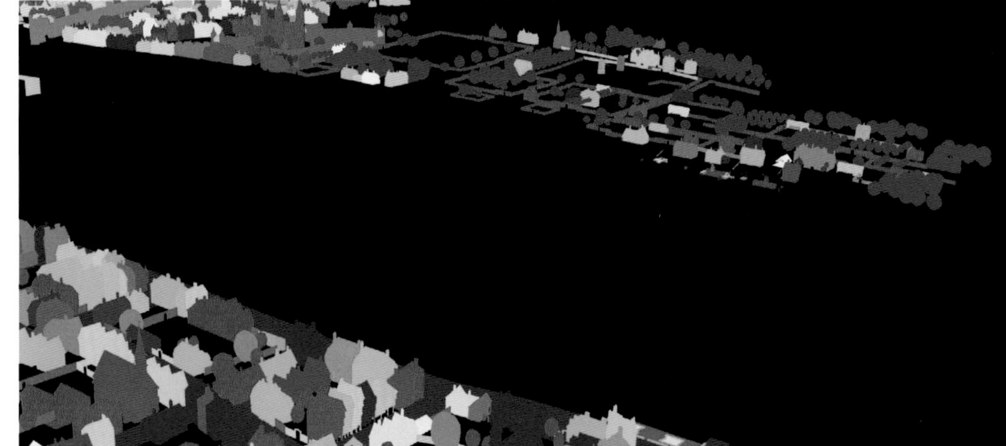

12. Perspective lines
I quickly made some perspective lines with the Line tool to guide me during my painting process, as I would normally do. I created these in very strong saturation so they could still be easily identifiable when I had them with a low opacity sitting on top of my painting.

13. Ground texture
I continued by creating a ground area on which the Animation Department would later place soldiers. The ground is a simple random brush paint layer with a two-color variation that I picked from the original plate to make sure I was staying within the color palette of the footage. Some updates on the fields had also started at this point. For this I cut and pasted chunks from photographs and color corrected them into the same world.

14. Tudor reference

I always try to use my own reference library before resorting to other sources. Usually VFX studios also have accounts at the popular image reference websites but I prefer to use my own whenever I can. Luckily I have a lot of random Tudor house photos that came in very handy during the production of *The Three Musketeers*. Most digital SLR cameras are capable of shooting in RAW format these days and I highly recommend using this function if it's available to you. I try to get as much out of their wide range as possible to preserve as much information as I can when importing RAW images into Photoshop. Where my images came short, I asked photographer Fabian Nagel for help, as he resides at the German-French border and I was able to specifically tell him the type of reference I was in need of. Strasbourg, the political, economic and cultural capital as well as largest city of Alsace, ended up being our main texture base with lots of Tudor houses featuring the studwork supportive frame structure of the walls visible on the outer façades and the dark, old beautifully weathered tile rooftops.

15. Re-skinning
Next I tackled the rather time-consuming task of face-by-face re-skinning. After I identified the lighting from the plate for light direction and intensity, I had to match to the plate because the lighting had already been established at this point.

16. RGB channel-based color matching
For integration I generally use a channel-based RGB color-matching method with only one Curves Adjustment Layer clip-masked to the layer of the specific element. I picked up this compositing technique when I was still using the program Shake and transferred it to Photoshop. I find Levels doesn't give me enough control, so I use Curves, and can add as many control points as I wish, and color match more precisely.

17. Brushstroke touch-ups
Despite all the technicalities of digital environment creation, I'm foremost still a painter. As such, I tend to implement a lot of brushwork in my mattes, relying on the photographic elements to provide enough realistic information for the brain. My Photoshop brush set has been the same for about six years, and I regularly use the same four or five brushes. It is important to know when to hand-paint something; I use my Brush tools intuitively whenever my paintings start developing too much of a computer-generated feel. This gives the image a more organic appearance and brings it to life. To stay within certain realistic color boundaries, I take cues from the plate itself and constantly sample colors from around the area I'm painting.

18. Balancing
As mentioned before, I did not worry about the area outside the bounding box because it was not visible through the final shot camera. I did another round of balancing, especially of light and dark shades interacting with one another. There was also a need for more foreground contact shadows, and I added grooves and variations to the streets to make them look used.

19. Building upgrades

In a way, matte painting is the art of determining how little is enough. It is an artform that has come into existence due to a specific need. In production there is very limited time for each task. As a result, here I was primarily upgrading elements that stuck out, such as some individual rooftops that looked too CG.

20. Refining the matte painting

Photons in the atmosphere create our depth perspective. Understanding this allows us as artists to mimic any type of atmospheric perspective we want to achieve. I tried to balance values all over my painting. The brightest whites and darkest blacks have to stay in the foreground while I can push the midground and background to wherever it feels comfortable to me. The foreground also needed a color correction for better integration with the rest of the image, and I tried to vary up the buildings a little more to avoid having the houses look too similar.

21. Checking with the plate

In such a shot, everything is dominated by the plate. I had to match the plate in perspective, color, value and overall feel. It is important not to fall in love with your work. The airship is the hero of the shot and the only part of the environment the viewer should be concentrating on is the front of the main building, if at all. It is rare that feature film matte painters would be trying to show off an environment. The point of this shot is an airship trying to land in the courtyard of the Louvre. If I had drawn too much attention to my matte painting I would have failed in my task.

22. Projection layers

After completing the base matte painting I had to export projection layers for myself to reproject it onto the geometry in Autodesk Maya. While exporting each layer I had to group my elements making sure houses didn't intersect with each other. At the same time I didn't want to create too many separate textures for efficiency reasons.

22. Projection layers
Continued …

23. Alphas
The alphas served as cut-outs to control the silhouette of each object. They allow more control; to avoid further technical issues by embedding the alphas in my texture files, I keep them as separate files corresponding with relevant parts of the matte painting.

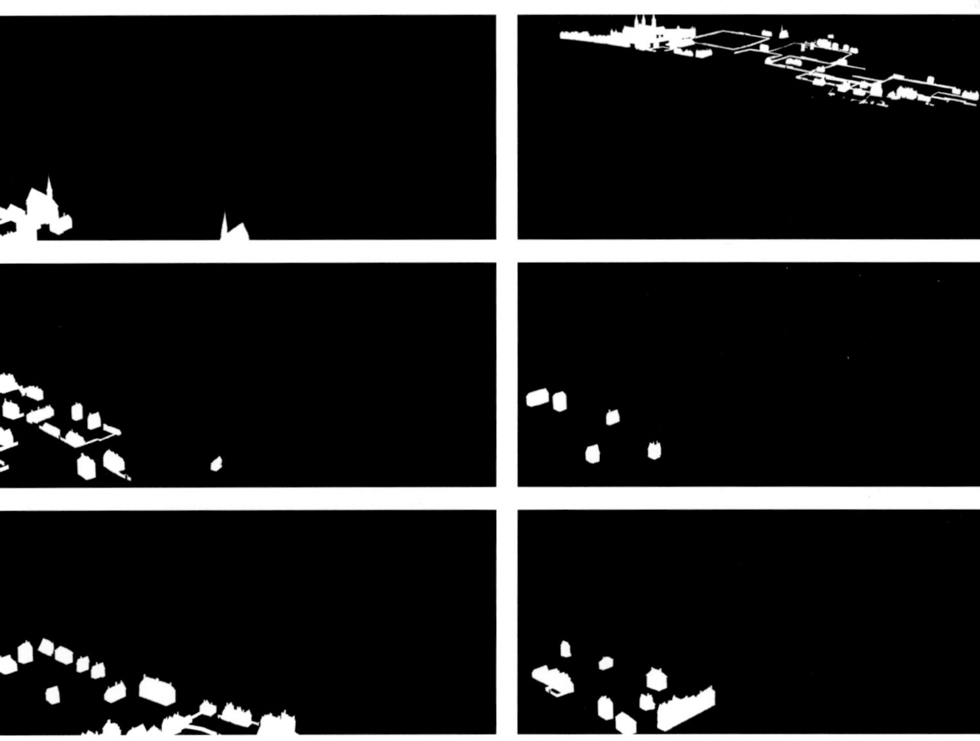

24. Stereoscopy

To achieve a stereoscopic image output, the final sequence needs to be rendered with two cameras. To match the proper distance to the camera all geometry that I was reprojecting my matte painting layers back onto had to be accurate in height and relative distance to the camera. The trees were particularly difficult in stereo because a wrong depth can feel strangely uncomfortable to the viewers' eyes and the shot doesn't work on the big screen. I modeled the trees as 3D spheres for the correct stereo result and kept adjusting their heights until the desired effect was achieved.

25. Foreground houses

Due to being so close to camera, the foreground houses needed some additional touch-ups and some projection fixing to work within the camera move. You can also see that I kept a lot of the original render, which at this point needed one final push. Once I see a shot moving, I always feel the need to improve certain details that stick out when it is in motion.

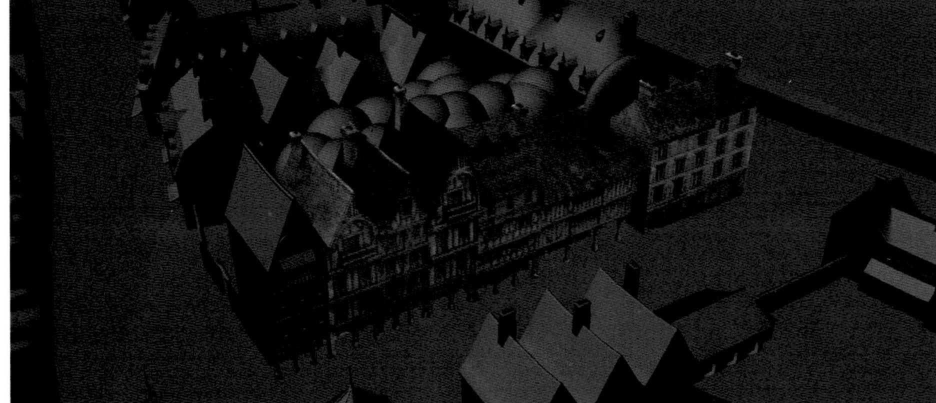

26. Taking the houses to MARI

In order to add more detail to the buildings on the left-hand side in the foreground, and to fix some projection issues, we decided to give MARI a try. MARI was relatively new at the time and we hadn't heard of it being used on any environment shots like this before. Since the models were UV-ed already, it was fairly easy to get everything in and out of MARI.

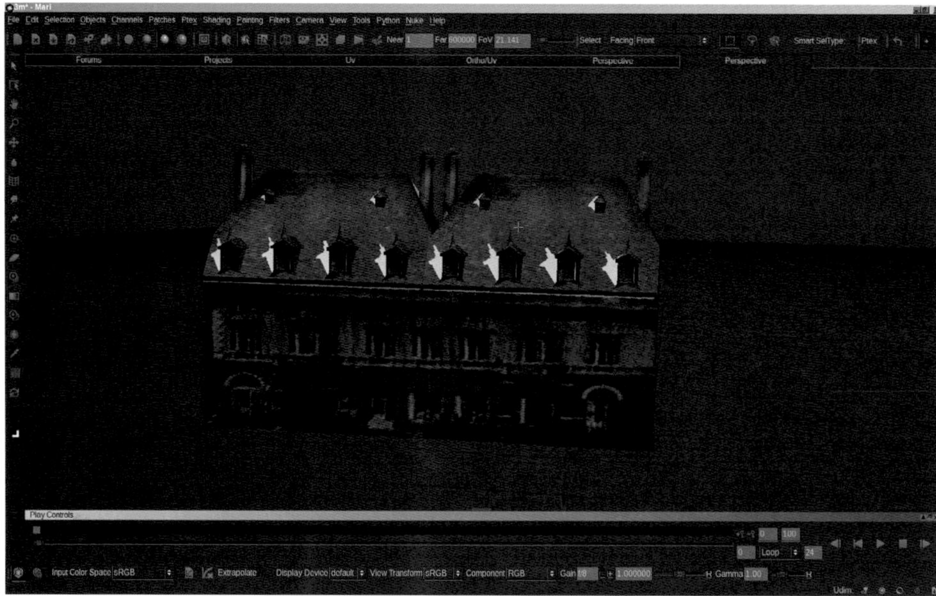

27. Maya mental ray render in stereo
I rendered the trees separately to give the compositor more control. At this point the shot also underwent a LUT color-grading session in the DI (Digital Intermediate) and I was given an ICC profile for Photoshop for any further work I had to do. The LookUp Table is the final color grade that is applied to the image sequence in the DI where a colorist and the director sit together and tune in every shot. The final product after that is what gets shipped. VFX studios get a working LUT provided during production, which the director either did prior to the final DI or is based on the color profile of the camera that the plate was recorded with. Softwares like NUKE have the ability to show images with a viewing LUT, helping artists to see what the color range the final image is intended to be in.

28. Final comp image sequence (left eye)
The compositor added further color corrections to my matte painting, lifting it somewhat and giving it the feel the director intended this sequence to have. The airship and soldiers were combined, making a successful final shot out of it.

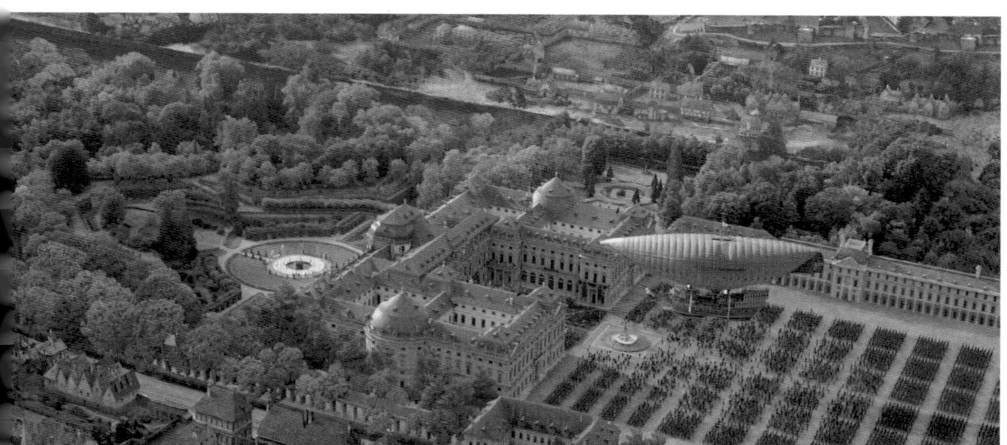

29. Stereo output

Stereo cameras converge in a rather cross-eyed way where the framing of the left eye displays more information on the right end of the screen and the right eye camera output shows more on the left side of the screen. Combined, this achieves the illusion of depth.

TUTORIAL 3: Resident Evil: Retribution – Times Square

Any successful visual effect must be invisible; especially matte paintings, which must appear real to be believable. Throughout my career I have found 3D paint-overs to be the most challenging matte painting work. A full CG shot without live-action elements often lacks the necessary connection to the world our eyes are used to. It is the matte painter's job to re-establish that link for the audience, using everything from cracks in a piece of concrete, stains on the ground or seemingly random objects like mail boxes, all the way to little pools of light placed by nature itself. Plate photography work gives you the necessary cues to all these, but CG has none of it, as it is 'perfect' and lacks the imperfection our brains are used to.

Being a 3D matte painter is something like a combination of a digital matte painting artist and an environment technical director. I love the painting part but I like to handle my shots all the way to pre-comp where possible. This New York Times Square shot from Paul W. S. Anderson's *Resident Evil: Retribution* movie represents a personal milestone in my digital environment creation process because it successfully makes use of The Foundry's texturing tool MARI.

I've been using MARI since my work on Paul W. S. Anderson's *The Three Musketeers*, and I took the time on *Silent Hill: Revelation 3D* to figure out some of its technicalities and establish a basic workflow. By the time I was setting up this shot on *Resident Evil,* my objective was to efficiently implement MARI into my matte painting workflow. I have been using this approach successfully on set extensions with implemented live-action footage, but this was the first time for me on a full CG shot. That said, MARI is not always the best solution. It is really shot-dependent and you have to weigh up which approach would be more efficient.

This tutorial should give you an idea how much it takes to fool the eye. It will also hopefully inspire you to get creative in your technical approach when creating large-scale environments for your next shot.

1. Pre-viz

The Pre-Visualization Department established the camera move, which had to go through an approval process before I was able to get started on the matte painting. In this sequence, gigantic tidal waves blast across several different environments. I mainly worked on the Times Square shots for this. My approach relied on getting this matte painting to work properly first and then recycling it for other angles.

2. Projection camera

Generally, matte painting projections are view-dependent. This way, I can efficiently preserve and use resolution. I started by setting up a projection camera that covers the entire move. Working in stereo, this typically means the widest frame with over-scan added to the camera scale.

3. Geometry
All the high-res buildings were provided to me by our 3D Department with their UVs already laid out. I saw that I would have to be modeling some background buildings myself, but that actually gave me more freedom for my matte painting.

4. Ambient occlusion render
I typically make use of the ambient occlusion pass whenever I can by multiplying it on top of my render or textures. Especially when working with such intricate architecture, I welcome this helpful render a lot. Whether or not you are proficient in 3D, let it help you as much as possible to achieve the best result. There are certain things such as this render pass that I recommend you obtain on a shot like this.

5. Color code
Color coding faces of your objects is a big time saver. It allows you to make selections without having to Lasso elements all over the place. Once again, the computer can really help you speed things up. This pass does not contribute to the look of your final image but it truly helps you get there faster.

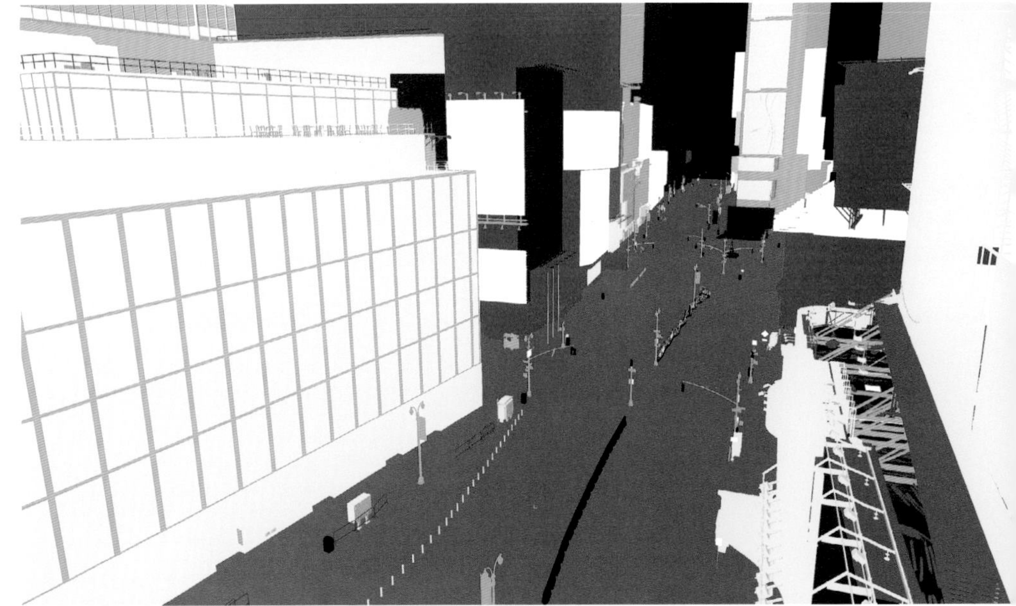

6. Photographic image reference

Mr. X Inc. sent out a team to take Times Square reference photographs in New York before I started this shot. I chose photos with similar perspective to my matte painting to avoid having to distort the images too much to make them fit into my painting. It was also helpful having uniform lighting throughout my various reference images.

7. Perspective lines

Besides establishing the usual perspective lines, I also created a second image with the help of the Line tool. When streets merge together, their view results in multiple vanishing points that should all still be sitting on the same horizon line. Quickly drawing in some outlines helped me lay textures underneath while being able to see the boundaries of each building surface. I could have used the wireframe render for this but my method makes it less convoluted, as I identify only areas I need one at a time. The multiple colors here all exist on their own layers, separate from each other.

8. First pass

This step displays a first texture bombing pass where a combination of basic textures and roughly placed reference photography gives a first impression of the shot. This stage made me realize that I had to research the traffic order in Times Square to figure out exactly how many lanes I needed to paint on the ground and which way each was going. Sub-tasks like this are part of a matte painter's duties and your audience will notice if you haven't done your homework.

9. Render passes

Once I had gained a first impression, I created a few lights to mimic the desired light direction, and applied basic shaders to the geometry. I put special emphasis on the foreground buildings because I was still searching for a good approach to handle all the railings and scaffolding close to camera.

Render layers:
Background
Diffuse
Lighting pass
Beauty
Global illumination
RawGI
RawShadow
Refelections

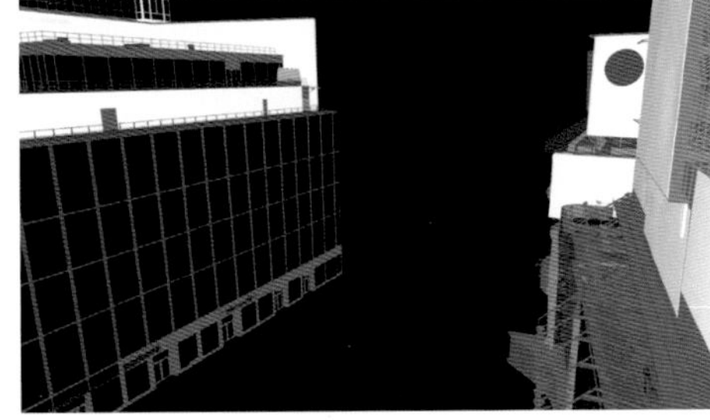

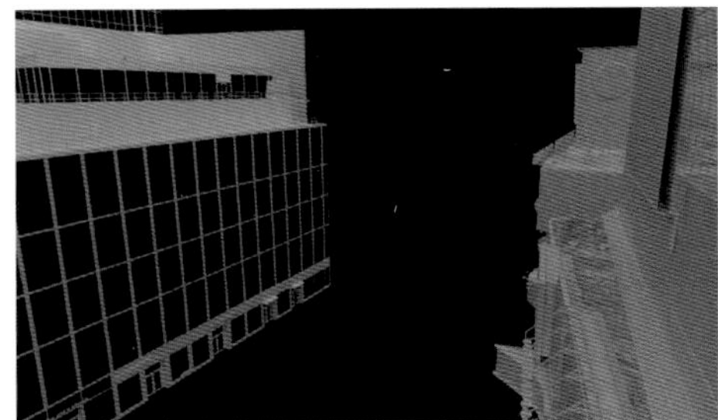

10. Dirt overlay textures

These are dirt textures I photographed myself. I used them masked on top of the concrete walls of the Minskoff Theatre. To achieve a weathered effect I switched the Layer Blend mode to Overlay and adjusted the dirt textures with Curves.

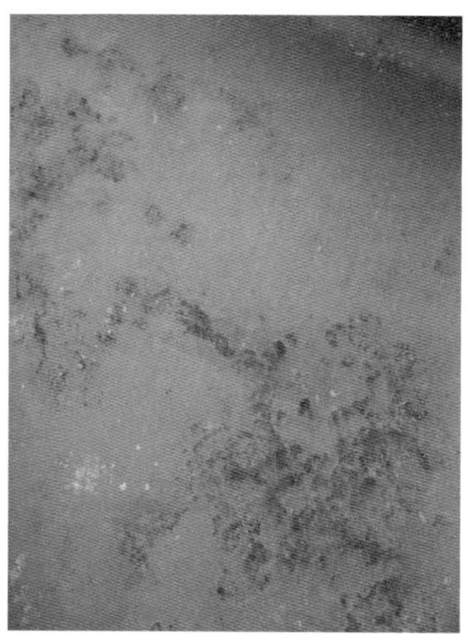

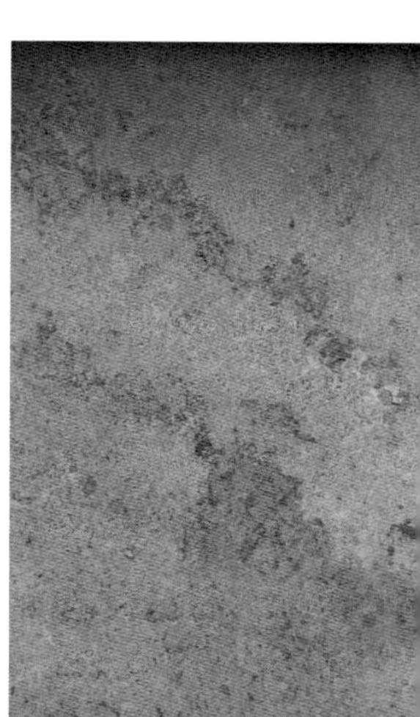

11. Matte painting version 1

Here is my first version of the real matte painting. It is not quite there yet but two weeks of hard work gave me a good understanding of where I was headed with this shot.

12. Refined version 2

A short while later I presented an updated version of my earlier painting, which also included a color correction suggestion to my original first take. Matte painting is a series of decisions that get you to a photo-realistc goal. While most decisions primarily lay in the hands of the artist, a lot of direction can also influence a piece as it's steering to final. As such, I was asked to clear off the side street in the back on screen left, removing two high-rise buildings in the process. I might have also gone somewhat overboard with my dirt overlay on the wall and I ended up toning this down. This version received a lot of overall small fixes in the areas of lighting and perspective.

13. No advertisements

At this point production also started to dance a legal tango concerning the advertisement space, as some logos are landmarks and others offered a chance for our own sponsors to use the billboard space. Knowing this, I started clearing off specific displays and posters, trying to find the least distracting presentation of an empty rectangle.

14. Layers for projection

Here are some of the original matte painting layers for my projection mapping set-up.

15. MARI

Once my single-frame matte painting was done, I imported the projection camera into MARI to add details and fix any texture issues. Generally, matte painting projections are view-dependent. Painting from a specific camera view helps to preserve and efficiently use resolution. MARI gives me a greater freedom to work with changes to the animated shot camera further down the line, creating less work for me in case somebody changes their mind about the camera move or angle.

16. Interior base

The FX Department was working on shattering the glass façade of the left building and I had to matte-paint the entire interior. I again applied some textures to the geometry, as before. To speed up the process of the environment build, Mr. X decided to purchase the Times Square model created for the production of *I am Legend*. Luckily for me, this building came with an interior. I set up a new projection camera just for the interior and painted over my base render in Photoshop before taking this part of the matte painting into MARI.

17. MARI interior

I won't go into technical detail about how I worked with and combined the Channels because The Foundry has, since I created this shot, completely reinvented their layering system. The new version is so similar to Photoshop that it is very easy to get used to MARI within a short amount of time. Overall, I try to use my Photoshop painting as guide and only add or patch the texture in spots, matching to the original matte painting. To keep visual consistency you can always zoom out and scroll through the animated shot camera in order to make sure your painting works as it did in Photoshop when it was a single-frame image.

18. UDIM

The UV space now goes beyond 0 and 1 and can be laid out better than trying to squeeze it all into one quadrant. The tiles are in rows of 10, with a sequence number attached to the file name. Most renderers nowadays understand UDIM and shaders can be set up easily with such exported textures of the baked matte painting.

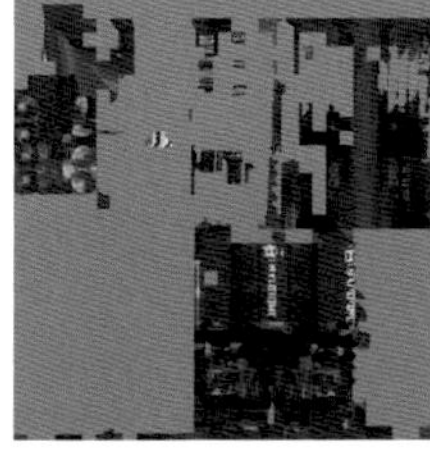
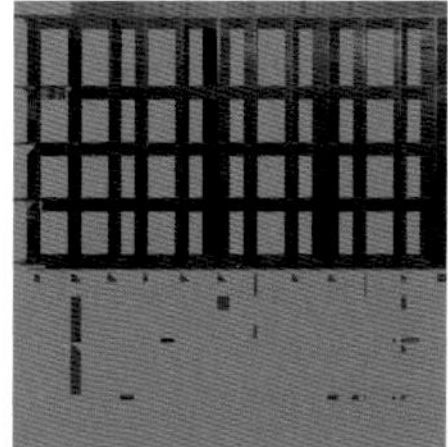

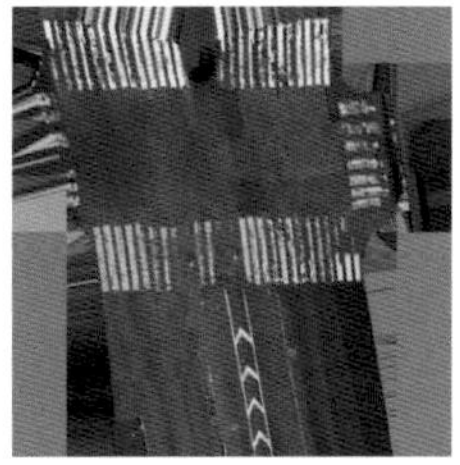

19. The railing

Some of the railings were actually not part of my projection and I used a black metal V-Ray shader for them. This was not required to be rendered separately because I didn't think the compositor would have gained any benefits from having this element as an individual layer.

20. V-Ray render

For the final render I used default lighting without any additional lights, and I plugged in the textures into self-illumination of the V-Ray shader. I rendered everything without shadows, as these are included in my painting.

21. 3D elements

Some of the 3D elements were full 3D objects created by our Assets Department. They were rendered separately and combined with the matte painting, and FX water later by a compositor.

22. Advertisements

Before handing off the shot, I masked out the billboard space so advertisements could be added to the moving matte. It is important to be able to pre-comp your own shot and therefore to possess compositing skills. It helps tremendously to supply the compositor with a script, especially because their department tends to get the busiest during the final stretch of production.

23. The finished matte painting

See the final clean matte painting overleaf.

The purpose of my work is not fine art but to help establish an environment, so I don't concentrate on trying to produce a pretty 'stand-alone' painting. A matte painting must look real. If the audience doesn't believe the shot I painted, then I did not succeed as a matte painter. I strongly believe that my paintings must be alive to be believable. There are advantages of knowing 3D but in my opinion it remains more important to have a strong artistic foundation. Matte painting is still what it has always been, only the tools have changed. It is still all about seeing and being able to sell a shot.

THE SUPERIOR
GRAB SOME BUDS
Reebok
Reebok
element
Billabong

GRAB SOME BUDS
Reebok
SMOKIN GEL
SQUARE
NYC
HERSHEY'S

TUTORIAL 4: Return of the Dragon Queen: Kiinu's Keep

My short film 'Return of the Dragon Queen' incorporates a flashback sequence. Back in the old world, when man and dragon had to share the planet, the earth was rich, the waters were clean, the skies free and all was good.

This matte painting specifically depicts one of the human strongholds at the end of this realm's Golden Age, before greed crept into the heart of man. Matte painters have always been required to have the broadest skill set within this industry. Most traditional matte painters were also very well-rounded special effects artists and today's digital matte painters still have to possess a good understanding of the overall picture.

With this tutorial I intend to show matte painting from a storytelling point of view, with a more illustrative touch of fantasy than my usual work portrays. As such, this matte painting is a mixture of photographic elements and brushwork.

I have about four to five regular brushes in my set but I mainly use the default soft round one with pen pressure. Some other matte painters completely disregard this function and toggle the opacity with the number keys instead in order to apply paint in layers onto the canvas. My painting technique heavily relies on pressure sensitivity, wherein the harder I press the more opaque my stroke becomes.

To get the feel of my painting right, I was using a lot of my own reference photos I took while living in England. During our time there, my wife and I went on short trips and took pictures of anything that might come in handy for our future matte paintings.

1. Original photographic images

I took these photos at the Nottingham Castle in 2007. These are the type of locations that you know as a matte painter will be useful at some point in your professional life. It is always a good idea to carry an extra memory card and take advantage of bracketing with your digital SLR if you happen to have a tripod with you.

2. The plate

After having carefully chosen an image, I started by reducing the digital noise on it with the Photoshop plug-in Noise Ninja. I then created a new file at double HD size with a dimension of 3840 x 2160 pixels, and I used the Transform tool to corner-pin the plate the way I wanted it to be. I paid special attention to it having proper horizontal and vertical lines by un-distorting the camera distortion with the help of the Warp function within the Transform tool.

3. Sketch

Matte painting is not concept art. You don't have the creative freedom to explore loose ideas because the brief you receive is already fairly tight. Although I was my own art director on this project, the shot has to serve the story and not the other way around. For my initial sketch, I painted over the chosen plate with an edgy oil brush set to pressure sensitivity. I was trying to keep the lighting interesting while creating attractive shapes. A reference image to a matte painter is similar to what a sculptor sees in a piece of rock. My main focus was to stay intuitive about it and quickly speed-paint through it, occasionally grabbing photo elements like rock textures without slowing down by thinking too much about what I was doing. As an artist I mostly make instinctive decisions to achieve my goal. This also gives me the benefit of seeing when I have made a wrong turn, and then being able to go the other way.

4. Perspective lines

Before bringing in actual reference images, I took the time to establish my perspective with accurate perspective lines on separate layers. Even though Photoshop now has some fancy Perspective Filter functions, I find that the Line tool is extremely straightforward and helps me to keep my workflow fairly simple while truly understanding the perspective of the image.

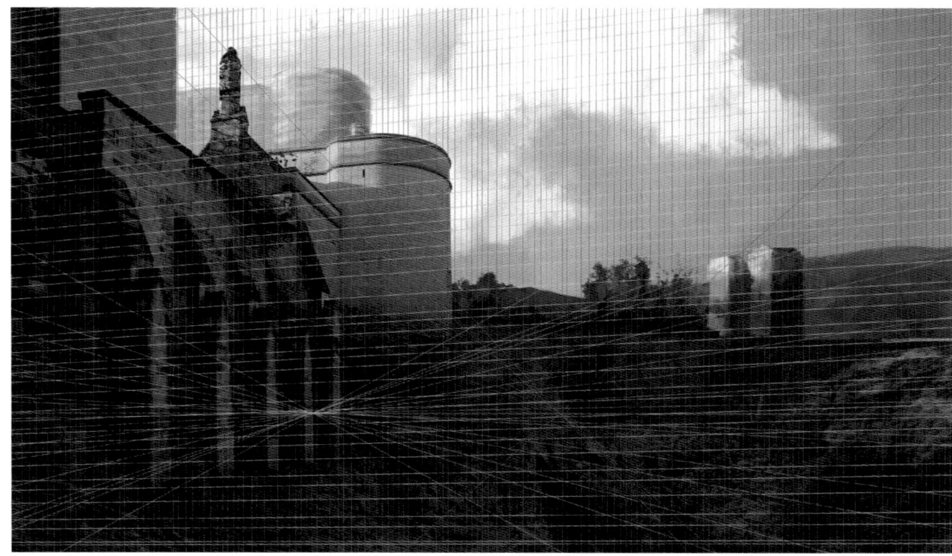

5. Importing RAW imagery

If you have access to a DSLR camera, it is important to be shooting in RAW format. For the highest usability in my matte painting work, I try to keep all my images fairly low contrast while importing. Within the Camera RAW settings I also dial the Highlights all the way down and turn the Shadows all the way up in order to get the best range out of the photograph. (These functions were called Recovery and Fill Light in previous versions.) I will later be using clip-masked Adjustment Layers to match this reference into my painting. However, I need to keep all the flexibility an image can offer me at this point.

6. Photo-real background

From a technical aspect I would always recommend to build your images back-to-front. Whenever I need some simple green rolling hills for one of my paintings I start looking through my personal library of the Black Forest. All modern imagery requires some de-modernization clean-up work but it is far more efficient than painting it from scratch.

7. Trees

I played with the idea of breaking up the strong horizontal line in my composition but decided against it. The way I imagined the final shot was with a character riding across the screen on a horse, rushing either to the keep or away from it. After bringing in each tree I had to bring it into the same world as the palette of my original sketch. For integration I generally use a channel-based RGB color-matching method with only one Curves Adjustment Layer clip-masked to the layer of the specific element. In the case of these trees, I concentrated on matching the brightest pixels of the new element to the white level of the destination, and the darkest darks to whatever I could identify as black in the plate. Doing this on a per Channel basis allowed me a procedural accuracy that I could trust.

8. Noise reduction

Some of the reference images I used were shot with a too-high ISO and have too much noise. As mentioned before, I currently use the Photoshop plug-in Noise Ninja for noise reduction. Being more of a photography tool, it does a better job with digital noise than real film grain. When bringing in bits and pieces like this, I generally try to match the quality to the destination material. With the wall texture, I paid special attention to not letting it become too soft while removing the color noise pixels.

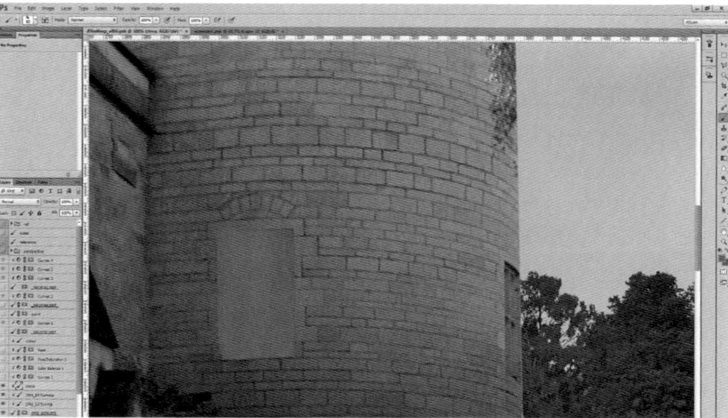

9. Paint-out

Instead of the Clone tool, I prefer to use the Healing Brush because it blends my paint-outs nicely with the plate and gives it a more natural touch. In the case of the turret window, I made a selection with the Lasso tool and painted in some solid color before healing the area. This technique is not specific to this tutorial but can be utilized as a generic part of your workflow once you have familiarized yourself with the tool.

10. Flipping the canvas

I find it important to keep refreshing my eyes. So, at this point I decided to flip my image horizontally. Throughout the painting process I continue to flip the canvas whenever I feel my eyes are getting tired. Some artists go to the extent of flipping the image in a vertical orientation to identify problem areas. This can be helpful when designing compositional aspects of your overall shot, but I find it less efficient once the painting is headed into a more photo-real realm.

11. Creating balance

Far beyond photo-manipulation, matte painting is not a simple Photoshop technique but rather well-rounded problem-solving based on a series of decisions from a painter's point of view. Due to matte paintings serving a higher purpose, the goal is always sitting in the back of your head, guiding you through the process. I used the big brick blocks on the bridge, from the sketch I originally painted, just as an opportunity to play with light hits for visual interest. They somehow happened naturally but created a strong compositional balance, without which the image would not work. The purpose of them was merely visual balance for my eyes.

12. Breaking up hard edges

Even though I eroded the outer edge of the blocks already, their silhouette still seemed too straight in full frame view. To solve this issue I painted out larger pieces using the Layer Mask of the group, staying non-destructive in the process. I kept zooming in and out to see if it was working overall.

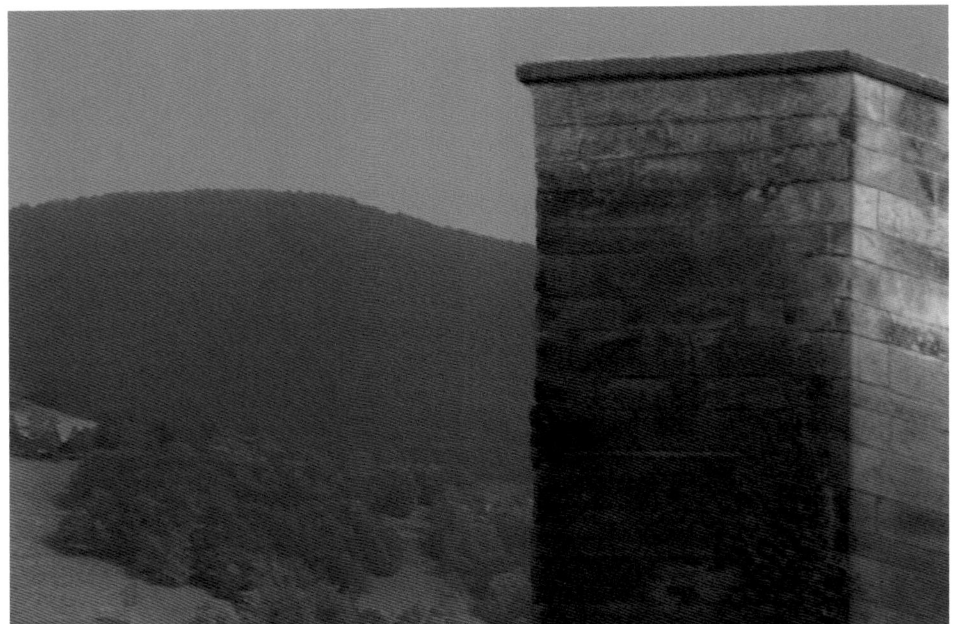

13. Adding a micro-composition back story

In the end I realized that I had no plausible logic behind these block-shaped structures, and I took a moment to think about their purpose. Ultimately I figured they would not have been placed there without having a function. Unfortunately, I maneuvered myself into this situation by letting my brush flow freely without thinking about it too much. The visual interest I created this way, however, was strong enough for me to try to find a solution. I came up with the idea that the blocks used to be an outer gate, and all of a sudden everything magically fell into place. This thought automatically answered many other questions and I was very pleased with my happy accident.

14. Clean up

By coming up with a back story of the outer gate having been destroyed and therefore explaining why both pillars were broken at such similar heights, I was able to happily move on to some clean-up work to get my painting to the next stage.

15. Dirt overlay

Another dilemma my back story solved was the question of what state the keep should be in. Now I knew that while the building might still have been operational, it was run-down at this point in time. I immediately felt the need to apply additional layers of dirt wherever the surface seemed too clean. For this I have a routine process I don't even think about anymore. I have a collection of photos of close-up dirt, cracked walls, plaster, pealing wallpaper and corroded metal. In this case I used a section of a dirty wall and masked it on top of the upper turret. Then I changed the Layer Blend mode to Overlay and adjusted the texture with some Curves to blend it better.

16. Building from scratch

Generally, I was bouncing around the painting addressing one note after the other in order of whichever offended my eyes the worst. When working for a client I recommend trying to keep a visual balance so that if you're asked to show a work in progress everything is at the same level. I try not to waste too much time polishing individual areas until everything is in place and well balanced. In respect to that, I needed to do some work on the bottom of the bridge as it had no texture at all. The Line tool helped me to block in the outline, and I used a brick texture that I warped into perspective with the Transform tool. For integration, I used my channel-based RGB color-matching method again, which I used on the trees earlier.

17. The cliff face

Left to right: Next I finally started to tackle the cliff face. The detail frequency of the rocks indicates the scale and because of that I had to make sure to use reference with the correct amount of information. In areas where the rock detail got too busy, I hand-painted over it with an edgy oil brush on a separate layer.

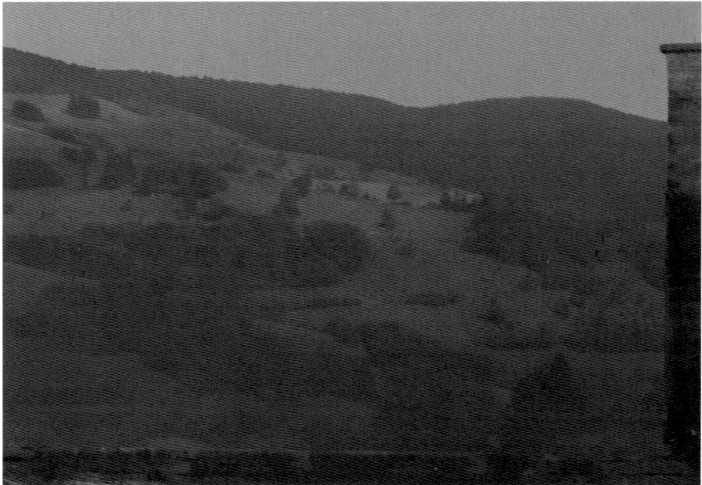

18. Atmospheric perspective

I regularly took a short break from the image to be able to refresh my eyes and return for a round of balancing. As part of this I added a solid layer of blue and dialed in the transparency at 30%. This is shot-specific and you have to judge it yourself depending on your scenario. The Color Picker helped me to select the right blue shade from the sky. These techniques are more than tricks but rather training your eyes to 'see' by pushing elements back and forth in distance to the camera or viewer. As such, atmospheric haze is your most powerful natural element to fake realism.

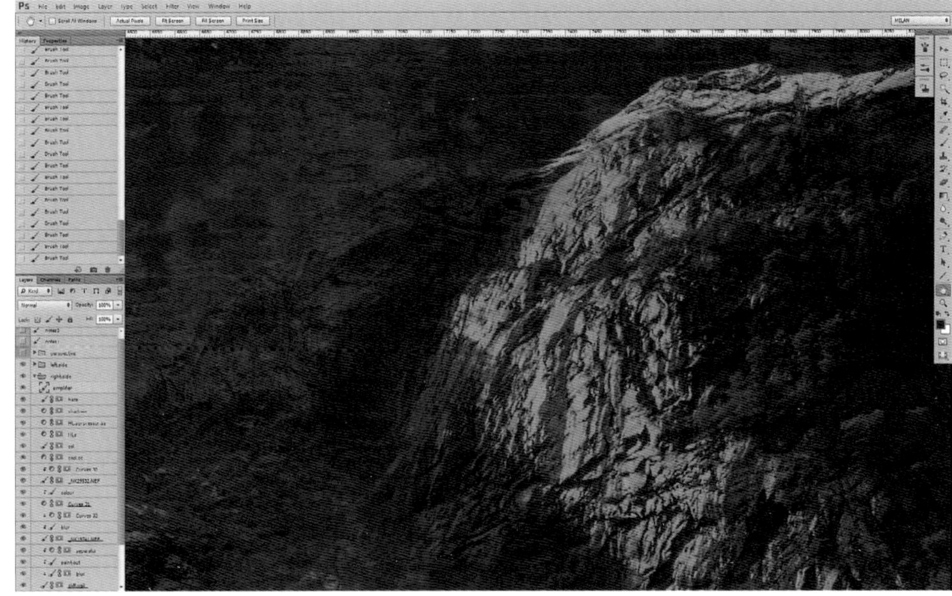

19. Interesting lighting features

To balance my painting some more I tried to play with some sun hits on the right-hand-side rocks, mimicking the way light could be reacting with the surface. I tried to motivate the lighting as if it would be breaking through a gap in the massive structure on the opposite side.

20. Adding real-life details

After another look at the entire image I started to add vegetation to break up the cold rock and to bring some life back into my hard surface environment. Since we don't always get much time away from the computer it is far too easy to forget how much 'life' there actually is in a dead rocky landscape. For an image such as this, I study lots of reference images of similar environments to create a place that could exist in reality. This much rock without enough greenery would mean we're most likely on an asteroid or alien planet, so I tried to swing the painting back into a more familiar world.

21. Matching Depth Blur

Although the final Depth Blur will be added in compositing (some compositors even request entirely sharp matte paintings with minimal depth of field), I prefer to reduce the details and Gaussian Blur my layers the further away a section is from the viewer. On some rare occasions, I get worried about taking it too far and I convert my layers to smart objects before applying the Guassian Blur. But this makes my Photoshop file heavier and I tend to try to avoid it when I can. On a piece like this I don't hesitate baking in the filter and committing to my decisions.

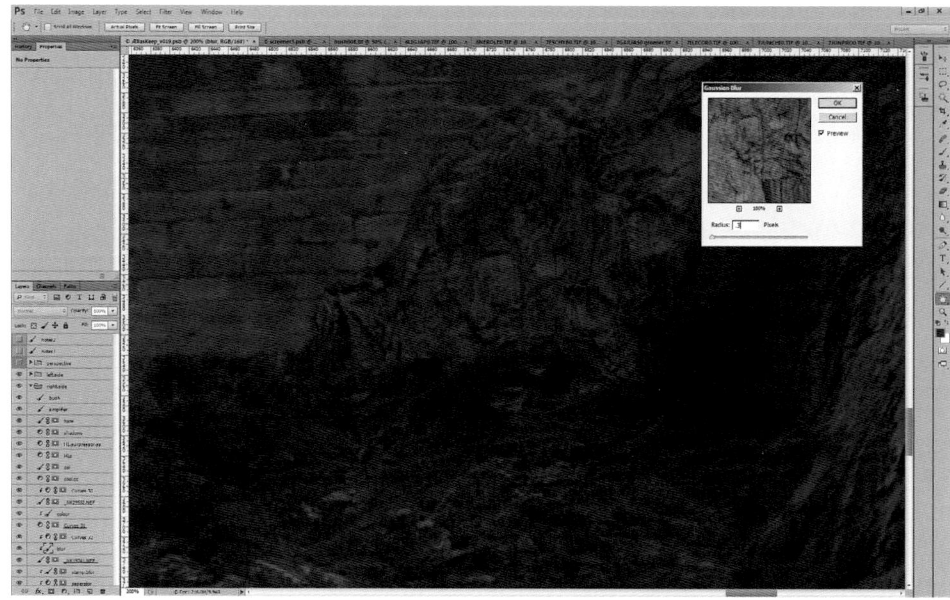

22. Mist at the bottom

At this point I was constantly going around the matte painting analyzing ways I could improve the shot, and I noticed that it was starting to feel somewhat static. This is something I don't usually worry about until I enter the pre-compositing stage, but for this particular shot I wanted to create a strong styleframe as visual guidance for what the final result should look like. In an attempt to imply movement, I used a random brush to paint in some mist at the bottom. I did not use white! With the help of the Color Picker tool, I found a bright color from the sky that worked great as water vapor rising from the running river in the gorge. I never add new colors by creating them out of nowhere; this is to avoid expanding the color range too much and breaking the color balance.

23. A new sky

The sky had been distracting me for some time due to the large simplistic shape I placed in the middle earlier. It was working alright for my sketch but the time had come to rework it for the final. The main guideline was to keep it in the same color spectrum and exposure level. I also wanted to further support the strong horizontal created by the bridge.

24. Re-lighting

Unfortunately, the large sun hit on the rock was implausible and I couldn't find a way to implement a break through the structure to motivate the lighting. The diagonal shows the accurate lighting angle and that there was no opportunity for the sun to break through. Furthermore, the large highlight play on such an unimportant piece of rock was distracting from the purpose of the shot and it made no sense to have the viewer's eye linger too long on something meaningless in our story. Any form of practical art is information transport, and most of the time less is more.

25. Implying movement

As one of my finishing touches, I decided to add Oriflamme banners and battle standards for implied movement. The idea was to have these animated with a warp in Comp. From an artistic point of view, I felt the need to color balance my painting. In color theory, red is a complementary warm tone on the color wheel as a color contrast to the overall tonality of my painting at this stage. I tried many different forms and shapes, arranged in a number of ways around the keep. In the end the image was getting too illustrative and starting to lose its matte painting quality. I had established a run-down, possibly abandoned environment, and the banners felt too uplifting and lively. They made me feel like they were clashing with the run-down look I established earlier.

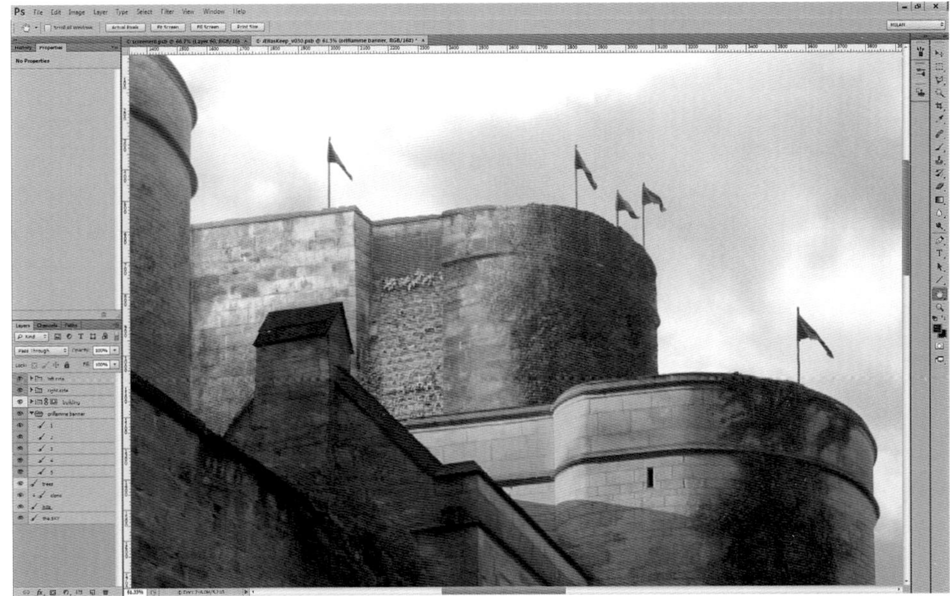

26. Notes

I recommend with any painting to keep flipping it horizontally. Even if your shot is set to play one way or the other, it helps to temporarily check it from the opposite side. When I flip one of my paintings it reads very differently and I can see things I did not notice before. By doing this here, I was able to write myself some final notes – to correct the higher turret's top curvature and to identify issues and problem areas regarding the global reflected light as well as local self-shadowing.

27. Final matte painting

The final shot reads left to right because my brain is used to taking up information in that order. This shot also ties into a sequence and I needed to keep continuity. My final task to round it off was a warm color grade. This is usually something done further down the line by the director or colorist in the Digital Intermediate.

TUTORIAL 5: The Bright Darkness – Escape

Matte painting is not simply painting pretty pictures. The artform has always been the most versatile position in the movie industry, even before CGI. A well-rounded matte painter must possess outstanding fine art skills while also being a well-versed graphic arts technician with an extensive understanding of cameras. It is important to know how to get your shot done in more than theory. Being a 3D matte painter requires a combination of the skills of a digital matte painting artist and an environment technical director.

I love the painting part but I like to handle my shots all the way to pre-comp where possible. I use The Foundry's texturing software MARI to help me improve and fix texture issues that can arise on such shots as this. For this tutorial my objective is to efficiently implement MARI into my matte painting workflow.

I want to demonstrate the possibilities of a 2D/3D combination workflow by walking you through a basic moving shot. However, MARI is not always the best solution. It is really shot-dependent and you have to weigh it up for yourself which software package would be most efficient.

On the visual side, I added Gothic details to the 9th-century architecture to please my own art direction because I enjoy combining different eras whenever I get the chance. Being the creative director of my own work allows me to explore avenues that would normally be taboo within an authentic period piece. As a visual style guide I tried to mimic a rainy French or German countryside for an initial impression of the environment in this sequence.

1. Original sketch

This shot started as a napkin sketch complete with camera move instructions on the back of a receipt while I was out running errands. I always carry at least one travel-sized sketchbook with me and am constantly working on multiple projects at the same time to keep my brain fresh. That way, when one flow of ideas slows down I switch my mind to another story. It's the same with my art – I like to work on multiple shots at the same time to be able to progress faster. For this matte painting I later did a cleaner line drawing but kept it traditional, trying to avoid digital influence at this point. My priority was to direct the viewer's eye with a storytelling emphasis.

2. Maya 3D render

After I had taken a photo of my still sketch, I put it on an image plane attached to a camera in Autodesk Maya. The perspective of such a sketch can not be completely accurately matched in 3D, but I set up an extremely wide focal length as a starting point. I then quickly modeled some simple geometry, matching my rough concept as close as possible in camera view. Even though I took some liberties with the 3D model, I made sure to respect the established composition based on the rule of thirds I originally put to paper.

3. Reference images for background

Having lived in both Germany and England, I have a fairly strong countryside reference library of photographs. I made sure to choose images based on their light direction because with diffused lighting in an overcast scenario like this I will either have to paint out shadows or limit myself to only using reference photos that were taken on a cloudy day. Basically, the greatest photo is useless if the lighting is wrong.

4. Perspective lines

One of the first things I do is create some perspective guide lines for myself. In this case I took advantage of the CG image and based my lines on the 3D render with the help of the Line tool. I dropped in my background reference under the horizon line to achieve an effect of being higher up and also to give me room to play with the wide angle, as well as to allow me to add more hills or to further change up the landscape.

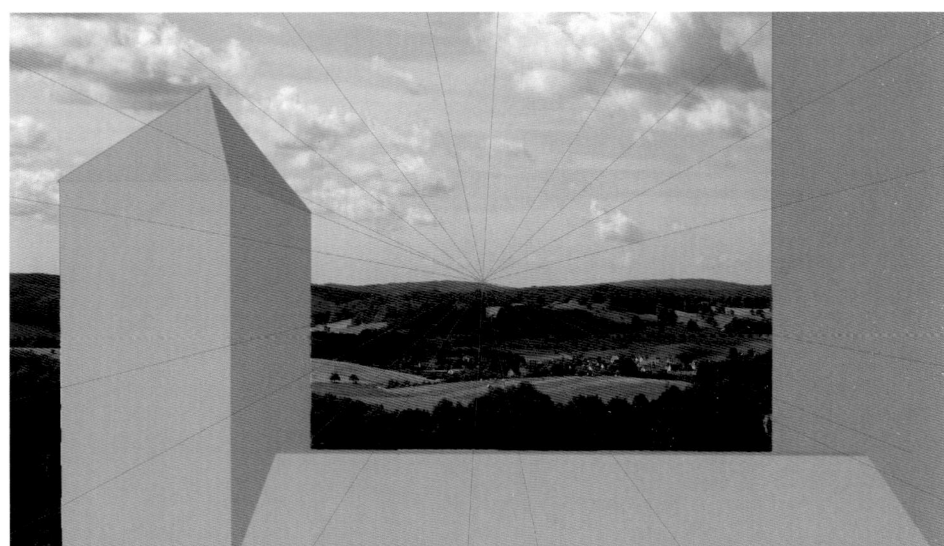

5. Back-to-front

Over the years I have established a working habit of constantly naming my layers and always building my Photoshop files back-to-front. After an initial color correction with the help of one Curves Adjustment Layer clip-masked to the background photo reference, I start layering haze on top. I also extracted the sky and kept it as the bottom layer of my Photoshop file. It is important to layer back-to-front (instead of painting on top of combined elements) to allow more flexibility for later. Changes happen way too fast in this line of work and I never want to limit myself by ignoring the power of Photoshop layers. In respect to that, each additional midground hill and level of haze gets its own layer. I like to set my background further back by adding more depth perspective and then toning it down to bring a more realistic feel to my painting.

6. Balancing

I took a moment to analyze how light changes across the landscape by zooming out because that way my eyes couldn't pick up details and I was able to evaluate the composition and values better. Generally, the image has to work as a thumbnail first before you can concentrate on specifics.

7. Foreground photographic reference

When working on period pieces, I take the time to familiarize myself with the appropriate architecture, materials used, and every type of detail I can find out. This being a personal project, and fantasy-based, I had more creative license, and I also took advantage of the freedom of creatively directing the piece by choosing aesthetics over historical accuracy. This is a luxury I'd never have when working for a paying client. I do not recommend attempting such risks without discussing it with a supervisor beforehand. Always do your research, or ask. It will save you time.

8. Foreground, midground, background, sky

Things closer to camera appear more red because of the wavelength of their colors, or, rather, the missing colors in the background. Especially for a narrow color palette as in this matte painting, it helps to add red in the foreground and reduce it further away. I also opened up the sky, setting the mood by doing so. My intention was to create an after-the-storm feeling, rather than the feeling of an approaching storm. My idea was that the highlight implies hope.

9. Decoration

There are no shadows due to cloud cover, but contact shadows always exist. I sometimes render myself an ambient occlusion pass to multiply it on top of my painting. Being a fairly simple structure, I felt that this wouldn't be necessary and I actually enjoyed painting in all the self-shadowing by hand. To be able to adjust it later if need be, I used a Curves Adjustment Layer and painted all shadows with a soft brush into the mask. For the overall lighting of the scene I established a weak directional light (there is still some light direction even in overcast weather).

10. Detailing

Digital matte painting, just as in traditional matte painting, is mainly a series of artistic decisions. To get an idea what particular characteristics of the foreground building should look like, I spent some time searching architectural terms online. I re-painted the tiles on the tower rooftop and added a spire. After researching bell towers, I decided to implement narrow window slits instead of big, wide, open ones as I had originally intended. The benefit of this was that I did not have to worry about the interior, and I saved myself about half a day of work.

11. LookUp Table color grading

Matte painters rarely have the opportunity to suggest a film look grade to the director. In my professional work environment, sometimes on full CG shots built from scratch, I do get to establish the color temperature as long as it ties in with the corresponding sequence. However, this is not a usual task of the matte painter. Since this shot was first to be finished in this sequence, I created the mood freely and will be using it as a style guide to narrow down the color palette in order to keep it believable for the viewer. I chose to take out some of the blue to reduce the cool feel, and strengthen a notion of hope.

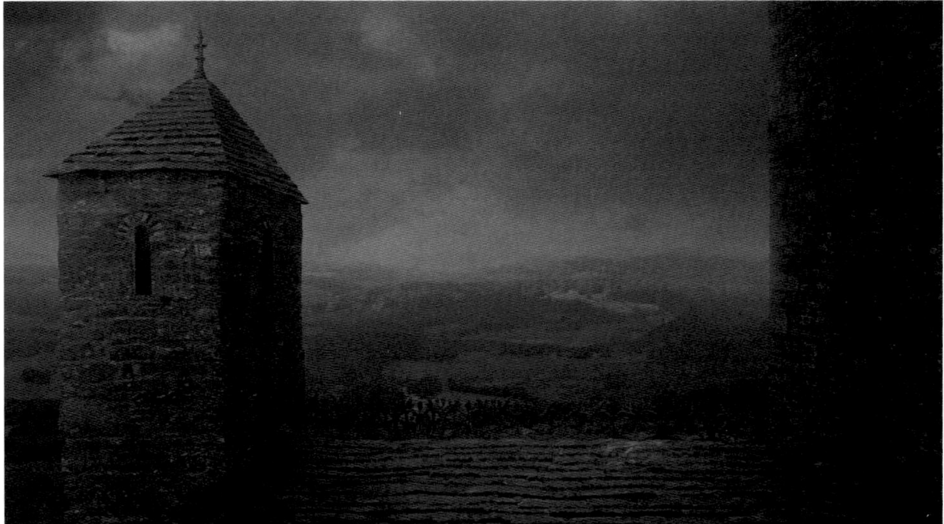

12. Fixing the window

The side window was wrong in perspective, and I used the front window as guide to fix it. This is some basic perspective that I should have got right the first time around when eyeballing it.

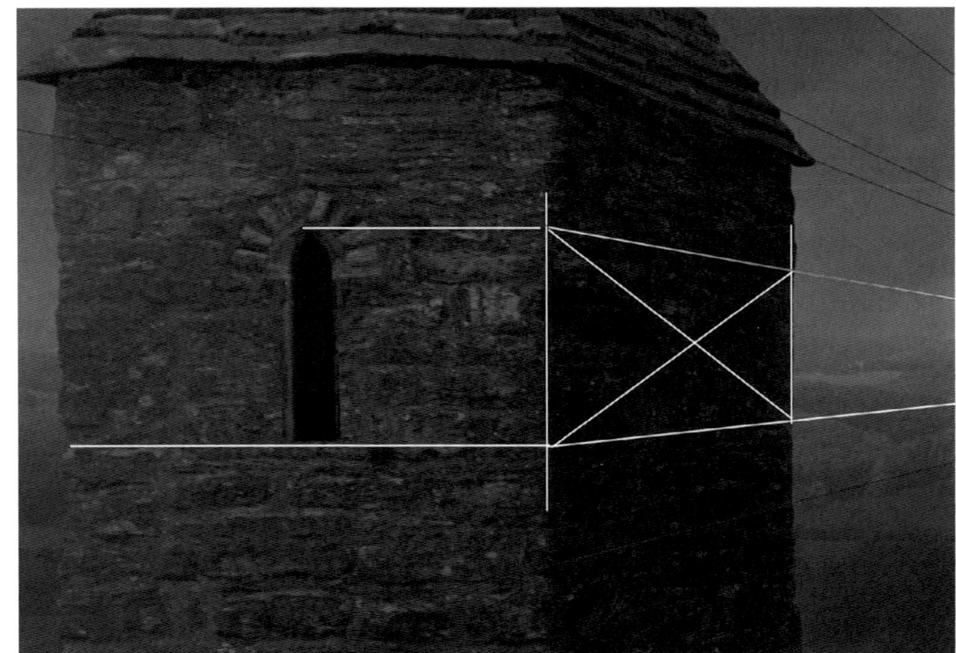

13. Fixing the roof tiles
Another oversight on my part was the angle of the main roof tiles. I judged these wrongly because when I zoomed out they appeared to be sitting above the viewer's horizon line, while the matte painting requires them to be below. The issue was quickly fixed with the help of the Healing Brush as I painted in more surface and reduced the side parts of the tiles.

14. Flipping
Flipping horizontally is the best method to identify problem areas. When I get stuck on a matte painting or a section of a painting, I look at real-life photographs. If an area is already not working I don't try to do what I think is right but try to analyze some relevant reference to fully understand the problem.

15. Exploring story variation
As an alternative direction I included a campfire. There is a camp in the story but I hadn't figured out yet if the environment would be too moist to get a fire going. In the end I decided to leave it as an option, since the fire would need to be a sequence in any case, with animated rising smoke.

16. Fixing the tower's roof perspective

Even though the tower's roof was completely 3D and had proper perspective, it looked 'off' and bothered me so much that I made an executive decision to correct it in 2D and make amendments on the model for it. This only works as long as this set-up is not used in other shots. As long as my matte painting stayed view-dependent I had the freedom to push some vertices around a bit.

17. Texture layering

I flipped back my matte painting before exporting the layers for projection because my original Maya set-up is oriented this way. It was important to paint in the background and have enough coverage when being revealed in parallax. If I kept this as a NUKE projection I could have prepared a simple PSD to use in conjunction with the Breakout Layers function, but for my Maya set-up I had to export individual files with separate alphas for the projection mapping.

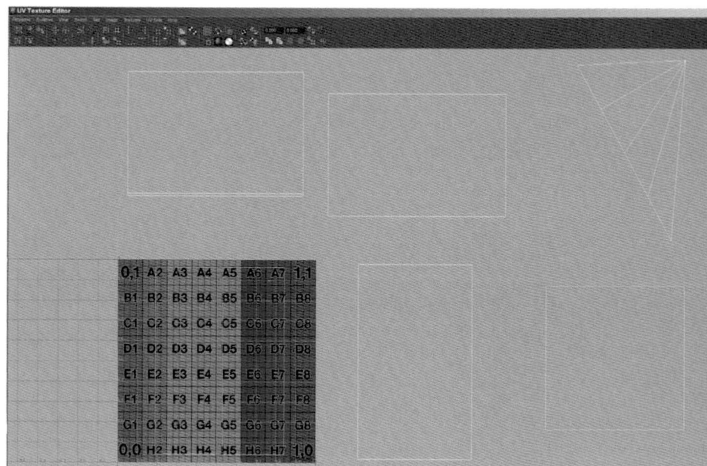

18. Preparing UV for UDIM tiling

In order to be able to take it to MARI, I needed to lay out the UVs, but I deleted the back faces which were not visible within the range of the shot camera. I also made sure to make good use of the UV space.

19. Maya projection shader set-up

This is the perspective view of my scene with the matte painting mapped onto the geometry through my projection camera. For rendering I prefer mental ray but also use V-Ray in certain situations, especially if I have to work together with other artists and I can't match the mental ray Motion Blur to the V-Ray one. For example, the biggest difference for my workflow is that with V-Ray I usually have to avoid using the Layered Shader node and instead build a shader using Blend Colors to combine textures when patching or layering.

20. Camera animation

I key-framed my projection frame and pushed in the shot camera on a later frame of the shot until I was happy with the final framing. This step shows the last frame of the camera move.

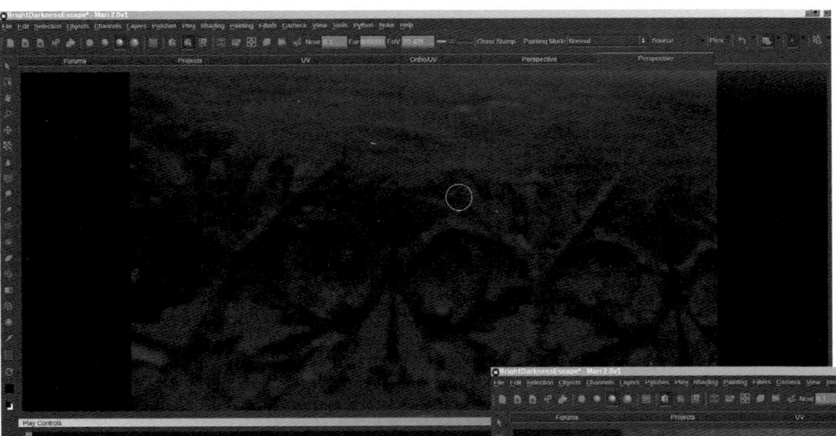

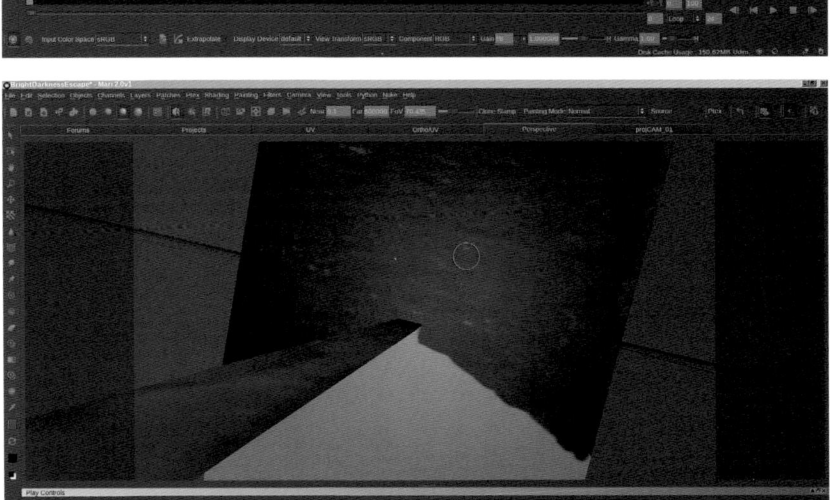

21. MARI fixes

MARI is not exactly a replacement for Photoshop because I can't create a matte painting from scratch with it, but for shots with camera moves it can be great for adding additional detail and fixing cloning tasks. I imported my image library and used the Paint-Through tool to bake and then add detailing touch-ups and fix stretching on the walls. It is not always necessary to resolve to MARI but MARI is great for quick fixes, especially if you're in Linux and would like to avoid rebooting. Situations where MARI is more necessary are with things like railings, scaffolding and, in this case, the ornamental decoration on top of the main roof for detailing. One important technical hint is to match the transform scale in the tool properties to the transformation scale of the projector.

22. Ropes

The story of this shot is our hero escaping the building in the foreground. That is where the idea of the ropes came in. The tower windows are too small for a human to climb through; I was also unsure about him being locked up in the bell tower, so I concentrated my main ropes on the large wall. I kept all ropes separate with alphas and individual shadows so they could be added in Comp with an animated warp to imply slight movement.

23. Final matte painting
After integrating four ropes I decided to remove all but one because the story features only one person escaping and there was no purpose for multiple ropes, even though it was visually stronger with more than one.

TUTORIAL 6: The Bright Darkness: Cornish Pasty in Shepherd's Bush

For this tutorial I chose another shot from my 'The Bright Darkness' pitch project that I am currently preparing in my free time. 'The Bright Darkness' is a period adventure with a fantasy twist that I have been developing over the past few years.

In production it happens every so often that a scene gets changed and the time of day in some shots has to be altered. While traditional matte painters had to start over or painstakingly re-light their painting in such a scenario, the benefit of the digital age allows us to keep our work flexible and make changes fairly easily.

It so happens that I had originally planned this shot as a night-time part within my story, but due to changes in the script it became an afternoon scene. In order to keep the mystical element alive I incorporated a very foggy atmosphere into the final version of the matte painting, making it daytime without having to compromise on the mysterious fantasy setting I was trying to portray in the first place.

1. Photo-merging the set photography

Usually an on-site survey crew would take photos of the film set or shooting location of a movie shot you're working on. In this case I utilized some of my own images I took during a weekend trip. With Photoshop's automated Photomerge, I stitched my images together to create a base for my matte painting.

2. Manual lens distortion correction

After creating some visual guides, which you can drag out from the rulers at the top and left side, I corrected the distortion by eye, attempting to make the stitched image as straight as possible in order to lose the feel that the frame had been assembled from multiple photographs instead of shot with one camera. The advantage of this is having a more comfortable way of working; not having to match or compensate for any lens distortion.

3. Filmback

At this point in the process, I cropped down the canvas to a 16:9 aspect ratio to bring it into a working format. My final framing was influenced by the information transport necessities of the matte painting, keeping the purpose of the shot within the storyline in mind. I chose to try to eliminate unnecessary visual distractions to be able to guide the viewer's eyes through the image to the main event. Additionally, I decided to flip the image horizontally because I believe it reads better from left to right this way.

4. Composition

With an approach such as this, the flexibility of the composition always stays within a certain boundary, which I try to use to my advantage. As part of my clean-up process I decided to replace the foreground building on the right instead of trying to re-build it from bits and pieces. Due to the already established perspective and lighting of the base image, I had enough visual cues to help me match another house into the painting. While bouncing around all over the painting, I also keyed-out the sky and put a solid color into the background for now.

5. Clean up

As part of the de-modernization I painted out anything that didn't fit into the period of the setting. For this I prefer to use the Healing Brush over the Clone Stamp tool because it gives me a more natural result. I also fixed the perspective issues on the foreground monument.

12. Warmth

This was my final image of the night version. The final day-to-night matte painting features warmer lights than before. This was meant to imply candlelight. The desaturated light sources from before appeared too modern and industrial, and this village has no electricity.

13. Mood change

One of the hardest lessons every matte painter has to learn early on in their career is not to fall in love with their work. You have to build your Photoshop file with enough flexibility to allow any changes to be made. In this case I had to change a portion of my script. Depending on the script writer, this can be very common, as we go through many versions of a script or screenplay during production sometimes.

14. Balancing

Once I had reverted my matte painting to the clean plate I was ready to go hazy. My intention for the new mood revolved around mist and fog. I started over with a minor color correction and a few new layers of painted fog. This was all done really quickly because now I knew exactly what I wanted.

15. Detailing

After quickly establishing the new look, I added a few details and tweaks here and there, such as the new lamp, and spent some time better integrating areas like the curb because the day scenario is slightly less forgiving than the night one.

16. Layering
Now, depth perspective was more important than ever. My back-to-front layering from the earlier Photoshop file allowed me to easily stack newly painted layers at different distances through the painting. There is a fine line between having too many layers and not enough layers. The key is to work clean and make constructive decisions. I always commit when I feel confident enough with an area, but leave myself the necessary control needed in case I have to address changes further down the line. This is also important in case one of your matte paintings comes back with notes weeks after you thought the shot was finalized. In such a case it can easily happen that another matte painter will have to take over, as you might be tasked on other shots by then. He or she will deeply appreciate a neatly organized Photoshop file with the necessary control still existing.

17. LookUp Table
I color graded the matte painting, dialing in a final look. This process is a combination of taste and purpose, while I had to pay attention that it still tied in with other shots in the same sequence.

18. Digital noise
Something I almost never do is add digital noise within my matte painting. This is strictly a task for compositing because noise and grain has to be moving frame by frame. The reason I chose to go this way here is because all of the reference photography I was able to find on the internet showed this photographic quality within photographs in this type of lighting and weather. Furthermore, I was unable to substantially remove the noise from my photo elements, and giving the clean parts the same imperfection helped integrate them better with the rest.

19. Final image
My final task was to add a subtle vignette effect to my shot. Once again, I chose this mainly because of personal visual preference, and it should not be done on professional matte painting work when presenting it to a client or supervisor.

The Beach
Photoshop
Anthony Eftekhari, USA
[above]

Milan: With this image, Anthony has created one of the most beautiful matte paintings I have ever seen. It is like the photo-real equivalent of a Romantic-era masterpiece. In my opinion, matte painting today is what Romanticism was in 1836 or Renaissance art in 1498. It is the most significant art form of our age and Anthony's 'The Beach' painting is at the forefront.

River
Photoshop
Igor Staritsin, RUSSIA
[right]

Milan: One key ingredient to matte painting is paying attention to detail. The unconventional format is possibly a result of a camera move, tilting up or down during the shot. It would be nice to see the water in motion. If I had the opportunity to art direct this piece, my advice would be to break up the tree line on the left of screen to make it more irregular, as nature tends to be.

Haunting of the Pearson Place
Photoshop
Client: MCM Films
Szabolcs Joseph Menyhei, GREAT BRITAIN
[far right]

Milan: Subtle light spill on the roof brings the digital backdrop and the house nicely together. The information transport works effectively as the audience immediately gets a sense of the horror/thriller mood conveyed in this delightful, down-to-earth matte painting.

'Haunting of the Pearson Place' ©MCM Films

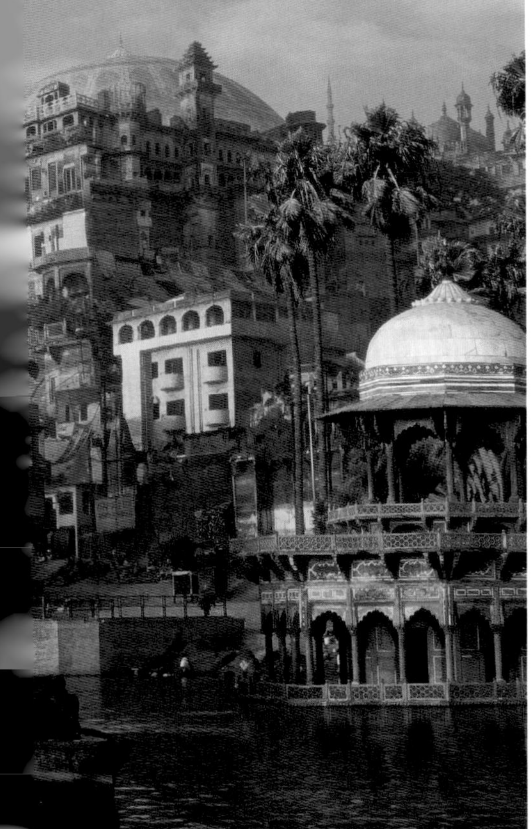

The River Bathers
Photoshop
Dylan Cole, USA
[left]

Milan: Dylan Cole is one of the authors of the original *d'artiste: Matte Painting* book and has been a great influence on my professional career over the years. It is an honor to be able to include some of his personal work within this book. This matte painting is a stupendous example of his artistry.

Home Sweet Home
Photoshop, Maya
Damien Thaller, AUSTRALIA
[above]

Milan: This is one of my favorite digital matte paintings of all time. Damien did a fantastic job. It is so well balanced and harmonious while being amazingly interesting at the same time. I would love to see the entire story that this piece has to tell. I can already picture it with a subtle camera move pushing in while a character comes around the corner.

Milan: Fabio is an amazing artist. This wonderful matte painting is like the CG counterpart to Peter Ellenshaw's iconic Rome establishing shot matte painting for Stanley Kubrick's *Spartacus* motion picture.

Ancient Horizon
Photoshop, 3ds Max, V-Ray
Fabio Barretta Zungrone, USA
[top]

'Resident Evil: Retribution' © Vision Globale

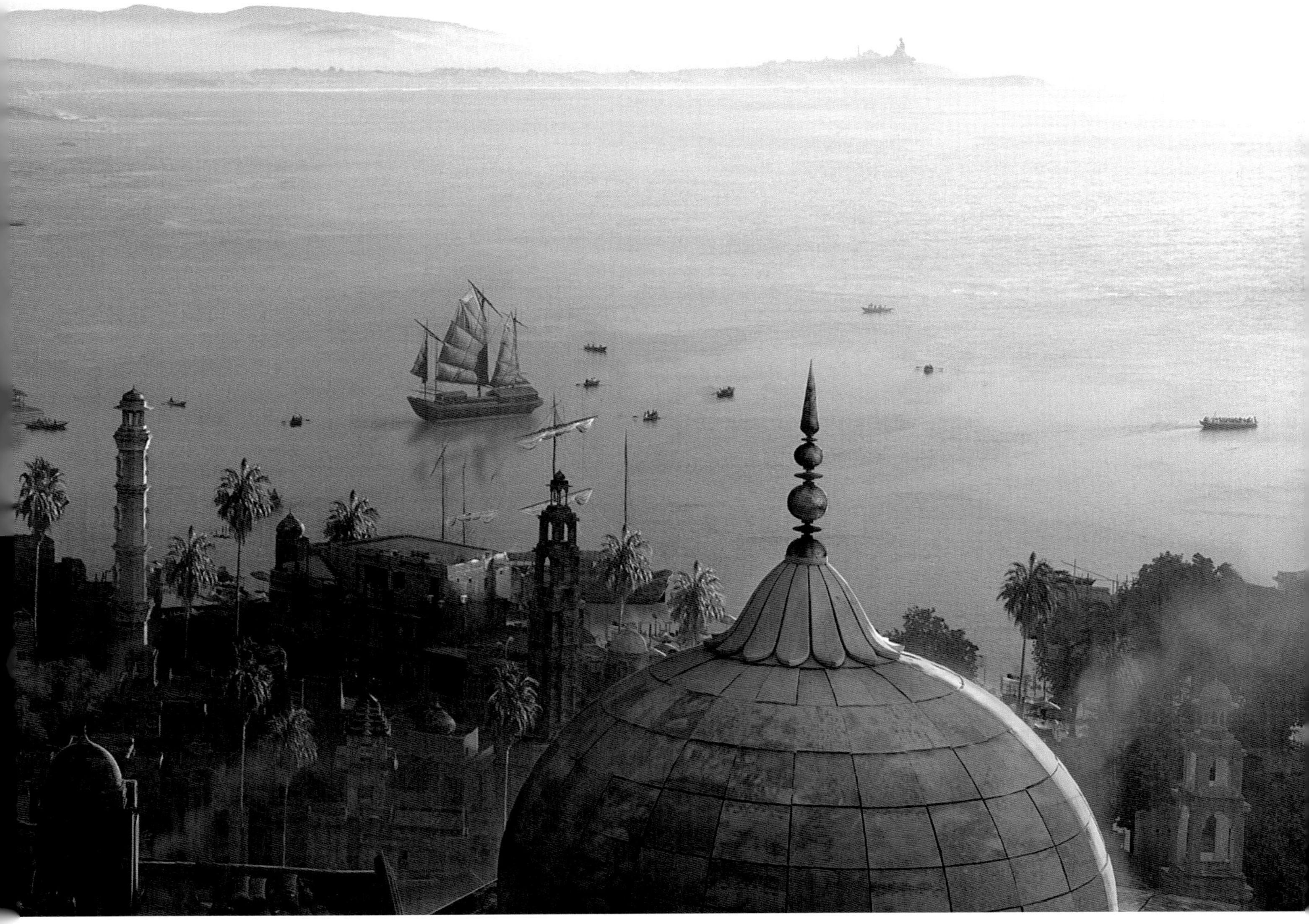

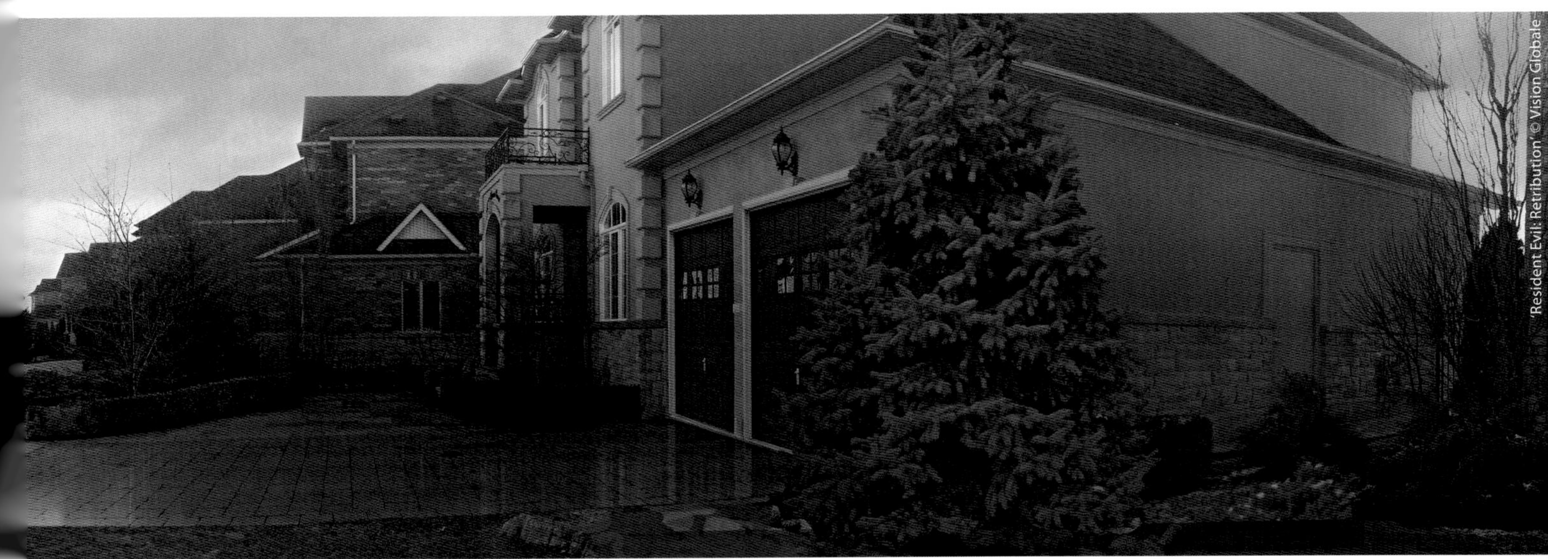

Milan: This image speaks for itself. I can not tell where the plate ends and which part of the shot is matte painted. Aesthetically, I like the after-the-rain wet look with all the reflections and highlights.

Resident Evil: Retribution (suburbs shootout)
Photoshop
Client: Vision Globale
Benoit Ladouceur, CANADA
[above]

'Dredd' © Prime Focus World/DNA Films/Reliance

'Dredd' © Prime Focus World/DNA Films/Reliance

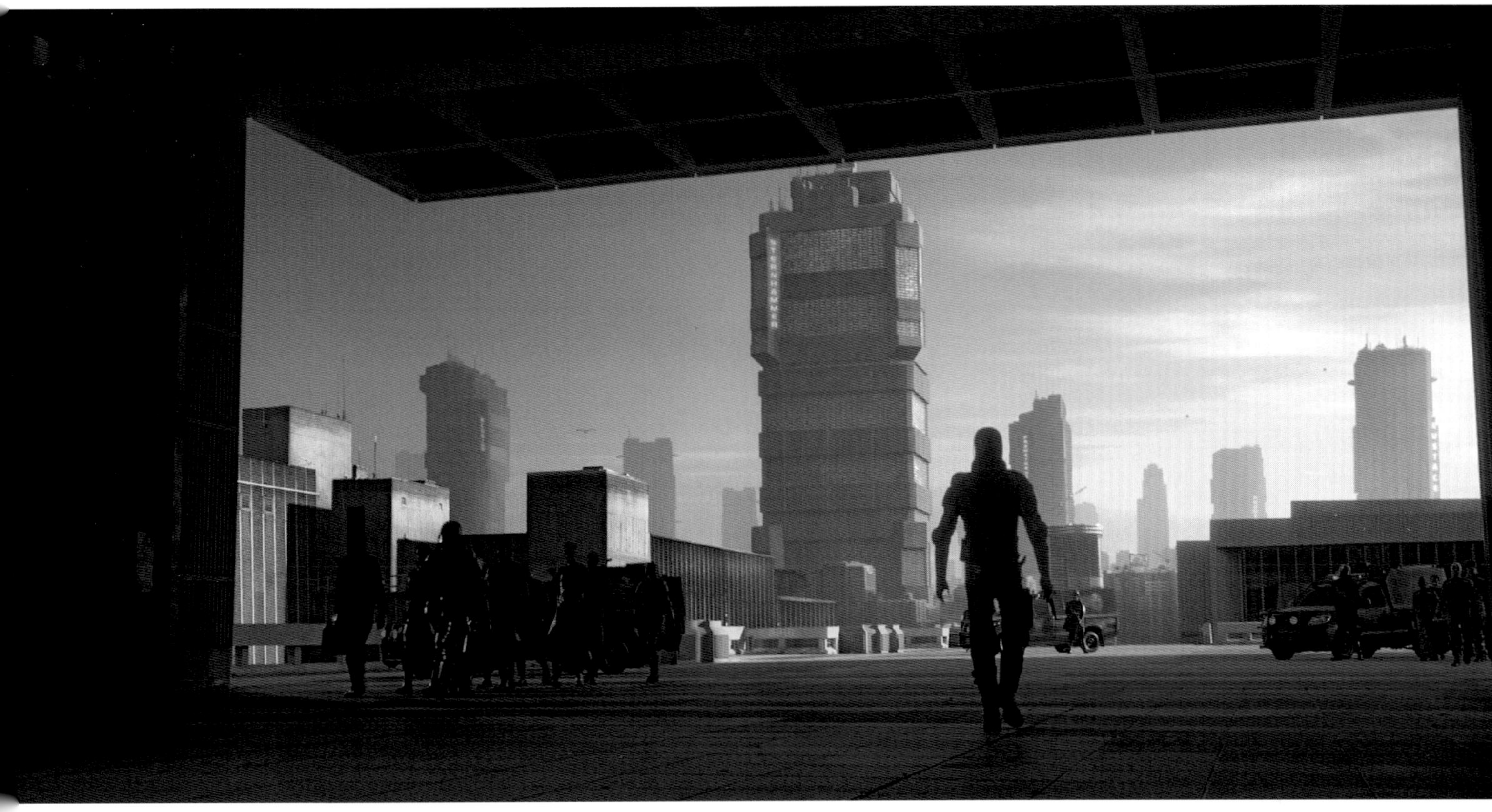

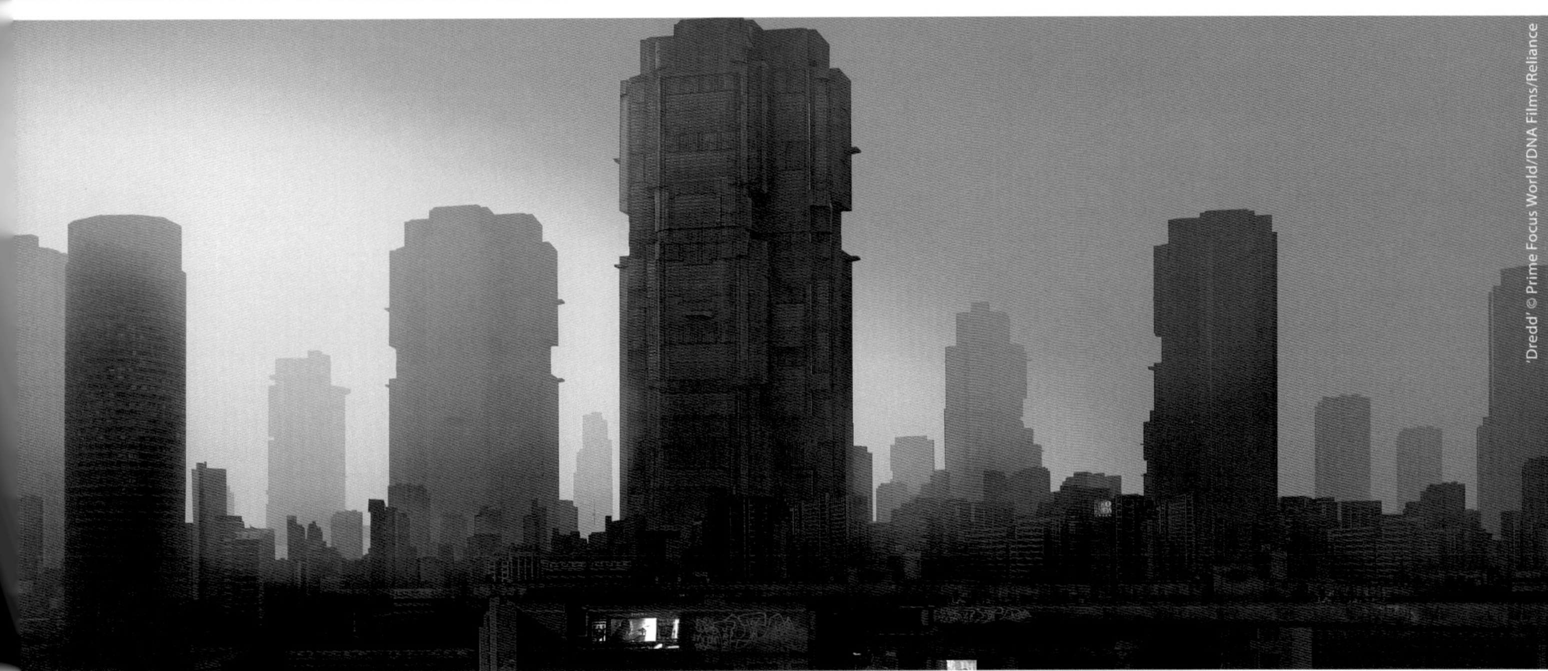

Misty Dawn on the Lake
Photoshop
Dylan Cole, USA
[facing page top]

Milan: I truly love the mood in this matte painting. Dylan is such a skillful artist – painting in any lighting scenario seems to come as a natural gift to him. Over the years, he has been a great influence on the matte painting community.

Babylonian Ruins
Photoshop
Wayne Haag, AUSTRALIA
[facing page bottom]

Milan: Production art such as this is invaluable for any project. Lighting, texture and the self-explanatory feel, created with strong contrast between the saturated foreground and the natural atmosphere in the distance, guide shots like this to a successful final result.

Dredd: Mega City
Photoshop, Maya, CINEMA 4D
Client: Prime Focus World/DNA Films/Reliance
Neil Miller, GREAT BRITAIN
[top & above]

Milan: Art directing is the perfect balance between matte painting and concept designing, developing the look of a movie, while being involved with some individual shots hands-on from sketch to finish. Neil took on the role of art director on *Dredd* when the project got into full swing. It was thrilling for me to see the final outcome and I was extremely happy with how Neil defined the appearance of Mega City.

'Season of the Witch' © Atlas Entertainment/Relativity Media

'Season of the Witch' © Atlas Entertainment/Relativity Media

Season of the Witch: The Rope Bridge Over Gorge
Photoshop
Client: Atlas Entertainment
Jiri Stamfest, UPP, CZECH REPUBLIC
[facing page: top and bottom]

Milan: These are two of Jiri's wonderful matte paintings from Dominic Sena's *Season of the Witch* feature film. They're so appealing to me because Jiri's work seems to have an enticingly traditional aura to it, almost like an Albert Whitlock original.

Asian City Extension
Photoshop
Jadrien Cousens, USA
[top]

Milan: Jadrien has created a very successful matte painting with this intricate architectural set extension. For the final shot I would very much enjoy seeing some people up on the higher balconies in order to balance the large amount of activity in the foreground plate.

Temple in the Mountains
Photoshop
Stephanie Kwok, CANADA
[above]

Milan: Strong foreground elements can carry a lot of weight in a matte painting. Stephanie created a well-defined foreground, midground, background separation and thoughtfully balanced atmospheric haze. Extracting those trees must have been painful but the result is rewarding.

Imohetp's Secret
Photoshop
Wayne Haag, AUSTRALIA
[top]

Milan: Wayne is one of the legendary traditional matte painters who successfully transitioned his craft to the digital realm. With his well-trained eye, Wayne is able to make the same decisions in Photoshop that he would have made when painting with oil.

Fragment in Time
Photoshop
Bobby Myers, USA
[above]

Milan: I'd almost call this an abstract matte painting if the term would make any logical sense. Getting such an alien landscape into a familiar enough and realistic world is an extraordinary challenge that Bobby has triumphantly accomplished. I especially love the direct sun in his perfect composition.

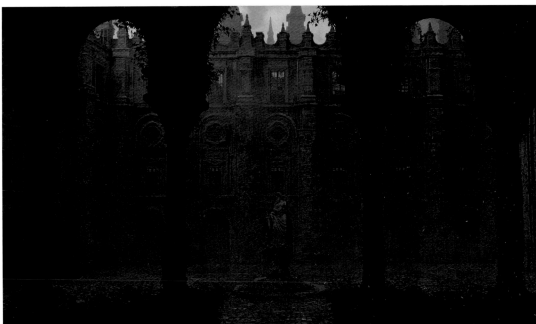

Spider's Web
Photoshop
Aziz Maaqoul, MOROCCO
[top]

Milan: Although this painting has evolved to a photo-real textural level, it manages to retain the organic feel of a concept art piece. That in itself is a respectable achievement. I believe that this place could really exist, and that is the ultimate challenge of any matte painting task.

Courtyard
Maya, V-Ray, Photoshop, ivyGenerator
Anthony Eftekhari, USA
[above]

Milan: I generally don't shy away from symmetric compositions with one point perspective. It is the most straightforward tool to point out the obvious. That's the reason I enjoy its efficiency and directness. Anthony is an outstanding artist with strong 3D skills and I believe he could have set up any angle for the base render of this shot, but he chose this particular one because he felt it would only strengthen the matte painting. These are the types of decisions a matte painter must feel comfortable making.

Aqueduct in Ruins
Photoshop
Jadrien Cousens, USA
[top]

Milan: The fictional Roman city in ruins sits well integrated in the realistic environment. Jadrien displays a strong understanding of keeping the connection to the real world within fantasy settings. As a final step I would take the lighting interaction further by adding some highlight hits on the top surface of the bridge created by the back-lit sky.

Way to the Mountains
Photoshop
Usama Jameel, INDIA
[above]

Milan: Usama successfully portrays the feel of a humid jungle. My main note for the future would be to lose the birds and avoid using them again in a matte painting.

The Gorge
Photoshop
Peter Baustaedter, NEW ZEALAND
[below]

Milan: This matte painting was done as an invitation to a party at Peter's house, which is situated on a hill. Peter took some artistic liberties in depicting the location in a Middle Earth type of way. The viewer's eye is lead skillfully to the focal point of the image, perfectly demonstrating the information transport of the piece. Peter is a master of knowing the right balance between brushstrokes and photographic elements, which allows him to play freely with light pools and have fun while producing astonishing imagery.

Totem
SketchUp, Photoshop
Peter Baustaedter, NEW ZEALAND
[bottom]

Milan: Peter's matte painting of these totems on an alien planet would be a bit like a photo space marines send home from their deployment. I am drawn to this well-executed painting because it tells the type of story I enjoy the most. The strong directional lighting with its large cast shadows adds special visual interest to the already powerful shapes.

d'artiste

MATTE PAINTING 3
d'artiste